IMAGES
of America

CLEVELAND

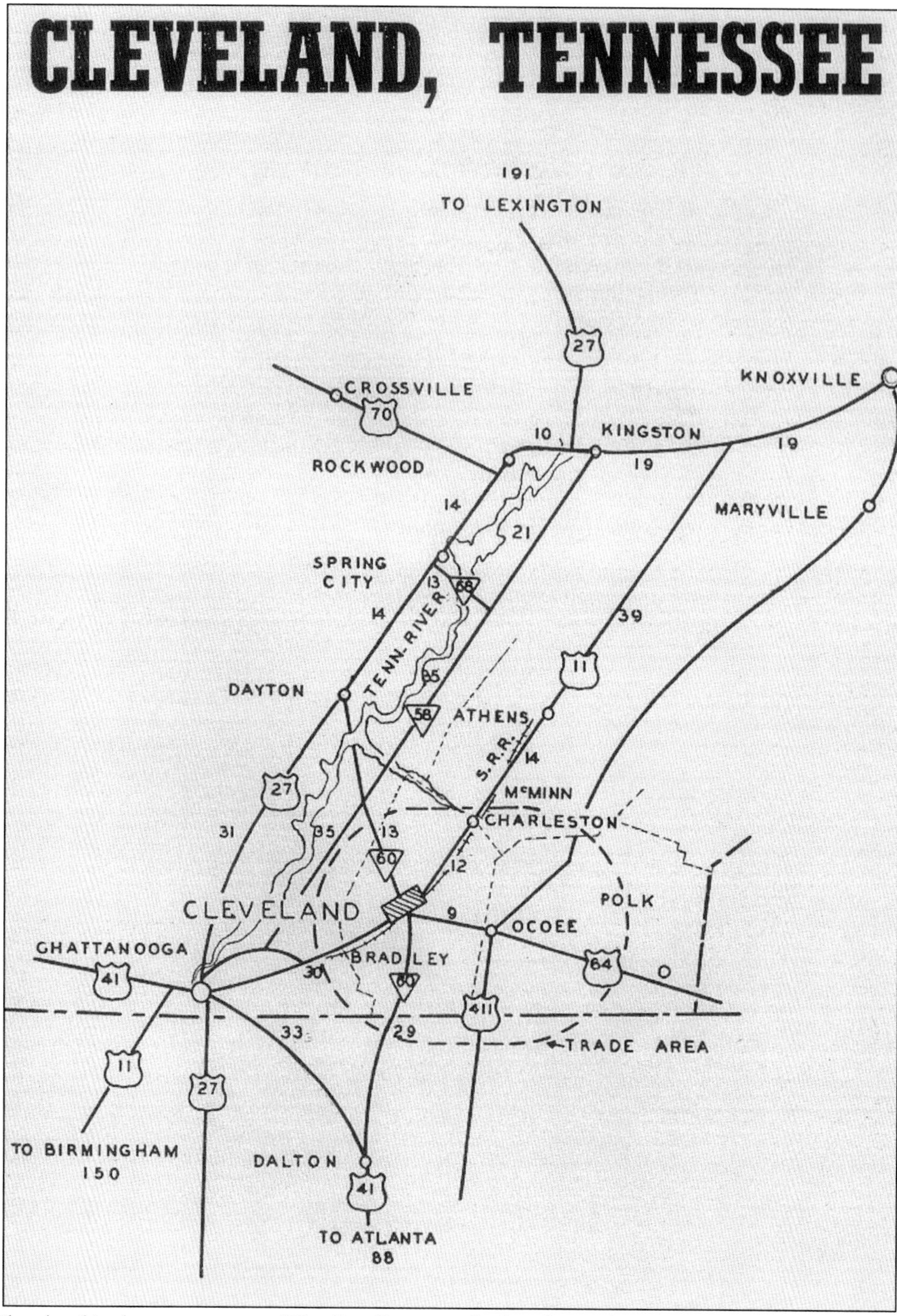

Cleveland is the county seat of Bradley County, which is located in the southeastern section of Tennessee. This 1957 map shows the Cleveland area, which is about 30 miles from Chattanooga, 80 miles from Knoxville, and 120 miles from Atlanta.

IMAGES
of America

CLEVELAND

Robert L. George

ARCADIA
PUBLISHING

ISBN 978-0-7385-0659-3

Published by Arcadia Publishing
Charleston, South Carolina

Printed in the United States of America

Library of Congress Catalog Card Number: 00107668

For all general information contact Arcadia Publishing at:
Telephone 843-853-2070
Fax 843-853-0044
E-mail sales@arcadiapublishing.com
For customer service and orders:
Toll-Free 1-888-313-2665

Visit us on the Internet at www.arcadiapublishing.com

This book is dedicated to my wonderful wife, Mary Lou,
and our daughters, Lauri Ann and Sarah Elizabeth,
who are the reason that Cleveland is home.

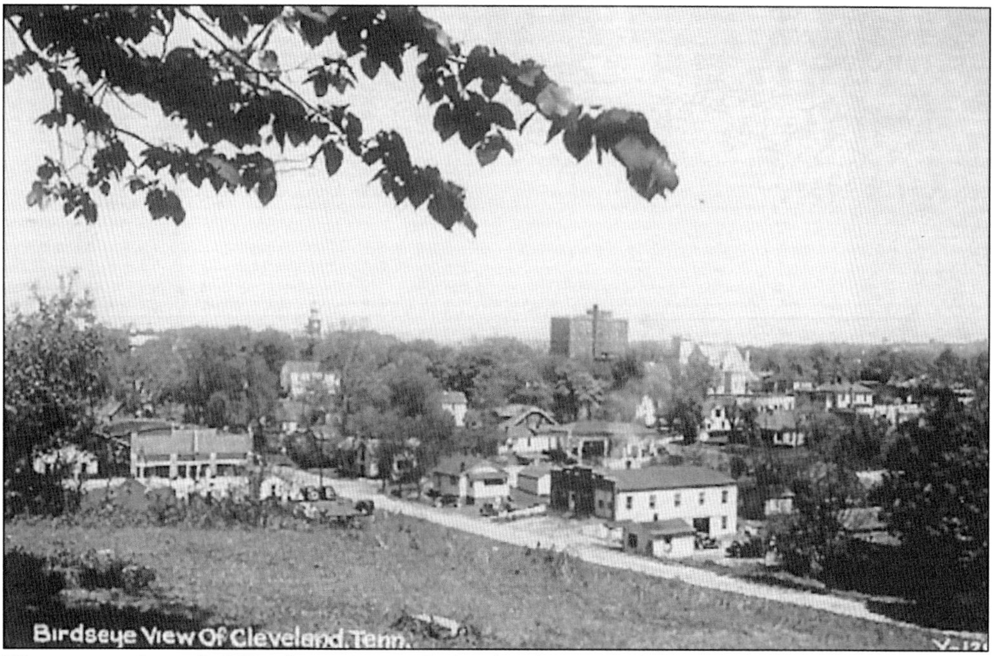

This postcard entitled "Bird's-eye View of Cleveland, Tenn." shows Cleveland in the 1940s.

Contents

ACKNOWLEDGMENTS

The author wishes to thank Jan and Bill Snell for all of their help, guidance, and understanding in making this book a reality. In addition, thanks for sharing pictures and information are due Barbara Fagen, Jim Gibbons, Kay Climer, Artis Hill, Harry Johnson, Mitchell Kinder, Walter Presswood, Norma Cate, Ileen Rucker, Lucille Curbow, Ramona McBride, Bob Osborne, Bobby Taylor, Jeanette Schlaeger, Jeff Morelock, Ann Cooke, Gerry Neely, Linda Watson, Lyle Wikre, Connie Green, Sharon Myers, Hazel Gannaway, and Howie Burger.

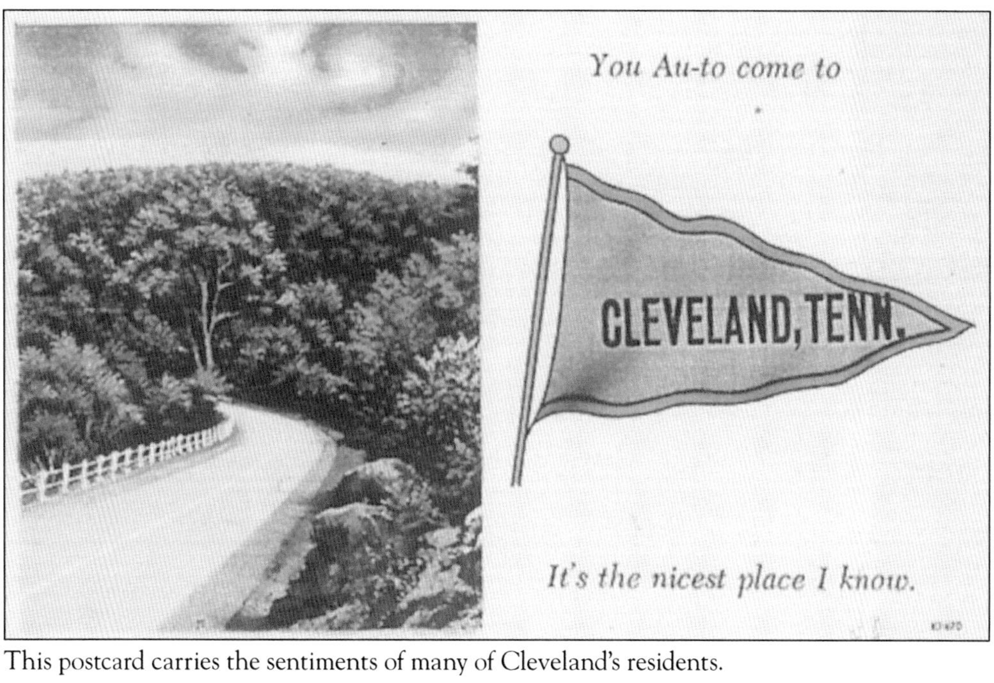

This postcard carries the sentiments of many of Cleveland's residents.

INTRODUCTION

The Cherokee lived alone in Bradley County until Andrew Taylor married a Cherokee and was granted a reservation at the present location of Cleveland. "Taylor's Place" was known by the early settlers as a favorite stopping place due to the many springs in the vicinity. In December 1835, the Treaty of New Echota was signed between the Cherokee and the United States Government whereby the Cherokee ceded the Ocoee District in Tennessee for land in Oklahoma.

The Tennessee State Legislature formally designated Cleveland as the county seat of Bradley County on January 20, 1838. Cleveland was named in honor of Col. Benjamin Cleveland of North Carolina, a Revolutionary War hero at the Battle of King's Mountain. The city of Cleveland was incorporated on February 4, 1842.

When the land office opened the first Monday in November 1838, Cleveland was a small lively village. The principal business houses consisted of four or five stores, several groceries or saloons, and two blacksmith shops. Col. R.M. Edwards described the Cleveland of 1838 as follows: "The courtyard was full of large oak and hickory trees, and all east of that was a swampy glade, full of pine and sweet-gum trees and bushes. Lea Street (now Broad Street) was the main 'big road,' as then called, from the Cherokee Agency at Charleston to Ross's Landing (now Chattanooga)."

In 1837 the Methodists and Presbyterians organized congregations in Cleveland; in that same year Oak Grove Academy was granted a charter to educate boys. The Ocoee Bank, chartered in 1854, was the first bank established in Cleveland. In 1866 the Cleveland National Bank was established as the first locally owned national bank. The *Cleveland Banner* was established May 1, 1854, by Robert McNelley. The East Tennessee and Georgia Railroad reached Cleveland in 1851. The railroad was responsible for Cleveland's first major industrial venture—a rolling mill used to process copper from the nearby Copper Basin. In 1855 a stock company built a steam rolling mill.

In 1852 Miss Rosine Parmentier of New York City visited Cleveland and provided the following description of the city: "This village is well laid out; the streets are wide and straight, many of them planted with trees. The courthouse is a square brick building with a sort of steeple. The most polite Negro whom I have seen during my travels certainly is 'Ned,' a servant belonging to Mrs. Inman, the lady who keeps the hotel."

The importance of Cleveland in the War between the States is shown in a message President Abraham Lincoln sent to Gen. Henry W. Halleck on June 30, 1862: "To take and hold the railroad at or east of Cleveland, Tennessee, I think is as fully important as the taking and holding of Richmond." For a period of time, the Confederacy was supplied with 90 percent of its copper from nearby Polk County, and most of the copper was loaded on the railroad at

Cleveland. The citizens of Cleveland were split about equally between Union and Confederate sympathizers. Both armies occupied Cleveland during the War between the States, and the people and land suffered severely from both sides.

Cleveland was described in 1877 as one of the most handsome towns in Tennessee. Its population was 1,658. The principal manufacturing companies were the Cleveland Woolen Mill, established in 1880; the Cleveland Stove Works, 1883; and the Cleveland Chair Factory, 1884. There were also extensive marble works established in 1875 and a sash and blind factory.

Around 1890, Col. R.M. Edwards reported that Cleveland could boast of 9 practicing physicians, 12 attorneys, 11 general mercantile stores, 14 grocery stores, 2 millinery establishments, 2 tinware shops, 3 furniture stores/undertaking establishments, 3 hardware stores, 3 drugstores, 6 butcher shops, 1 shoe store, 7 licensed saloons, 2 hotels, and 3 livery stables.

At the turn of the 20th century, A.J. Tomlinson, a birthright Quaker shoe salesman from Indiana, came to Cleveland and became the General Overseer of the small holiness sect known as the Church of God. The church grew rapidly and held an annual assembly in Cleveland to conduct its business. A publishing department, school, and church offices were established. In 1923, a major division in the church occurred resulting in two Pentecostal Churches of God headquartered in Cleveland. Later, further divisions would result in five church groups calling Cleveland their world headquarters.

Education has been important to Cleveland since its founding in 1836. The Oak Grove Academy for boys and the Masonic Female Institute were early efforts to provide an education. Central Grammar School was started in 1885, becoming a high school that merged with Bradley High School in Charleston to form Bradley Central High School in 1916. The Cleveland public school system started Cleveland High School in 1966. Centenary Female College, Bob Jones College, Lee College, Tomlinson College, Kent College, the National School of Business, and Cleveland State Community College all sought to provide education at the college level.

As throughout the New South, industry has been important to the growth of Cleveland. The stove foundries, cut and sew plants, and hosiery mills employed most of the workers through World War I, the Great Depression, and World War II. Then the economy changed drastically with new industry moving down from the North. American Uniform moved from Minneapolis to Cleveland in 1949. Bowaters, Olin, Mallory Battery, and Bendix were to follow.

Cleveland is a great place to live. The citizens have always had a special spirit of cooperation and resourcefulness. The Cleveland Associated Charities began in 1938 and later became part of the United Way of Bradley County. The chamber of commerce will celebrate its 75th anniversary in 2000. In 1997, Bradley County's population was 80,220 and Cleveland's population was 33,755. Cleveland is Tennessee's eleventh largest city and the second largest Cleveland in America.

One

Street Scenes

I proceeded on, and my horse being in a tolerable willing humor, we at length reached an American settlement called Cleveland, newly made on the road from Calhoun on the Hiwassee, in Tennessee, to Gainesville in Georgia. Being now on a stage road, and no longer being embargoed, I inquired for the best tavern, and was directed to a clean house kept by a person named [Major James] Berry . . . Twelve months ago there was not a building of any sort here; but such is the activity of these people that already they have got a street and a square, and a tavern, and stores upon the plan of the older settlements.

—George W. Featherstonehaugh
July 28, 1837
A Canoe Voyage up the Minnay Sotor (pp. 220–221)

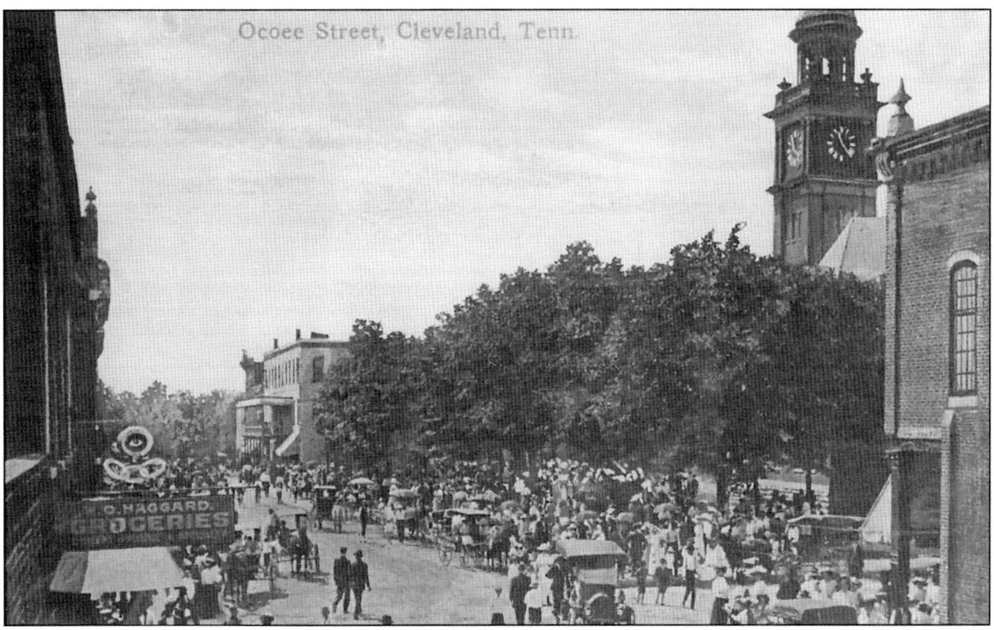

The courthouse square is the center of activity for a county seat. Cleveland was no exception. Shown here is what could have been a typical Saturday on the courthouse square about 1910. Notice the unpaved streets, the horse-drawn buggies, the striking courthouse clock, and the Odd Fellows sign above W.O. Haggard's grocery store.

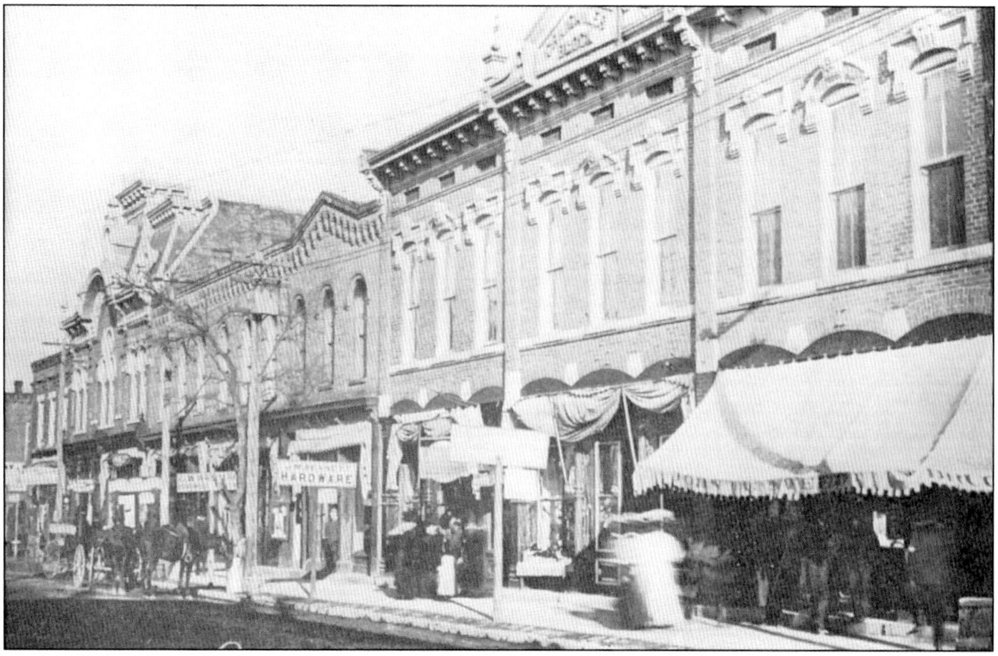

Around the turn of the 20th century, a photographer named Russell made a series of four photographs of Cleveland. Here is the "Craigmiles Block," including the opera house with its majestic facade, the hardware stores, and the Craigmiles Building.

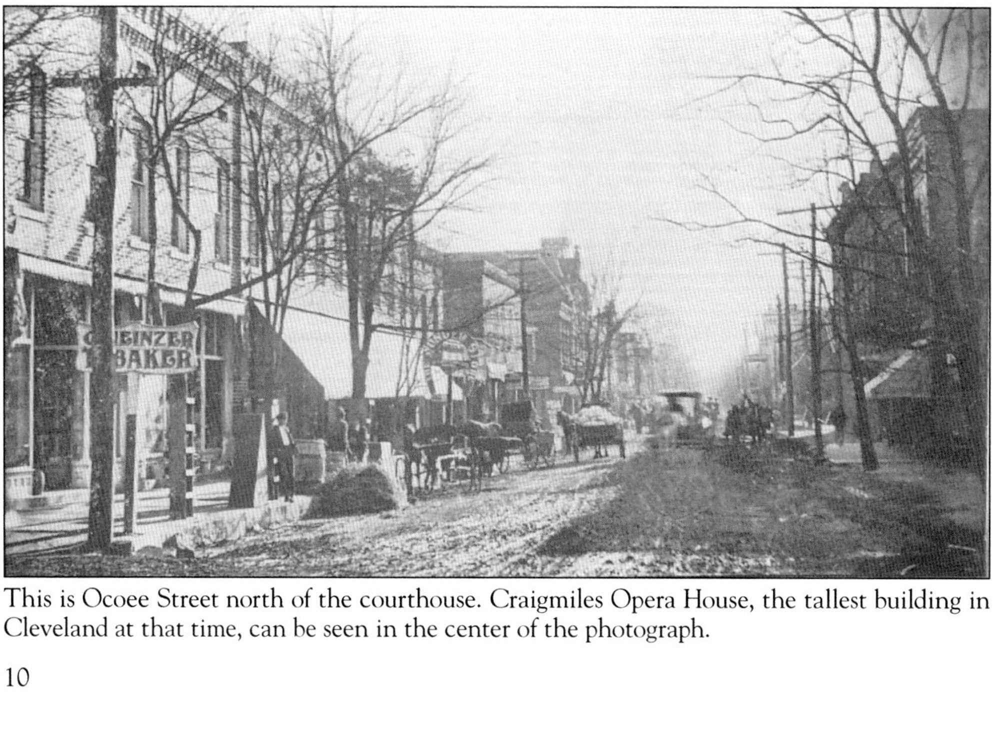

This is Ocoee Street north of the courthouse. Craigmiles Opera House, the tallest building in Cleveland at that time, can be seen in the center of the photograph.

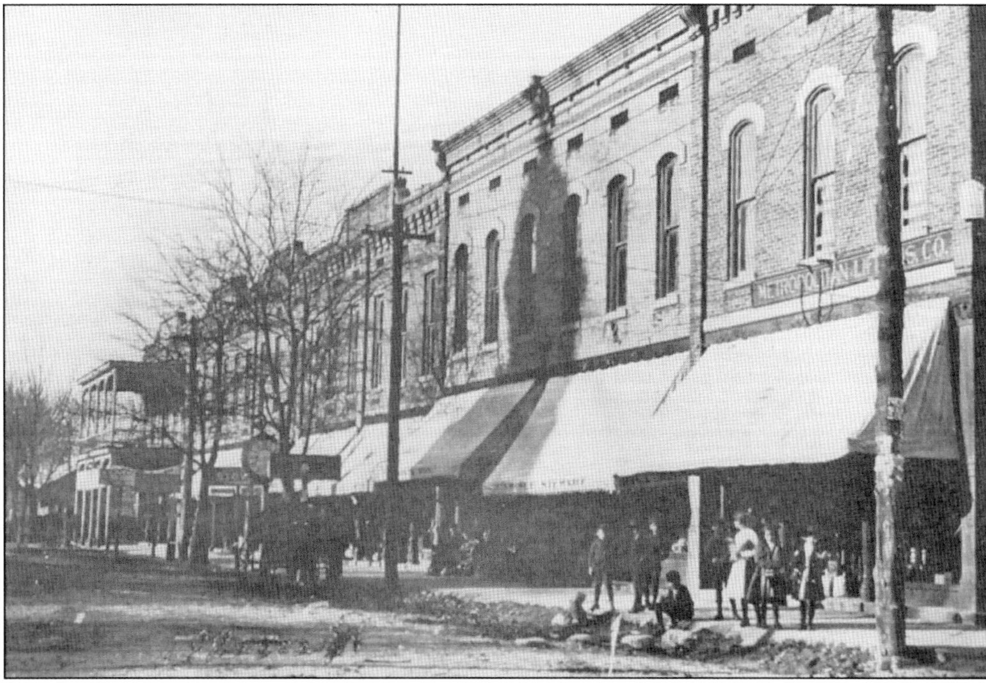

North (later Second) Street is the northern border of the courthouse square. The Ramsey Building is seen with a two-story porch. The Metropolitan Life Insurance Co. occupied the upstairs of the right corner building.

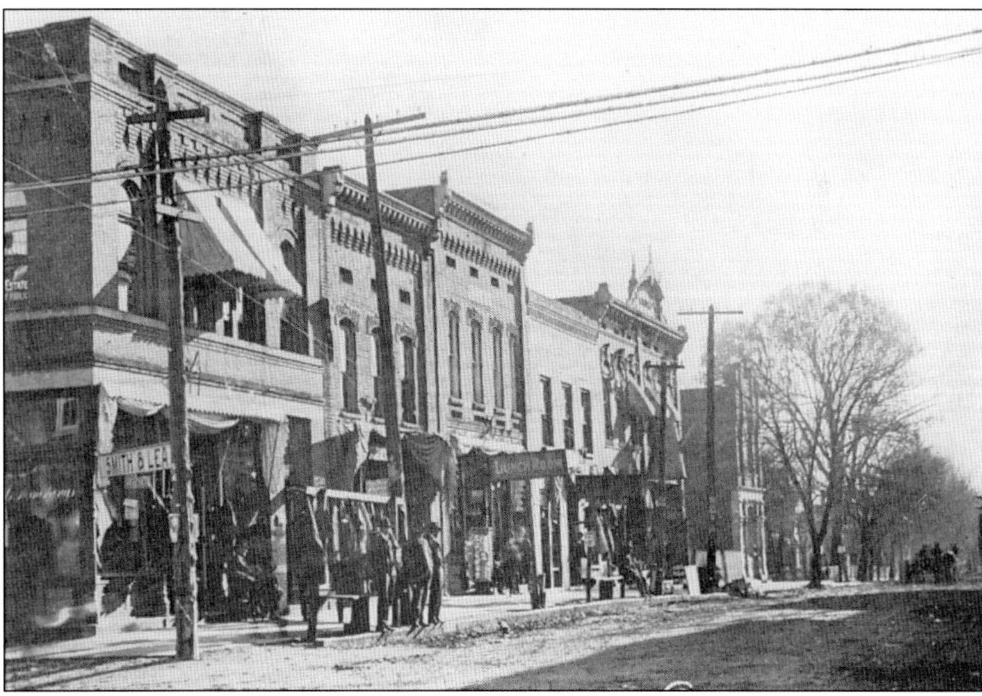

This part of Ocoee Street was unpaved until after World War I, but had several fine retail establishments.

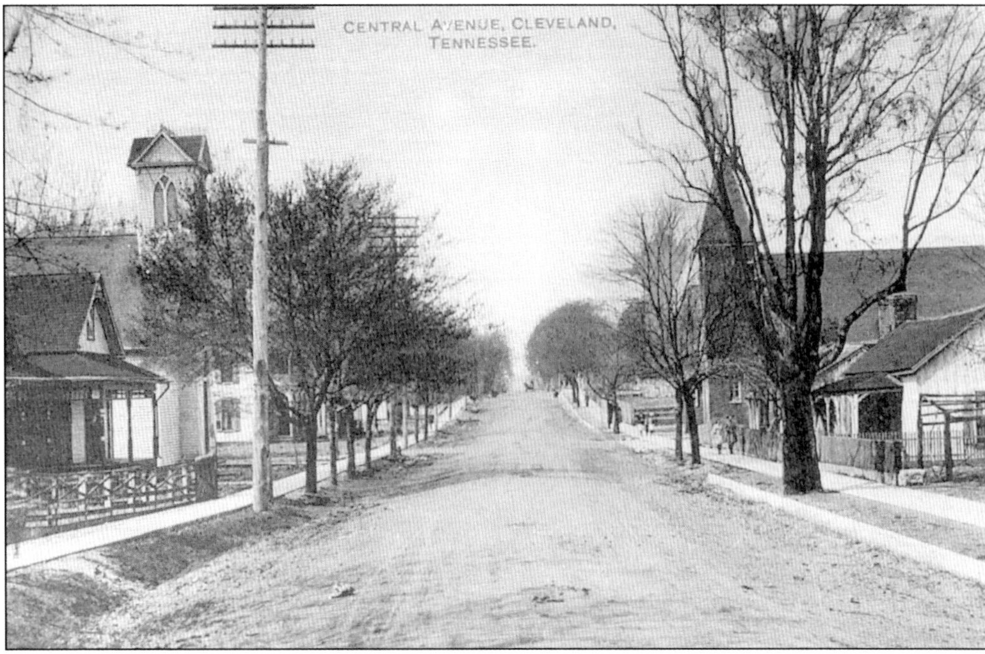

A scene about 1910 on Central Avenue (formerly Berry Street) shows the First Christian Church on the left and Berry Street Baptist Church on the right.

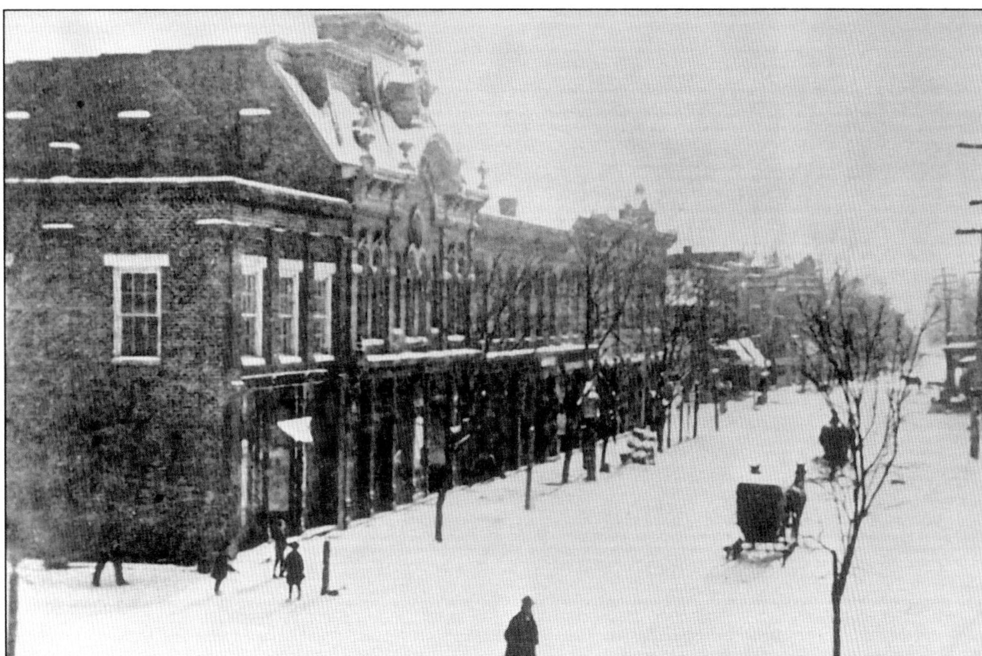

Snow on Ocoee Street makes a lovely winter scene. The horse-drawn buggies were on runners rather than wheels.

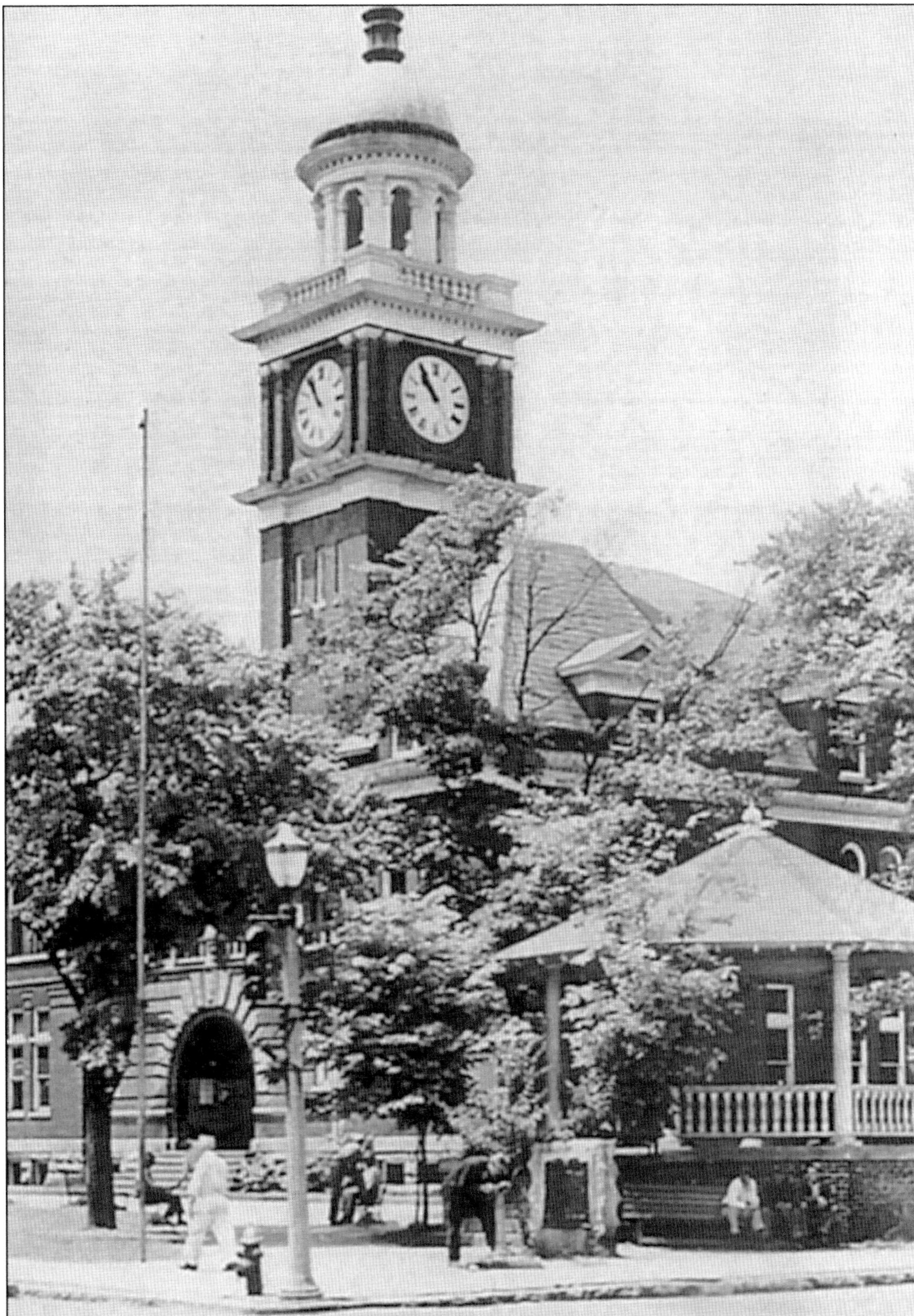

The third Bradley County Courthouse was built in 1893 at a cost of $75,000. It was considered by many one of the most picturesque courthouses in Tennessee. This building was replaced in 1964 with the current structure.

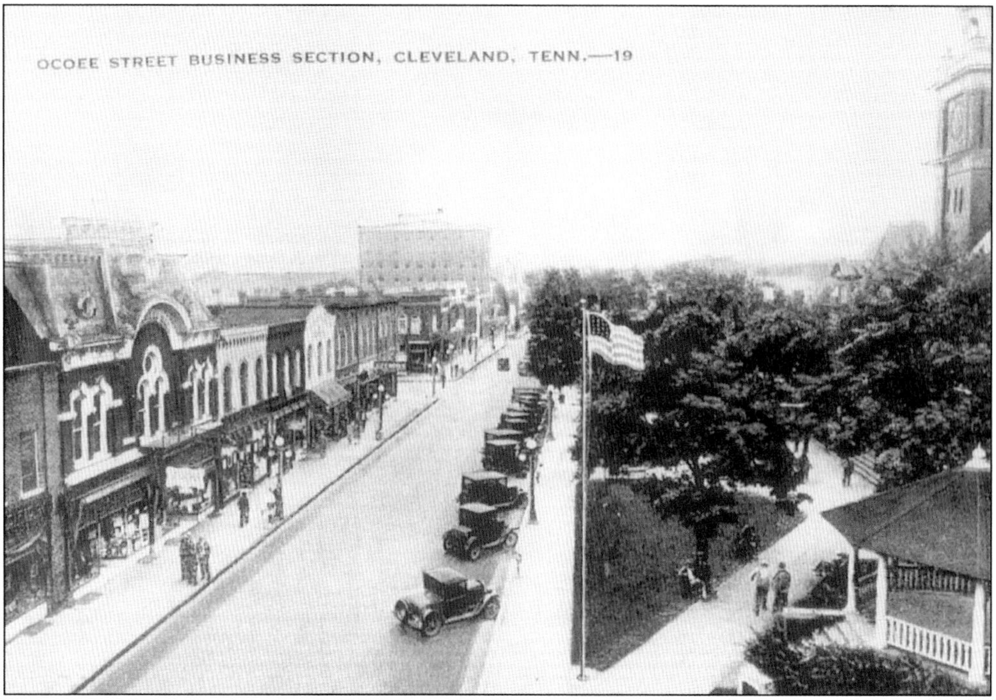

This postcard shows the courthouse square with the bandstand on the right. The tall building in the distance is the Cherokee Hotel.

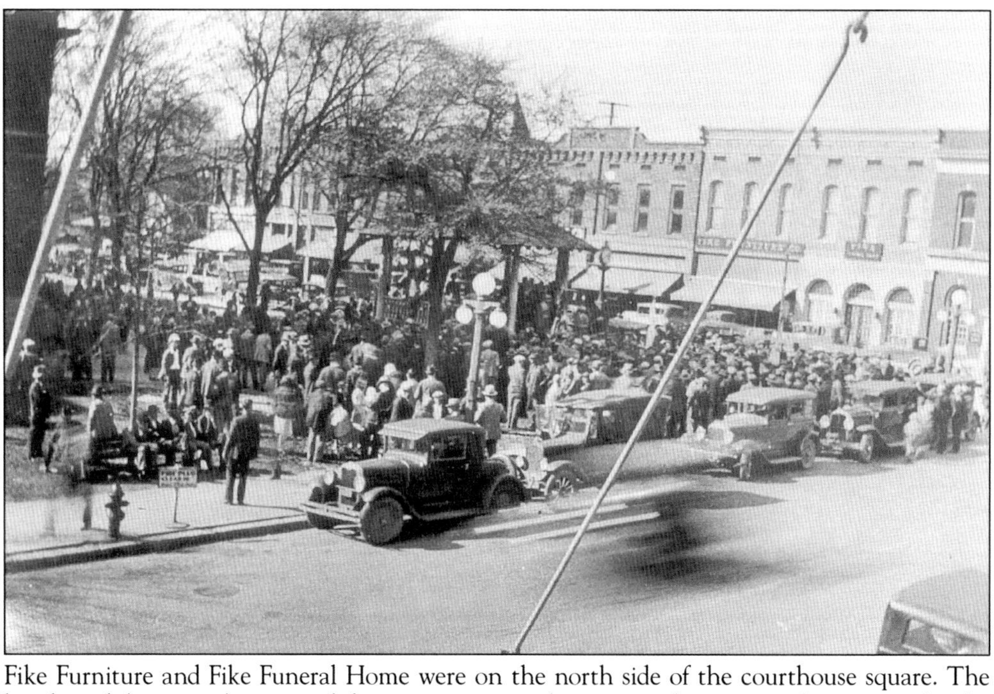

Fike Furniture and Fike Funeral Home were on the north side of the courthouse square. The bandstand (in center) was used for community gatherings, such as musical concerts. In the 1940s snake-handlers preached scriptural holiness from the steps of the bandstand.

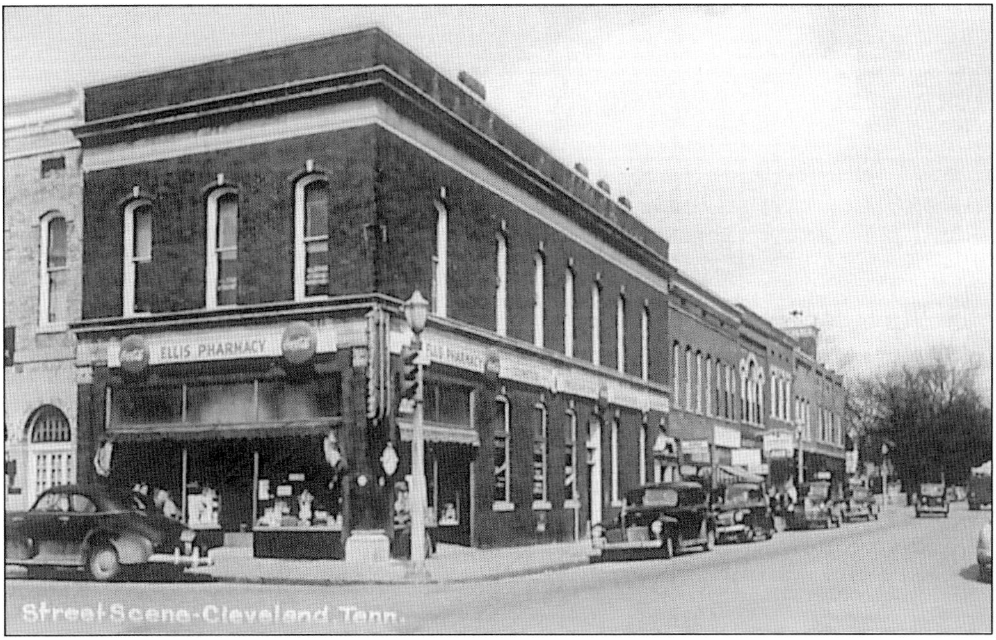

This postcard shows Ellis Pharmacy, former home of the Peoples Bank. The bank opened in September 1911. Its doors were closed in 1931, when the firm went into receivership with patrons receiving about 75 percent of their accounts.

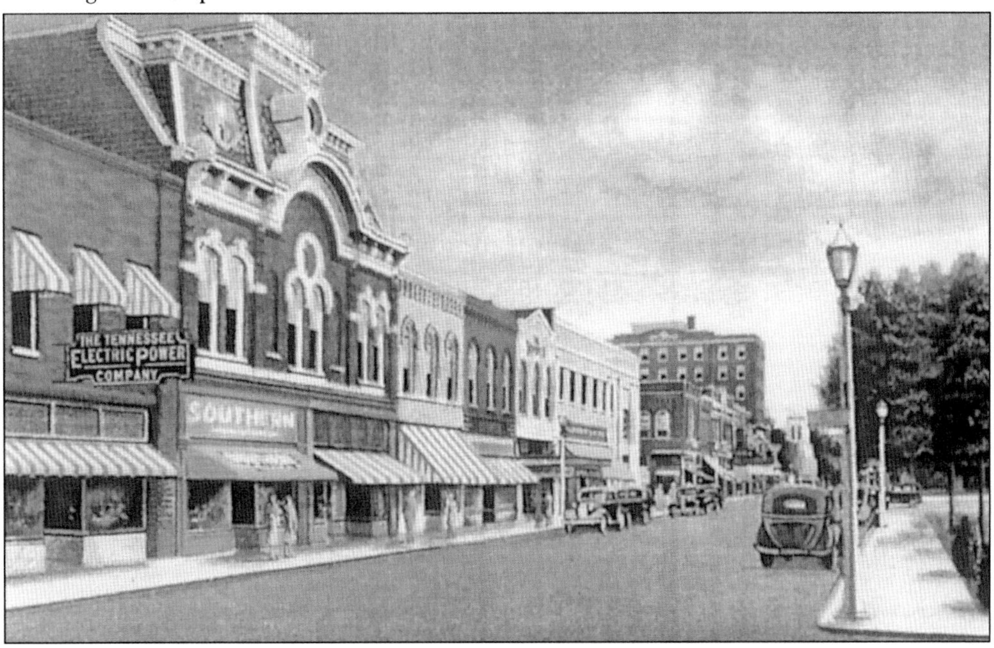

Shown on this postcard is the Tennessee Electric Power Company (TEPCO) office next to the Craigmiles Opera House building. TEPCO, the privately owned power company, had its home office in Cleveland during the building of the two powerhouses and dams on the Ocoee River. Cleveland was the third largest city in the 1920s served directly by TEPCO, being surpassed only by Nashville and Chattanooga. TEPCO was taken over by the Tennessee Valley Authority in 1939.

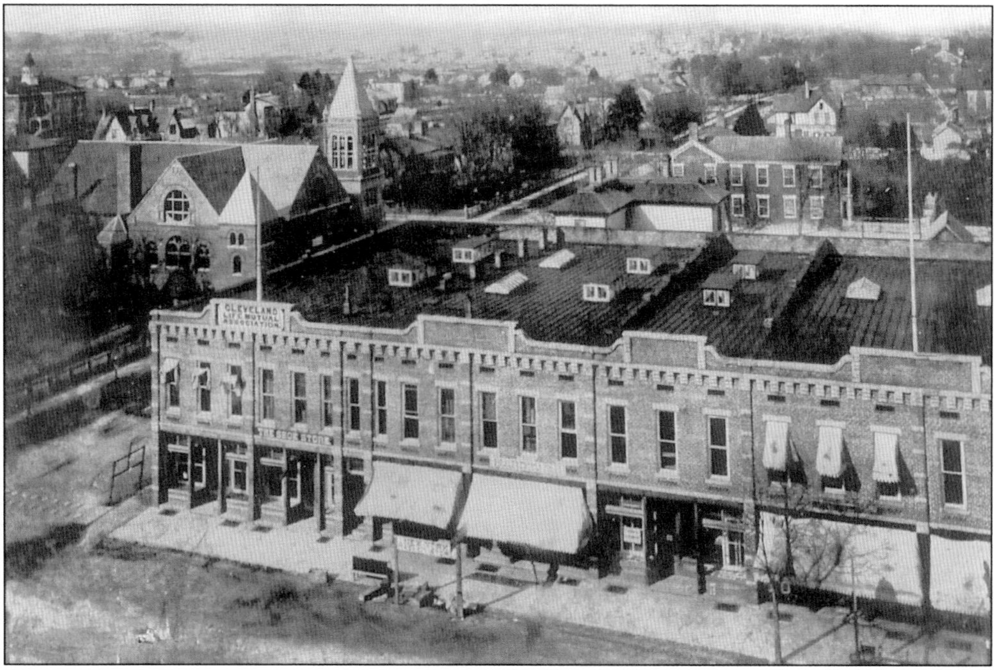

As pictured in this 1893 scene, the Ramsey Building on the north side of the courthouse housed several prominent businesses, including the following: The Shoe Store, New York Racket Store, and Cleveland Life Mutual Association. The church on the left is Broad Street Methodist Episcopal Church, South. The building on the left with the cupola is Central Grammar School. Notice the blocks of granite used as stepping stones to aid in crossing the unpaved street.

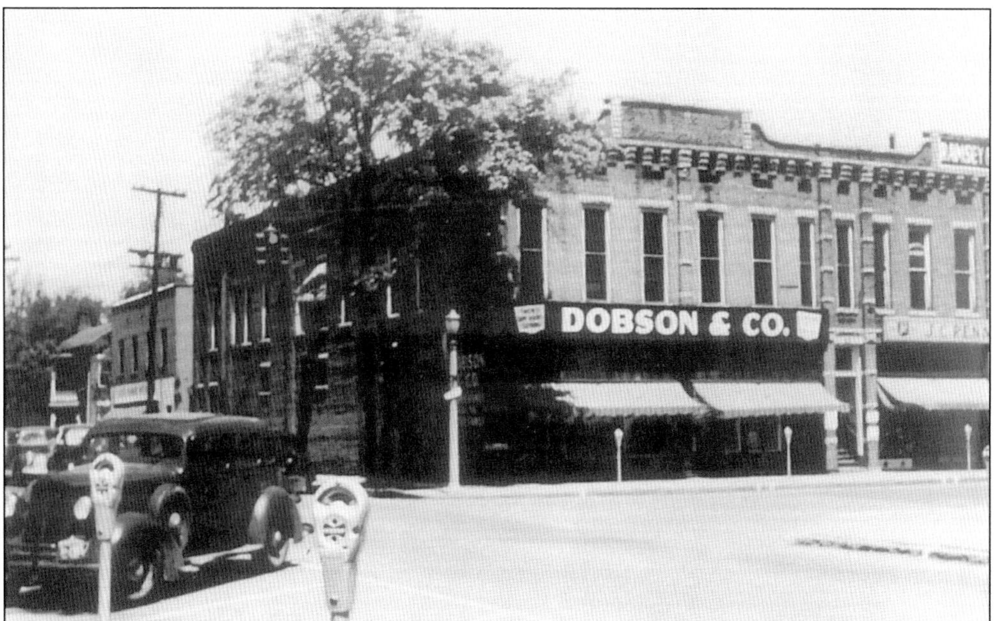

This is another scene of the Ramsey Building, but with new tenants, Dobson & Co. and J.C. Penney. Notice the parking meters, which were used from January 1947 until September 1974.

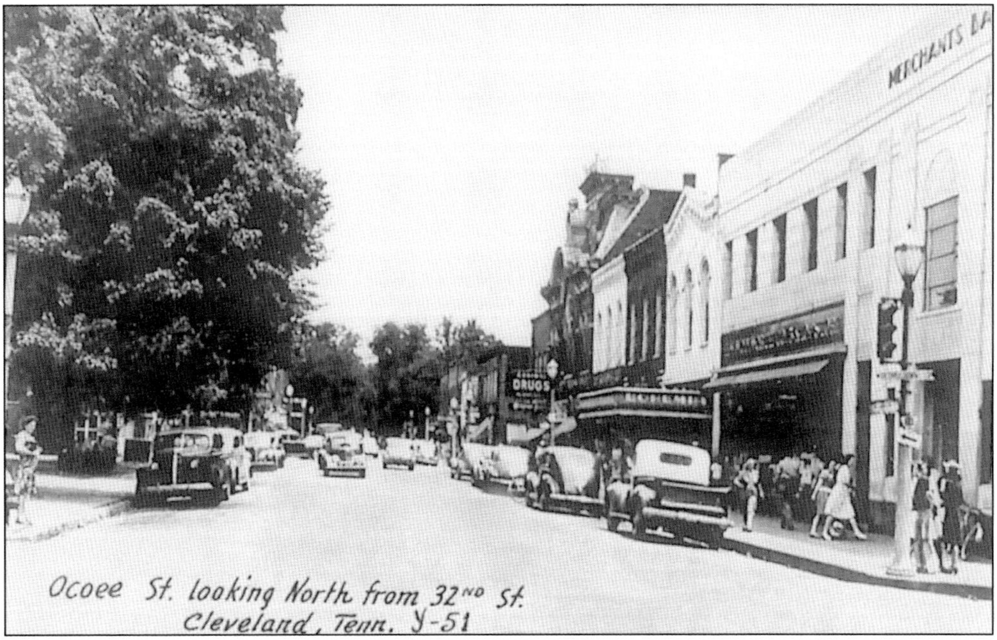

Next door to S.H. Kresge was the Bohemia Theater, which opened with silent films on February 11, 1911. The theater closed in 1955. When it closed, the price of admission was 15¢ for a child and 35¢ for an adult.

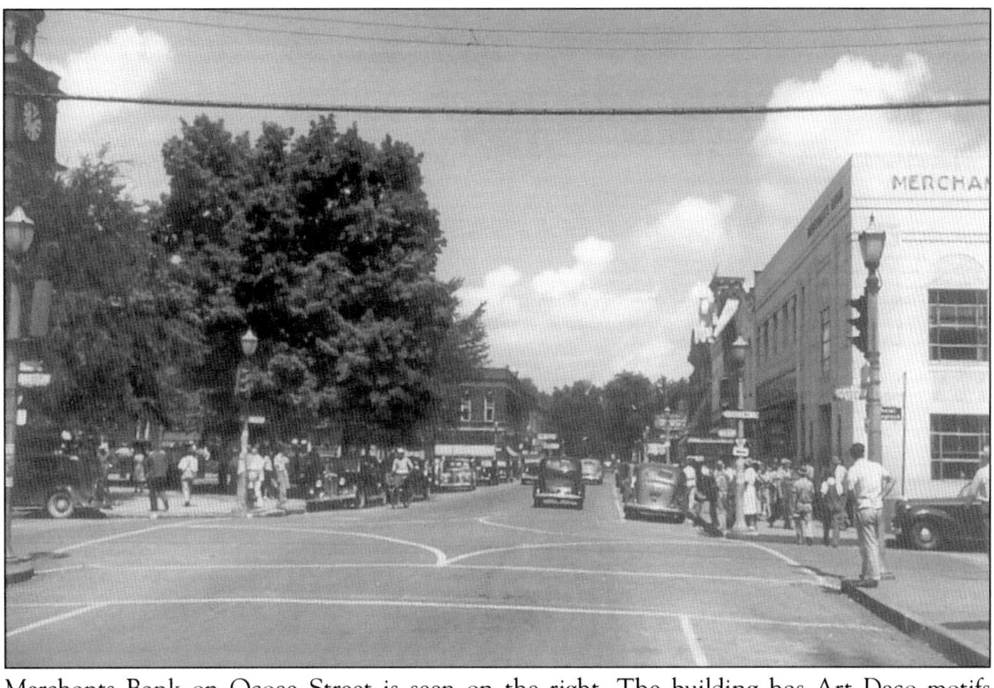

Merchants Bank on Ocoee Street is seen on the right. The building has Art Deco motifs enhancing the solid granite face of the exterior. Ocoee Street had two-way traffic at this time (1933–1967).

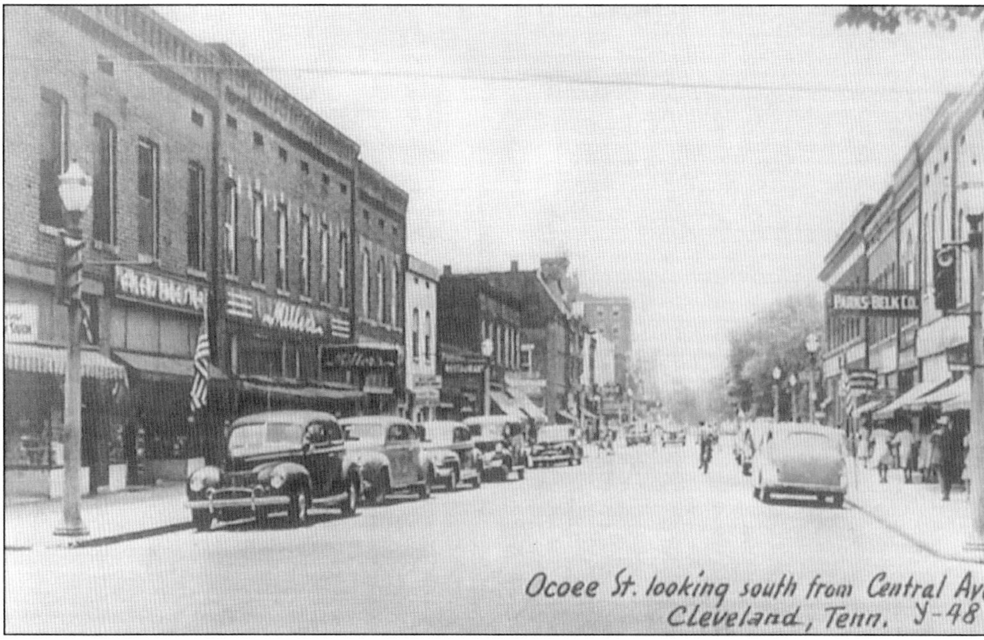

The block of Ocoee Street north of the courthouse housed many fine businesses in the 1940s and 1950s. Parks-Belk Co. is on the right. Apler's Shoe Store and Miller's are on the left.

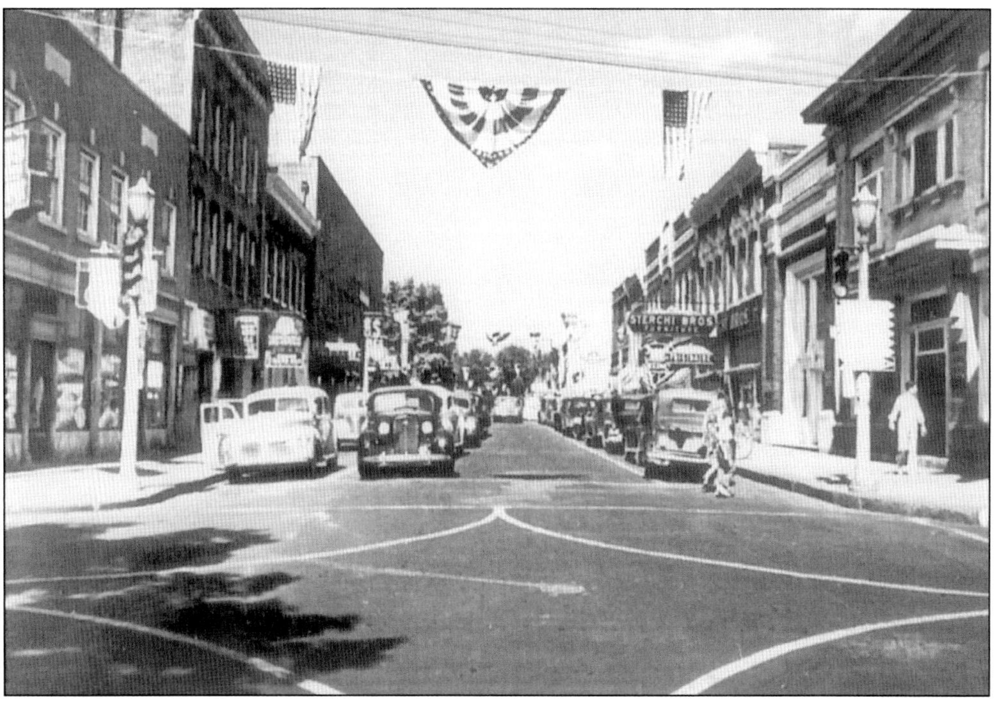

On Ocoee Street south of the courthouse were located Sterchi Brothers Furniture Store, Cleveland National Bank, and Cleveland Bank & Trust Co.

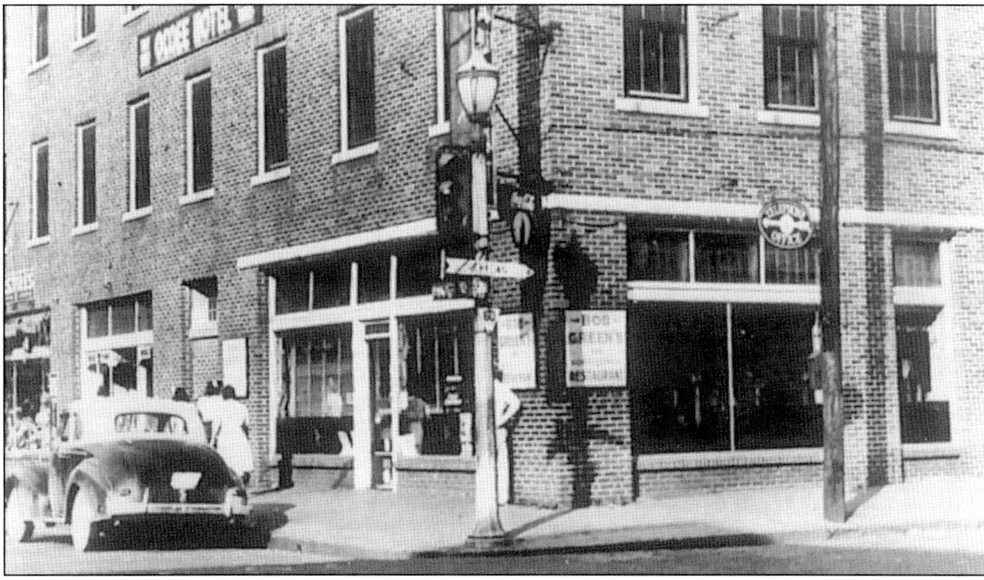

Bob Green's Restaurant was located in the Ocoee Hotel Building. Called the Ocoee House, it was built by Cowan and Tibbs and was the tallest structure in East Tennessee at that time. A three-story brick building with 50 guest rooms, dancehall, and large dining room, the hotel became a favorite stopping place for salesmen and tourists. During the Civil War, this building was used as a hospital. A horse-drawn carriage was operated from the railroad station to the hotel. The Ocoee House was demolished in 1964 for the construction of Merchant Bank offices.

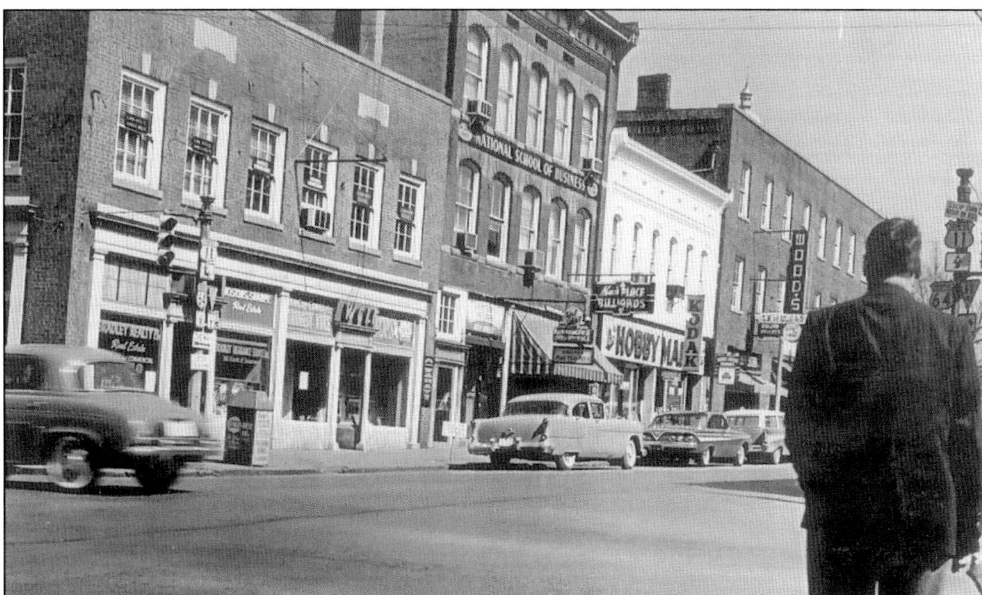

The three-story building in the center, constructed by Calvin Hardwick, housed The Spot, a famous local eatery for several generations. The National School of Business advertised that it occupied "the entire third-floor." During the 1980s, with many veterans receiving the GI Bill, National had over 800 students. The Hobby Mart and Wood's Jewelers were in adjacent buildings.

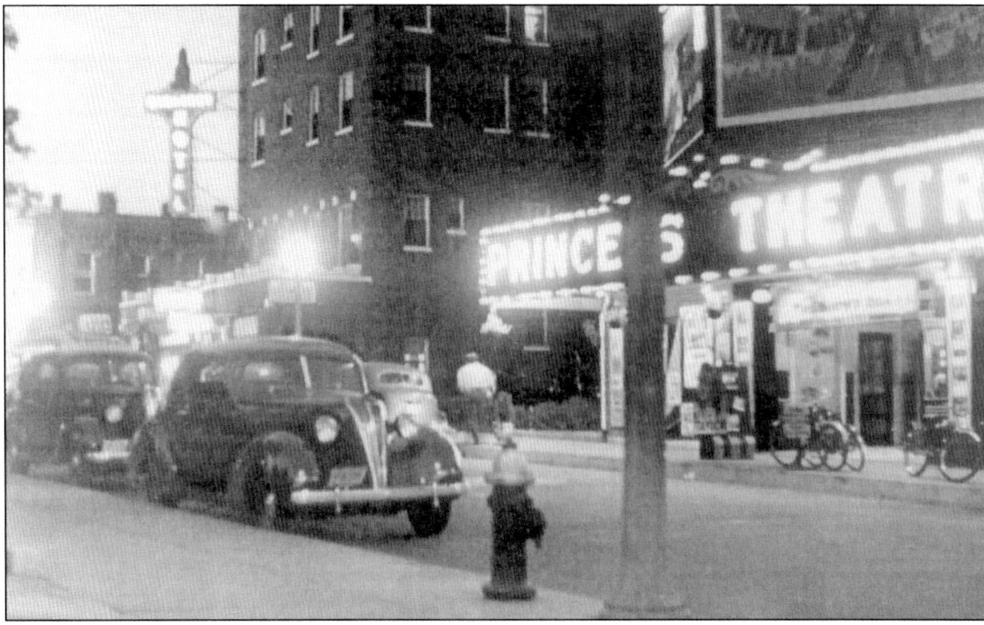

The Princess Theater was located on Ocoee Street across from Johnston Park. Built in 1927 at a cost of $115,000, it was state-of-the-art in building design. Opening September 3, 1927, with the program "Red Raiders and Smoke Eaters," it was the first theater in Cleveland to have "talking pictures."

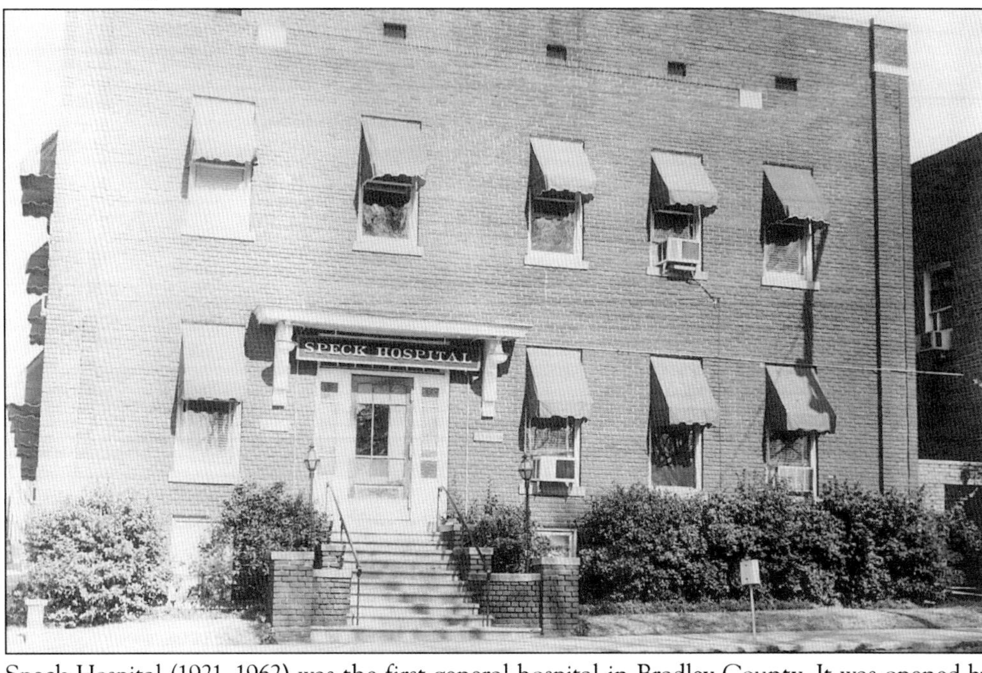

Speck Hospital (1921–1962) was the first general hospital in Bradley County. It was opened by Dr. Carl T. Speck Sr. when he returned from the Army after service in World War I, and was located in a new two-story building constructed at the corner of Inman and Broad Street. The hospital was also known as Cleveland General Hospital. By 1929, it housed 36 private rooms and two wards of four beds each.

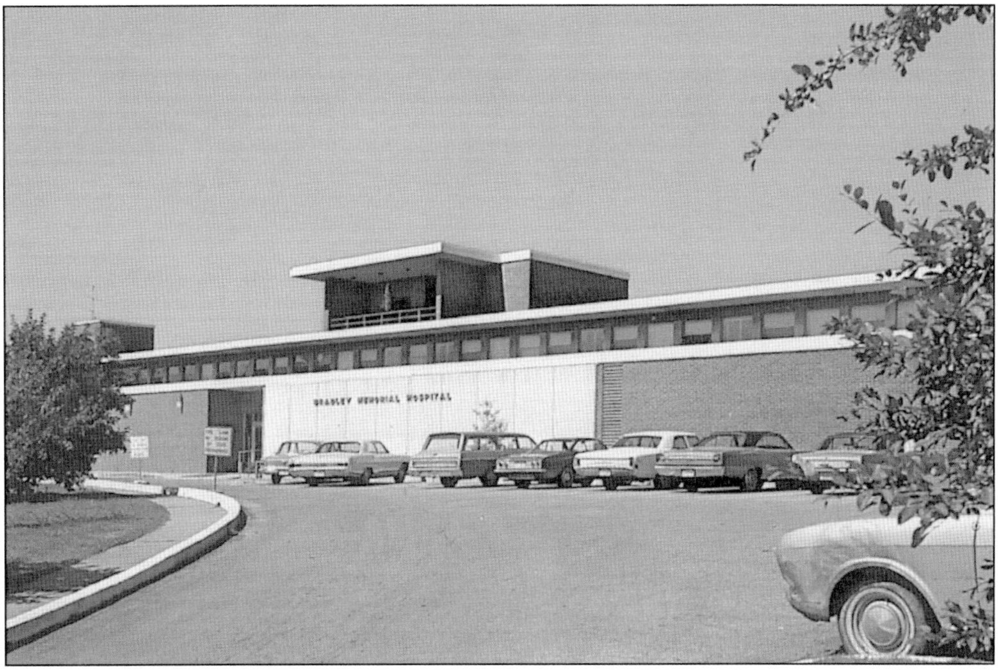

Bradley Memorial Hospital on Chambliss Avenue opened on December 31, 1952. The 52-bed hospital was hailed by the press as "a twentieth century hospital . . . trim, clean-cut, efficient, but harmonious and rhythmical."

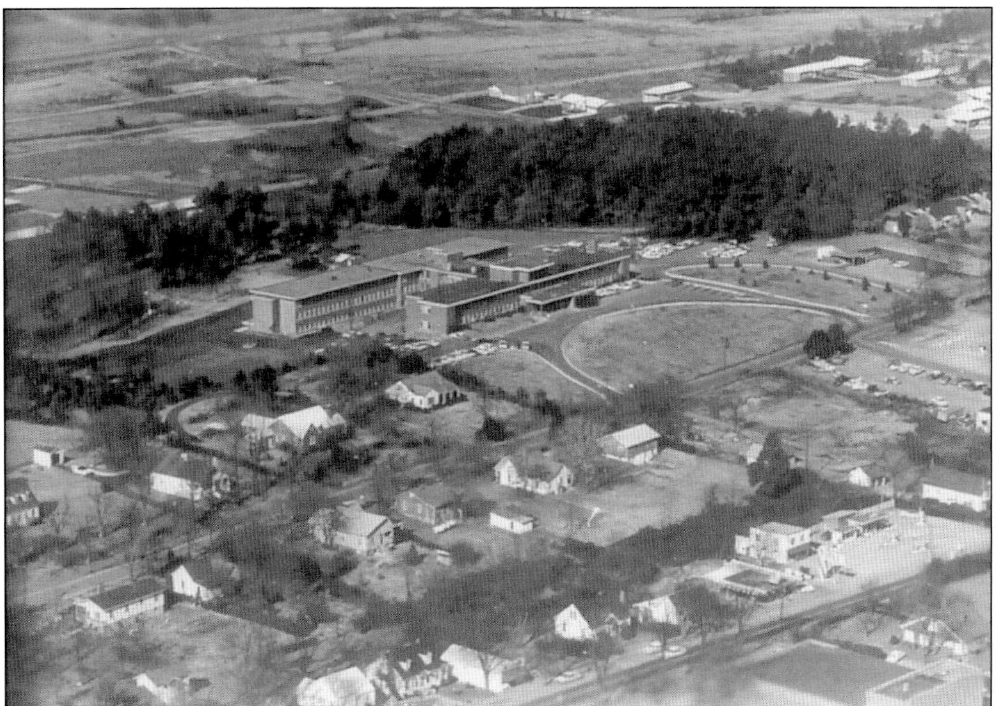

This aerial photograph of Bradley Memorial Hospital in December 1962 shows the expansion of the hospital in ten years. Note the abundance of farmland available in Cleveland at that time.

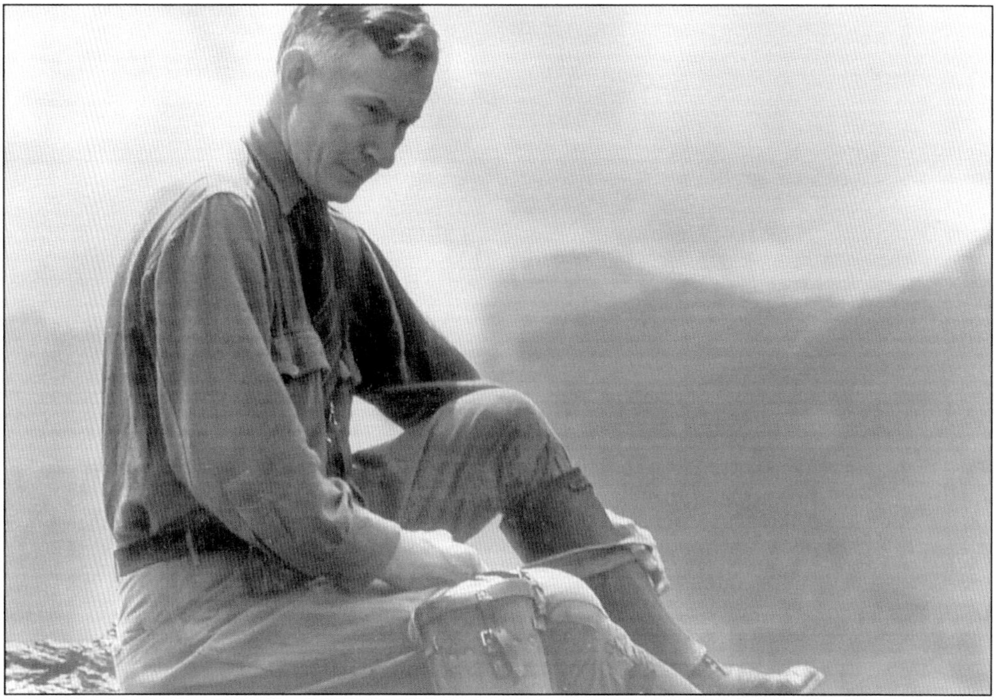

Seen here is D. Wilger, a photographer in the 1930s, who made the following series of aerial photographs of Cleveland in 1939.

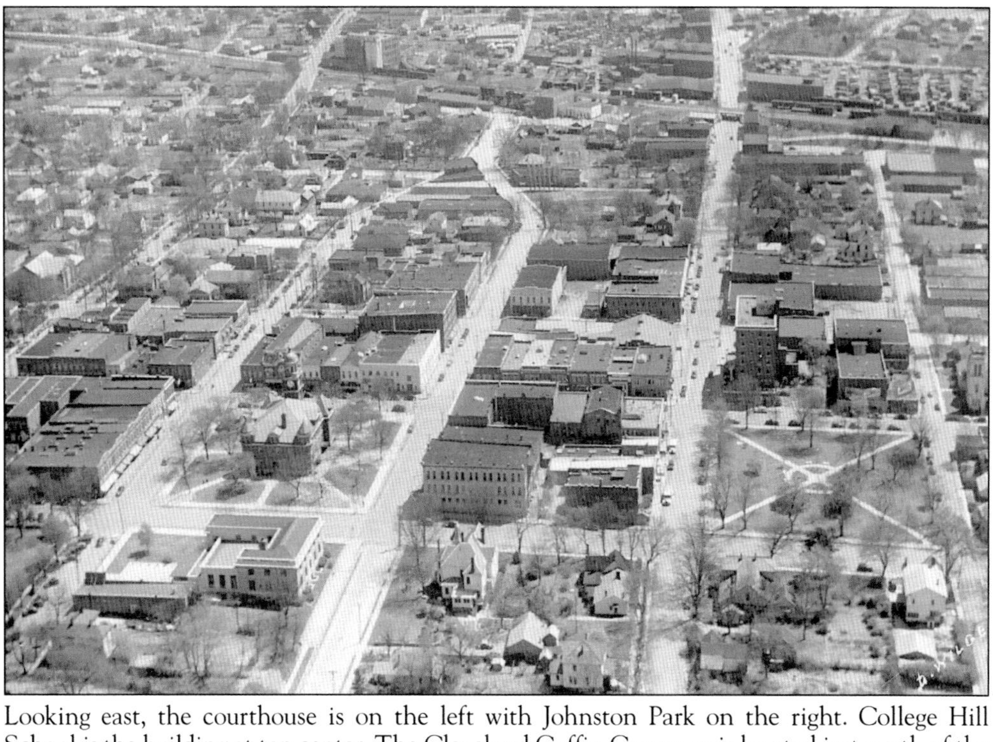

Looking east, the courthouse is on the left with Johnston Park on the right. College Hill School is the building at top center. The Cleveland Coffin Company is located just north of the railroad overpass.

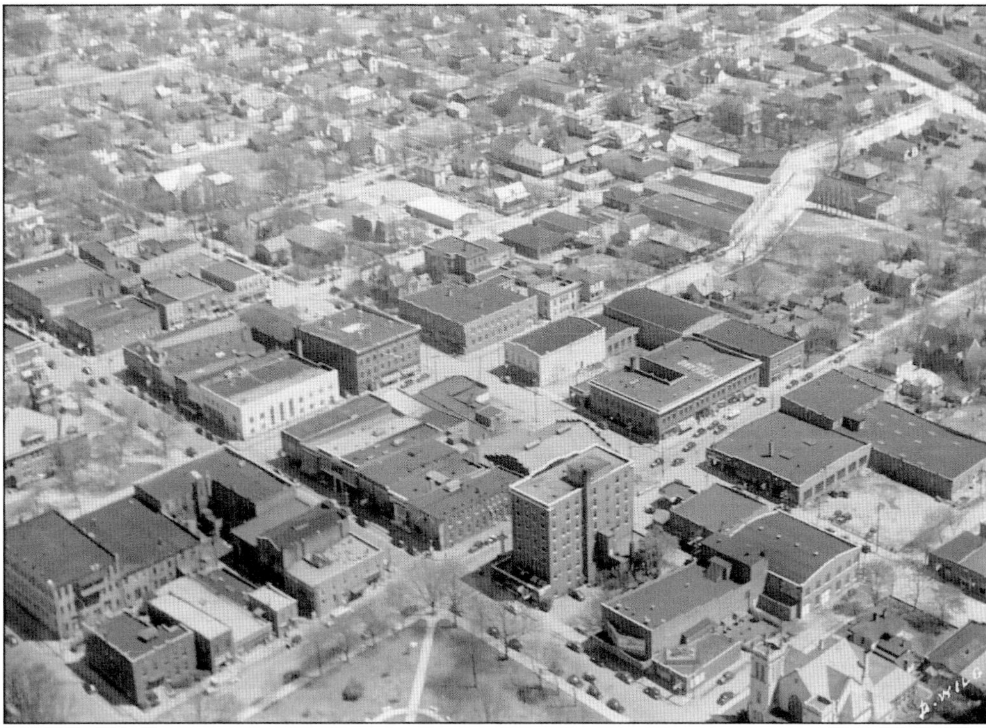

This view is from the south looking north. The Cherokee Hotel is the tall building at the lower center; First Methodist Episcopal Church is located at the bottom right; and the Cleveland Milling Company is located at the top right.

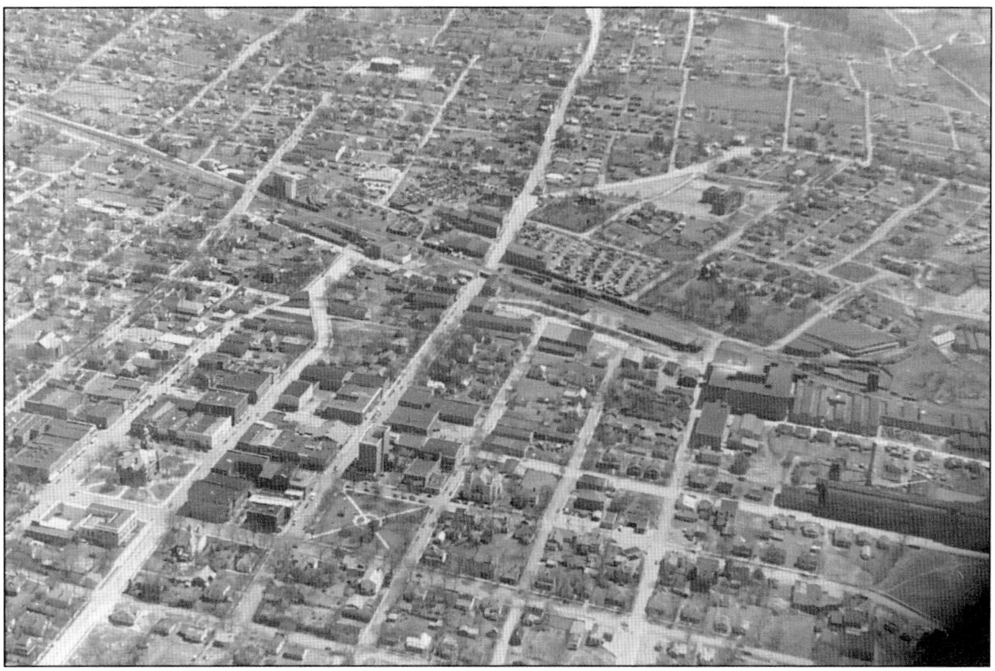

This photograph shows Inman Street in the center. At that time Inman Street began at Worth Street. The Hardwick Woolen Mill and Hardwick Stove are on the right.

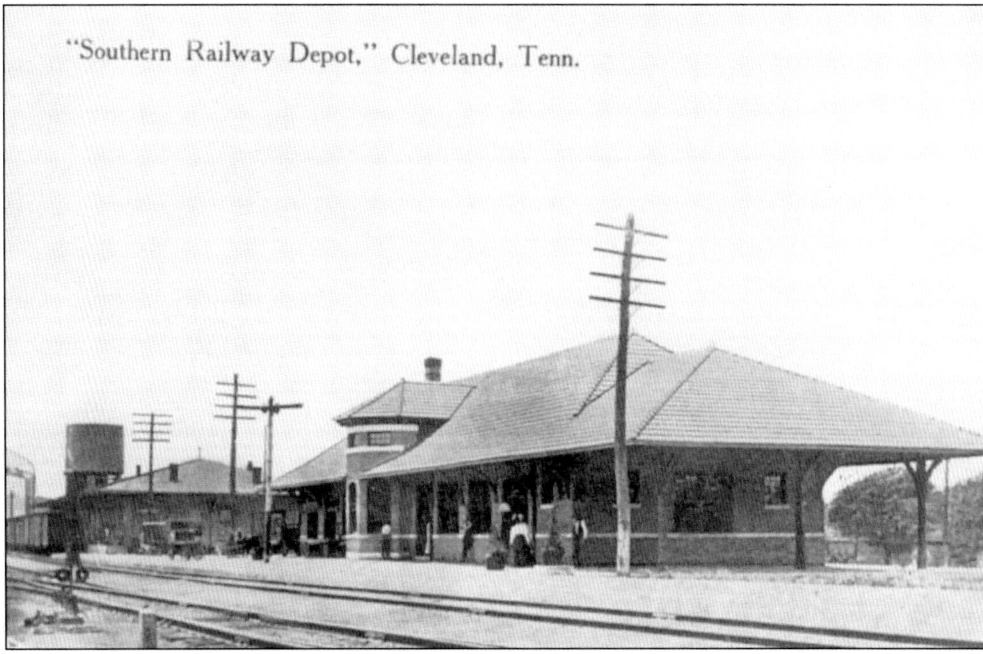

The Southern Railway Depot was very active until the 1970s. The building on the left was used during the Civil War to house prisoners awaiting rail transportation. In more recent years, it became the offices of the Cleveland Plywood Company.

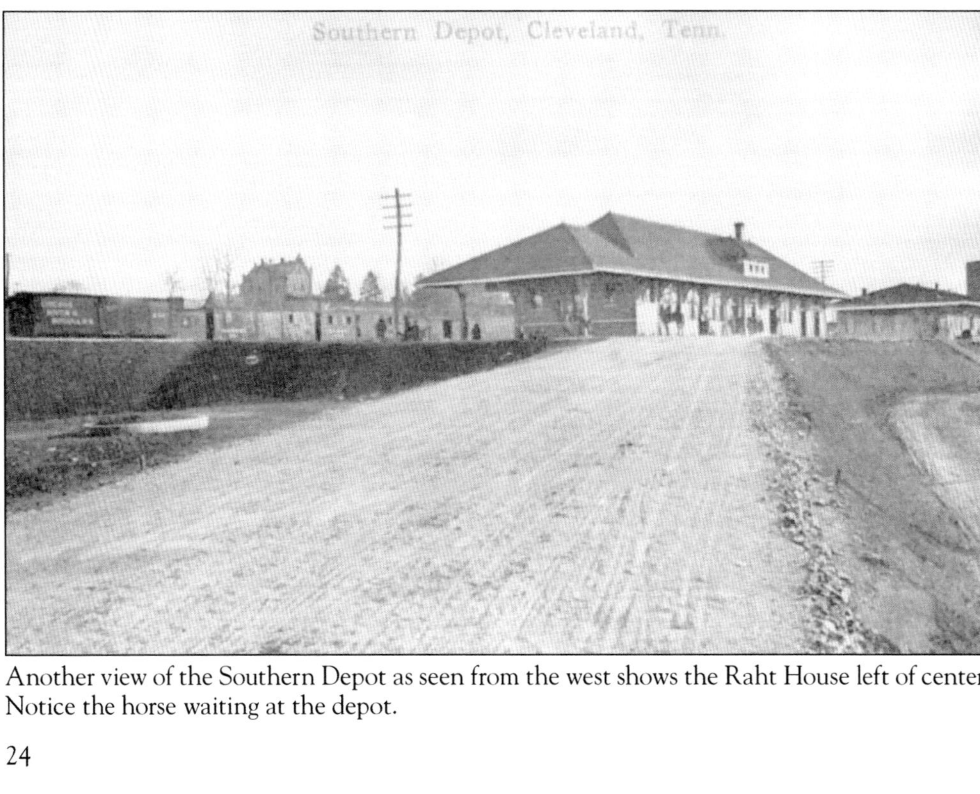

Another view of the Southern Depot as seen from the west shows the Raht House left of center. Notice the horse waiting at the depot.

Two

RESIDENCES

The people of Bradley County have always offered a cordial welcome to all moral, honest and industrious people seeking homes and a place for investments. The healthfulness of the locality, the salubrity of the climate, the beauty of the scenery, and the hospitality of the people make the section one of the most desirable places in which to build a home that can be found in the South. The church and school privileges are not excelled anywhere, and there is a ready and convenient market for all the products of the farm.

—Theodore L. Rogers (1859–1950)
Real estate agent and Cleveland city booster

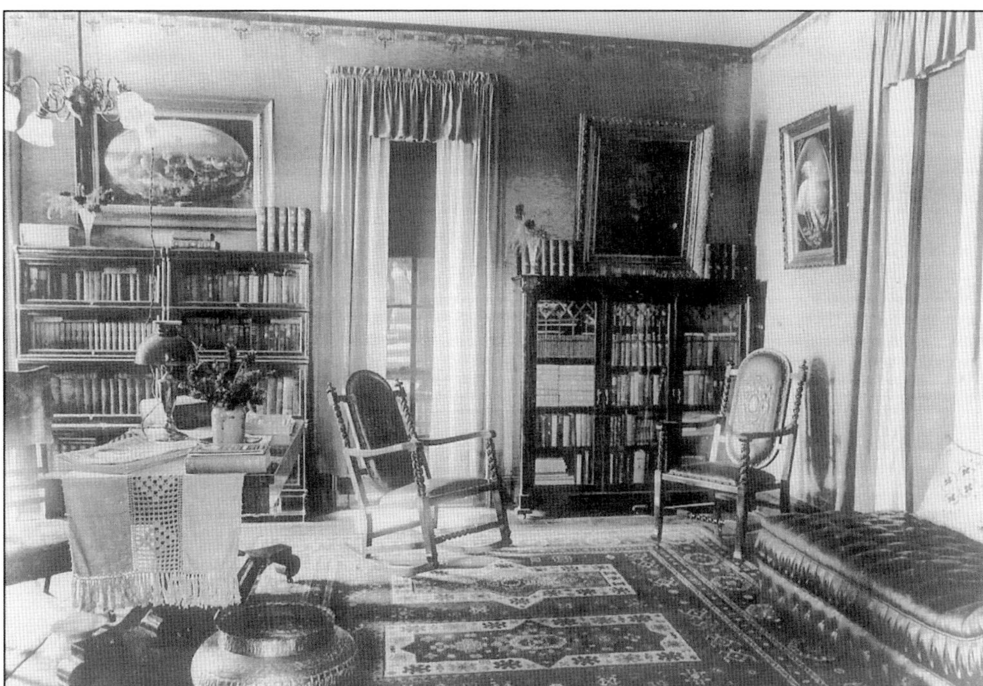

The library was an important room in the Victorian home. Here is an example of one of Cleveland's finest.

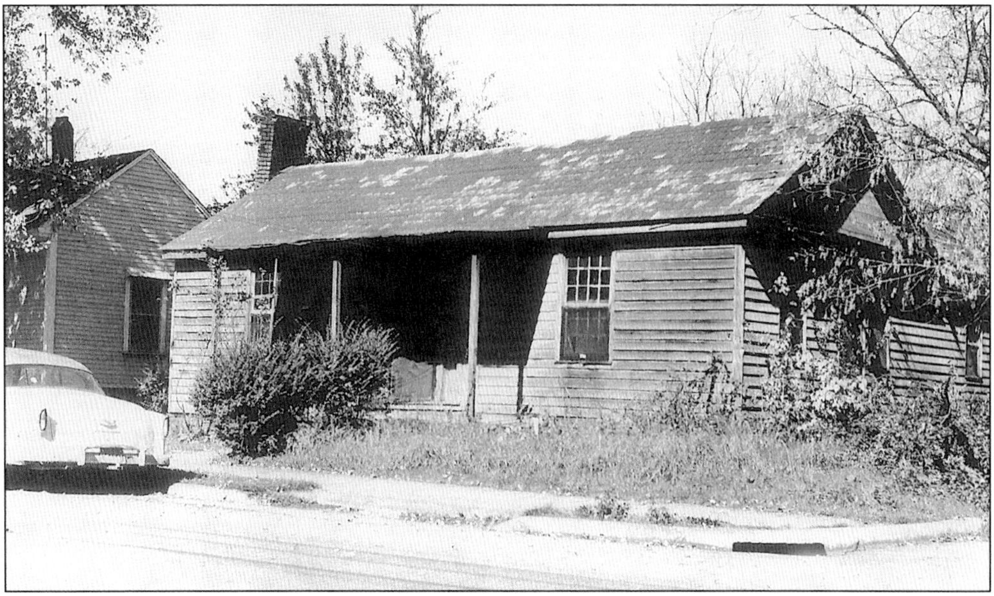

The Hall House, built in 1838, was located on the corner of Second and Spring Street Northwest. Mazie Steed Nevin was born in this house on October 10, 1881. It was demolished in 1959 for a parking lot.

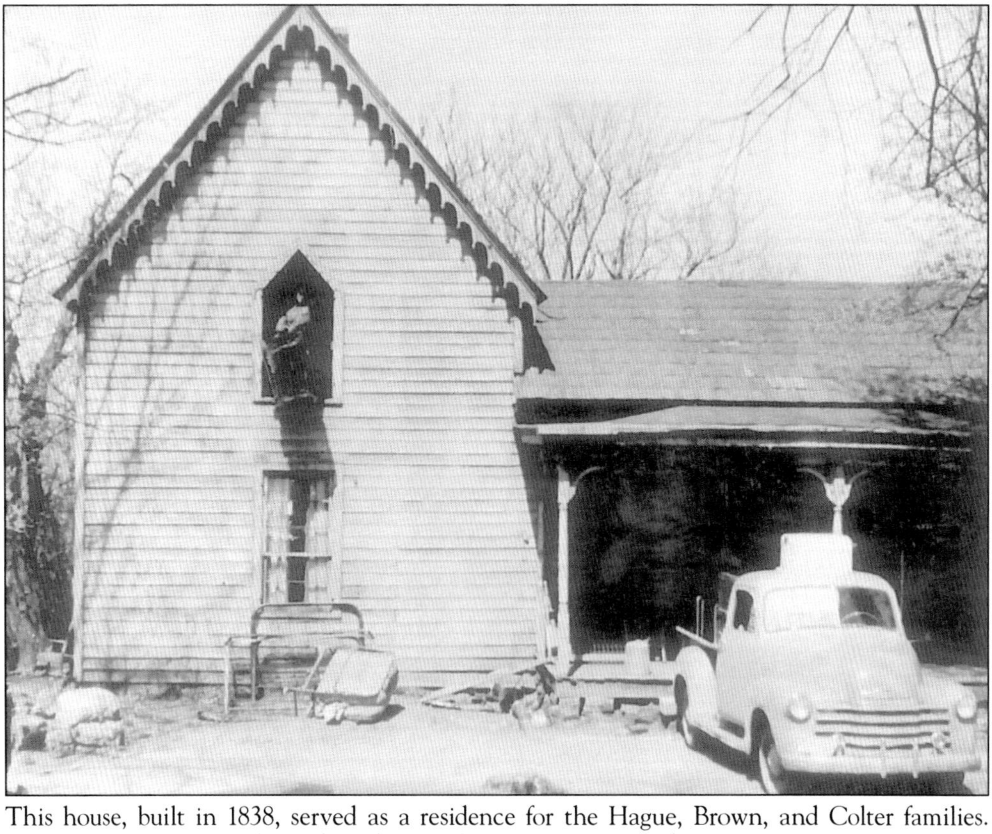

This house, built in 1838, served as a residence for the Hague, Brown, and Colter families. Located on the corner of Worth and Second Street, it was torn down in 1955.

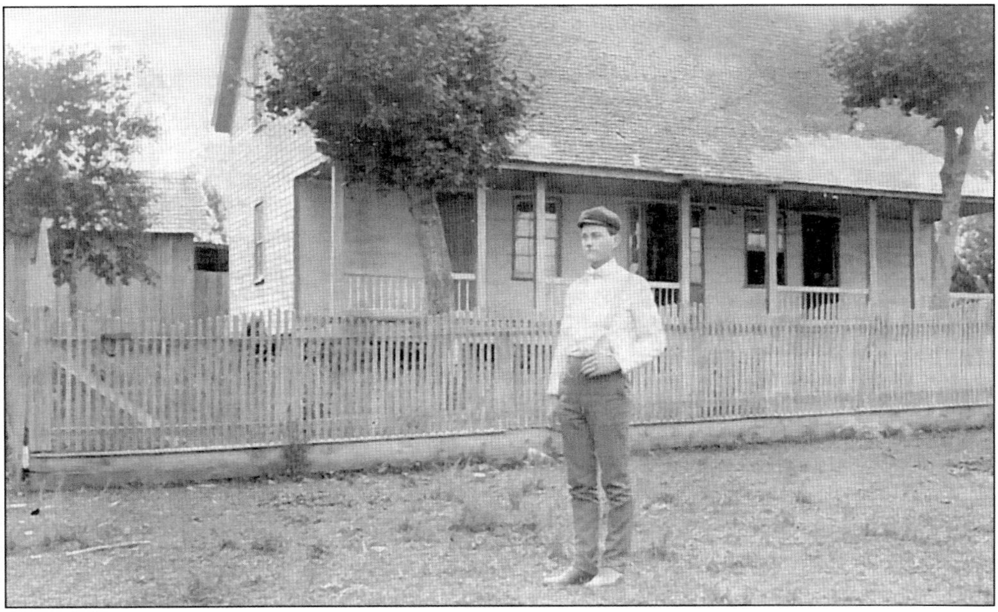

Most of the early homes in Cleveland were of wood construction. Here Frank Simmons is seen in front of a typical home.

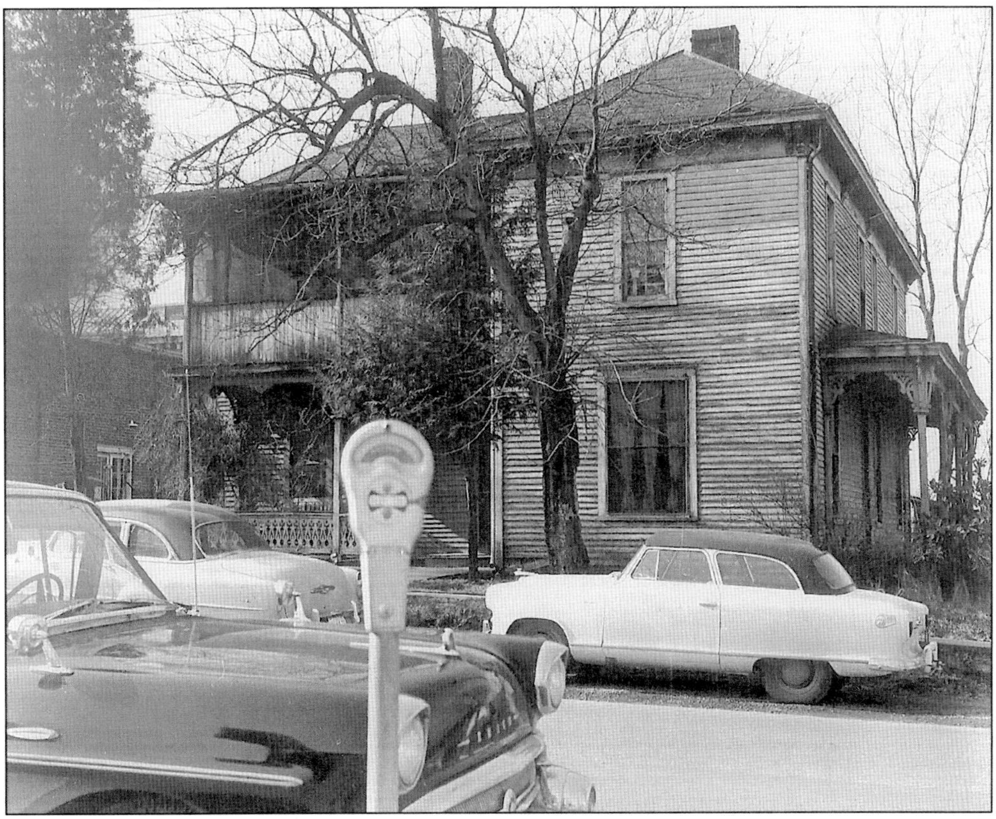

The Lucy Cate Boarding House was located at Worth and Second Street Northwest. This photograph was taken on March 16, 1958.

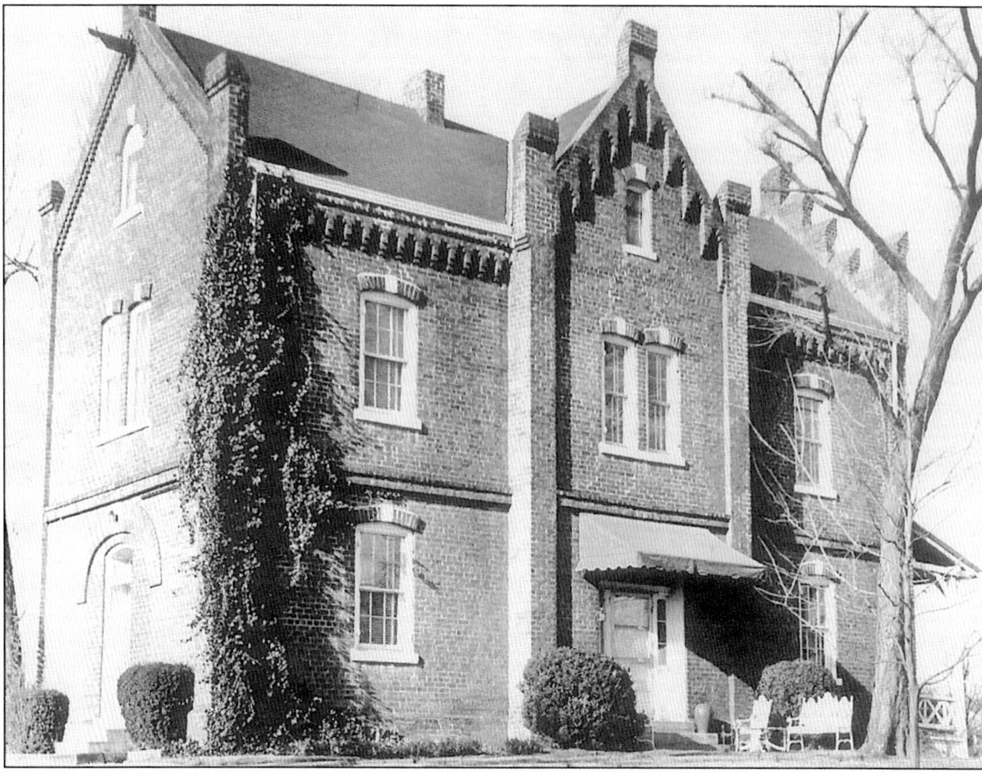

In 1861, Thomas H. Callaway constructed this house, fronting on the Southern Railroad, east of the track and depot. J. E. Raht bought it in 1861. It served Raht as his home and office while he directed the operations of the Ducktown Copper Company. Notice the hook at the roof line on the left side of the building used for hoisting supplies in and out of the building. Legend has it that during the Civil War a tunnel from this house ran west to the railroad station and was used to hide Confederate soldiers and supplies.

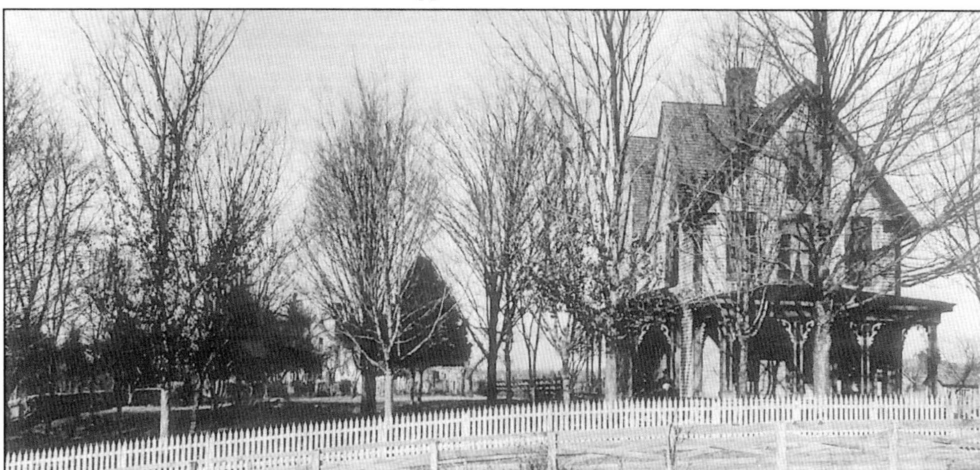

This home, located above Wildwood Avenue, just off Inman Street, was purchased by A.J. White from J.E. Raht. The house was later razed by H.E. Haggard and replaced with a brick residence.

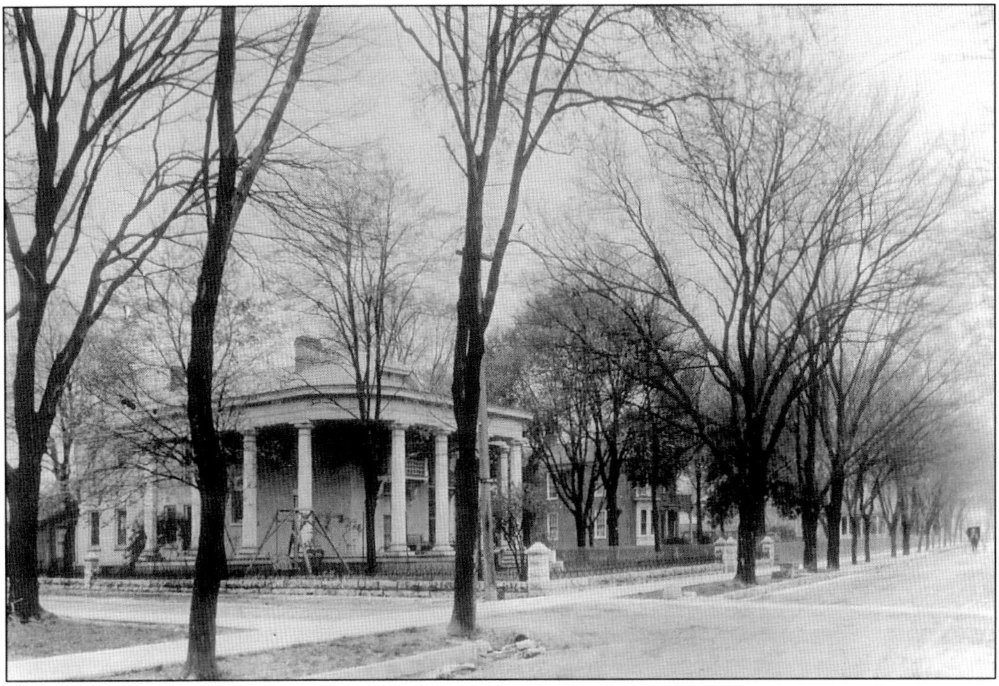

The Jarnigan House was built in 1883 by Col. J.H. Hardwick, founder of the Hardwick Stove Company. Originally a wooden frame house, it was later bricked, with great columns and other classical details added, resulting in a stately brick structure of the late Georgian architectural style. In 1940 the Jarnigan family remodeled extensively. In August 1987 this historic structure became home to the Cleveland Public Library. Notice on the right side at the street edge is an "upping block" used by Victorian ladies to enter their carriage.

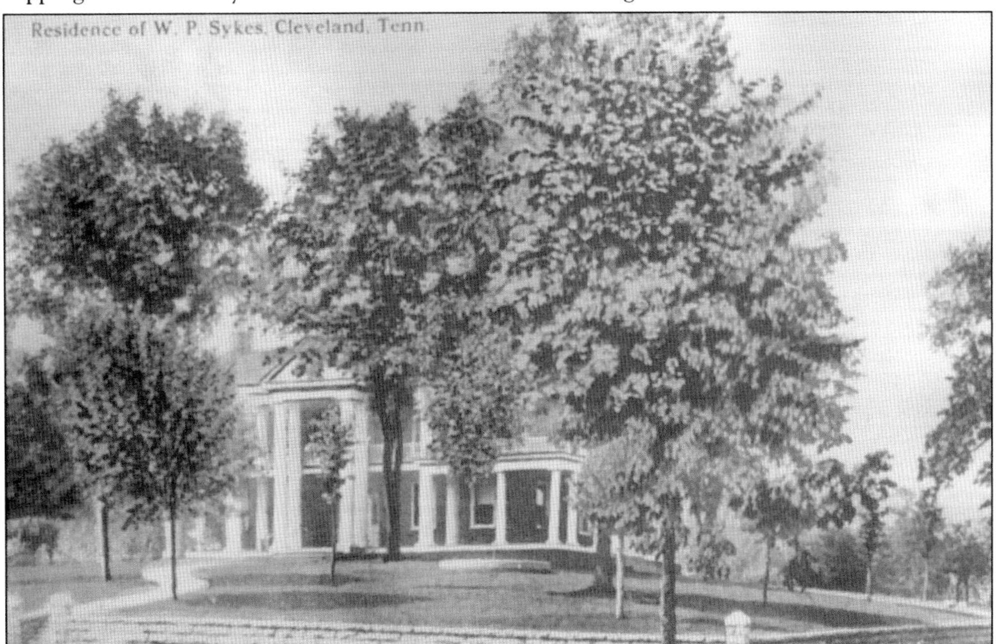

This is a postcard of the stately mansion of W.P. Sykes, owner of the Sykes Milling Company.

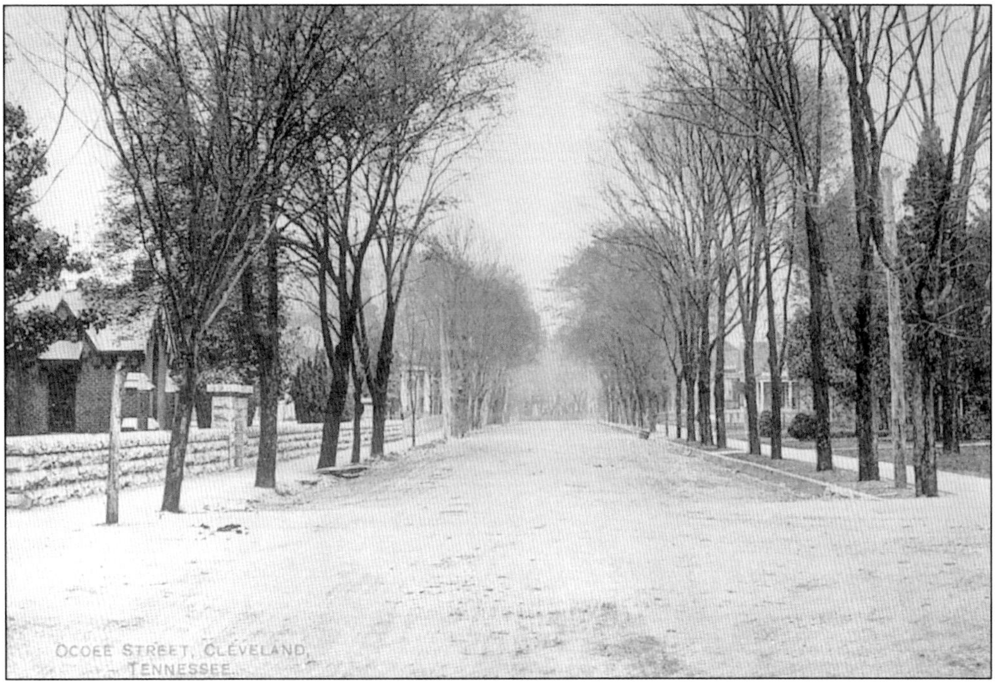

Cleveland became well known for its beautiful tree-lined streets and stately homes. Shown here is North Ocoee Street, one of the main north/south thoroughfares.

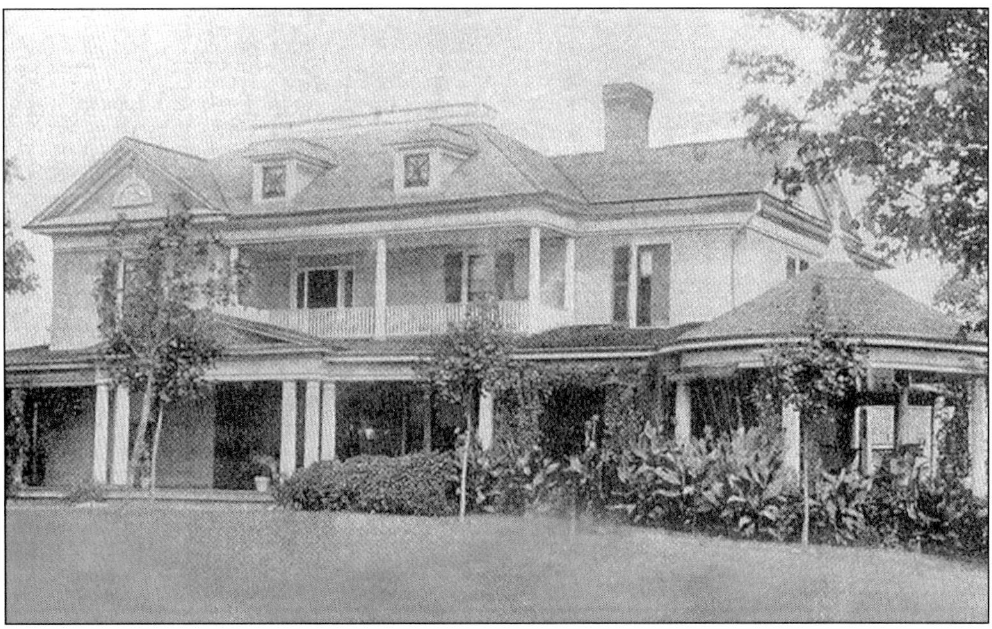

Located on Seventeenth Street, this was the residence of the well-known Methodist evangelist George R. Stuart. In June 1904, Stuart's daughter Mary invited her sorority, Zeta Tau Alpha, to hold its second national convention in her home. The spacious home was described by one of the members attending as follows: "It was the ideal home for the fraternity house party, with its wide, cool halls, broad verandas, and smooth, sloping lawns, made even more fair by the gold of those perfect June days." Faith Memorial Church was built on this site in 1959.

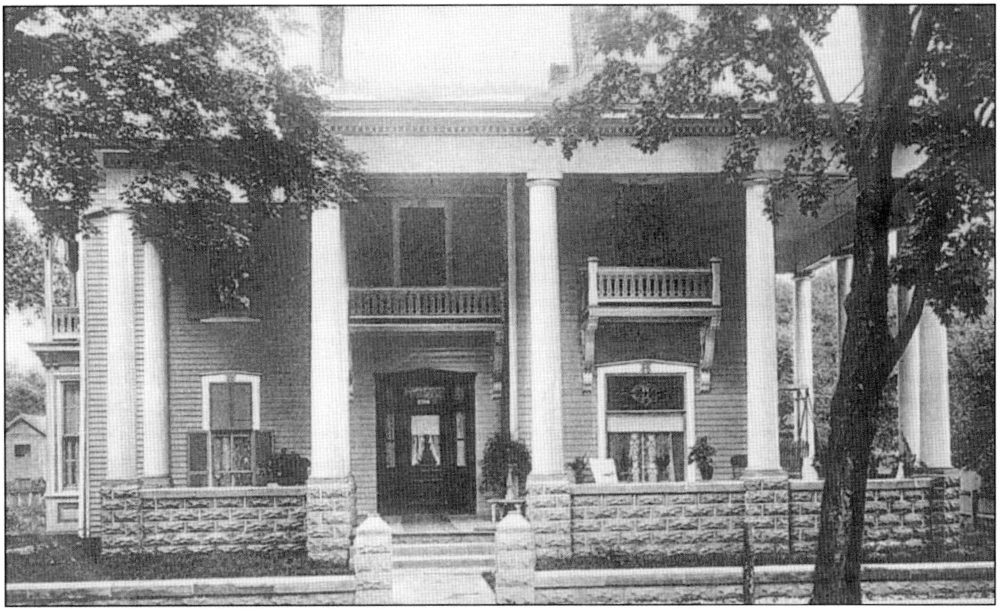

This was the residence of J.J. Harrison at 2709 Ocoee Street.

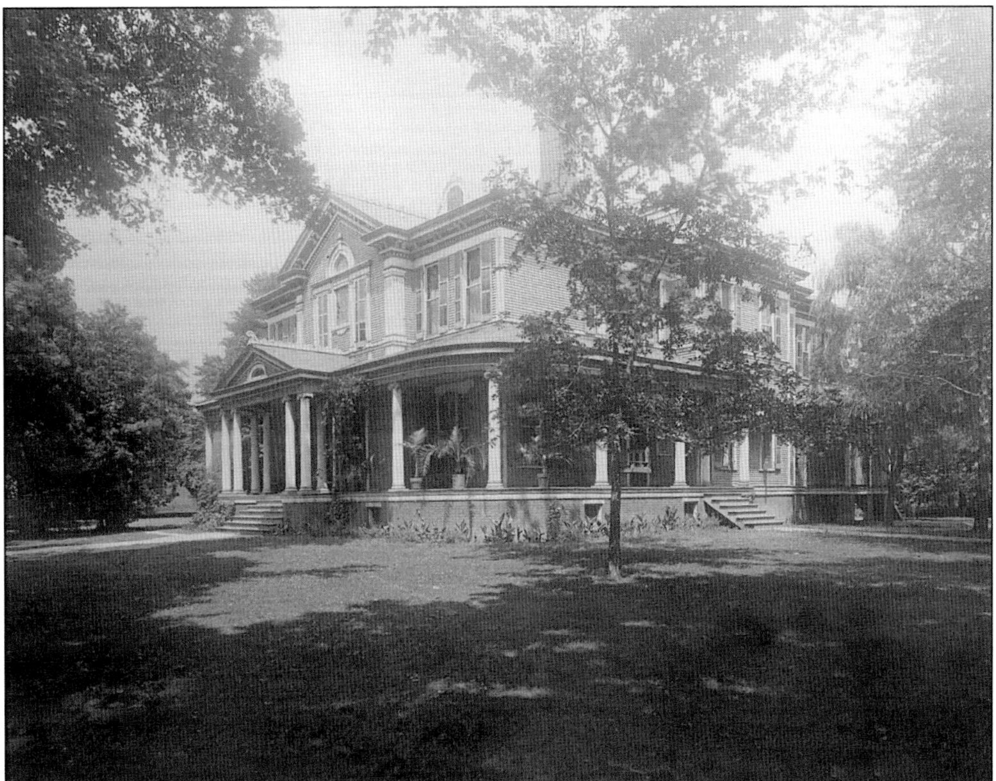

John H. Craigmiles built this 14-room house about 1900. Adelia Craigmiles sold the home to George L. Hardwick Sr. in 1904. The stately home had ionic columns and a wrap-around porch. At one time this building was the Prater Motel. It was razed in 1947.

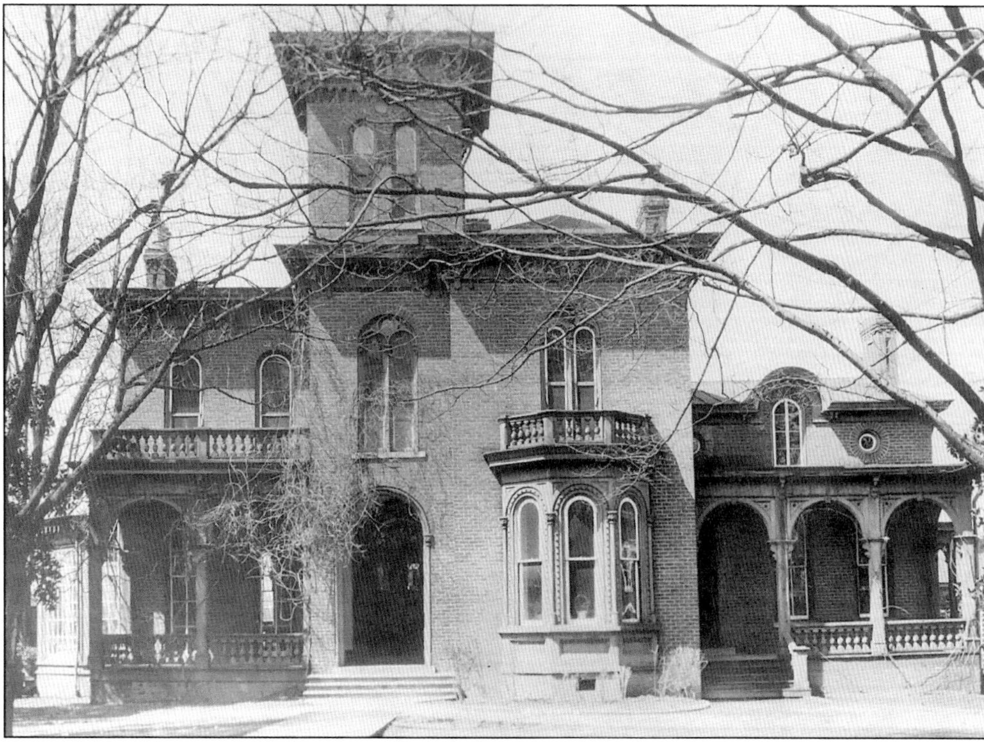

Pleasant Craigmiles built this home for his family in 1866. It was modeled on the Italianate architectural style of the mid-1800s with a flat roof, tall windows, and a highly symmetrical design. In 1923, Sarah Tucker's family donated the residence to the city of Cleveland, along with 4,000 books, for use as the community's first public library. Today it serves as the history branch of the library. In 1975, the Craigmiles Home was placed on the National Register of Historic Places.

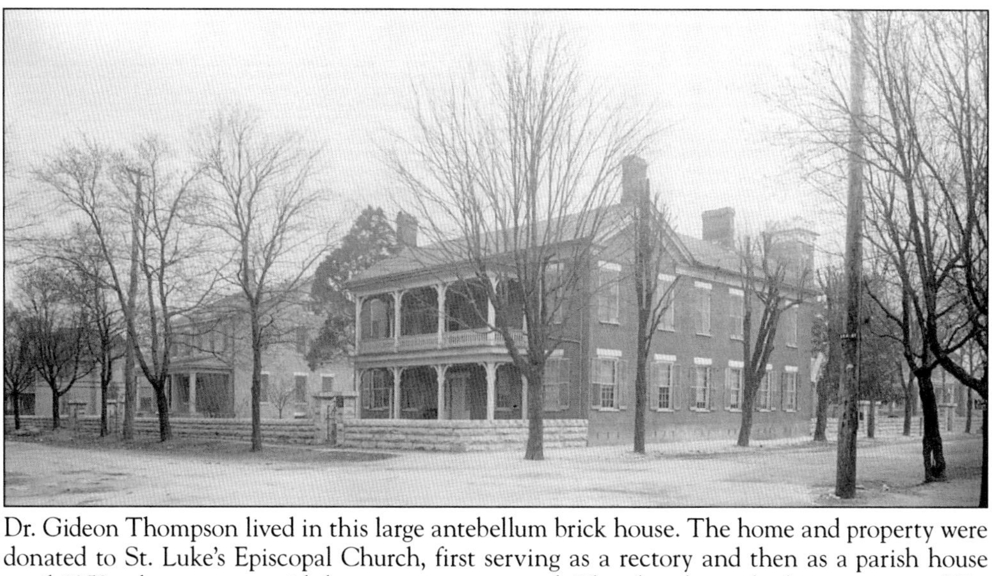

Dr. Gideon Thompson lived in this large antebellum brick house. The home and property were donated to St. Luke's Episcopal Church, first serving as a rectory and then as a parish house until 1958, when a new parish house was constructed. The church was built in memory of Dr. Thompson's granddaughter, Nina Craigmiles.

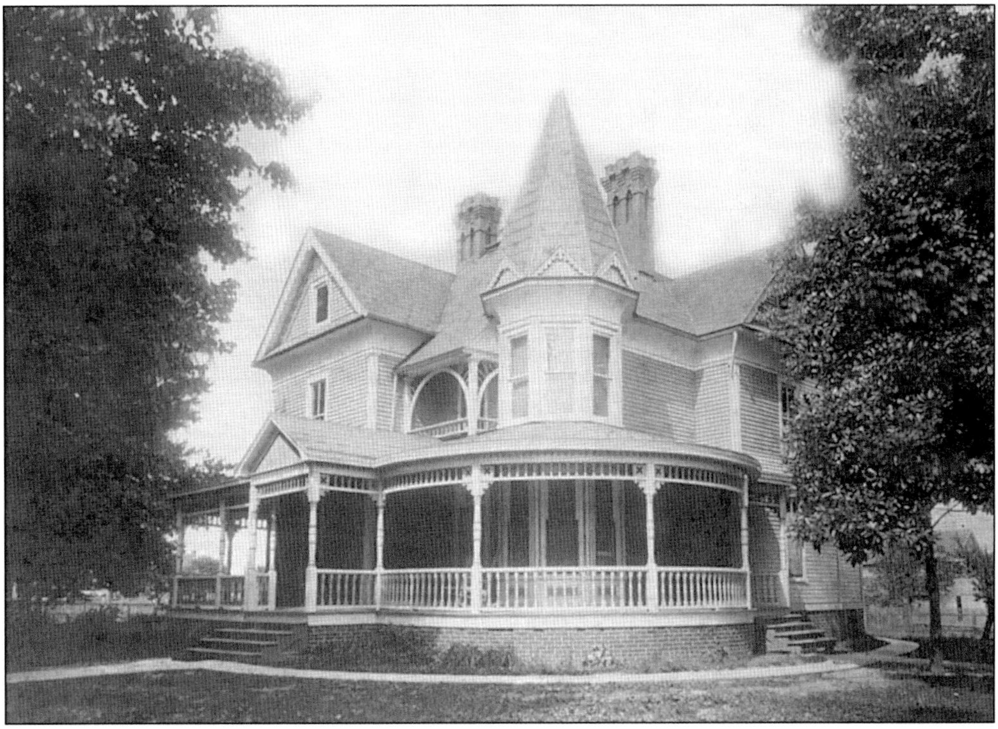

This residence on Ocoee Street was built in 1876. Over the years it has been owned by George Hardwick, Adelia Craigmiles, J.M. Ewings, Ella M. Jones, E.H. Bartlett, M.V. Jones, Mattie Moore, B.H. Williams, and Dr. Keith Mills.

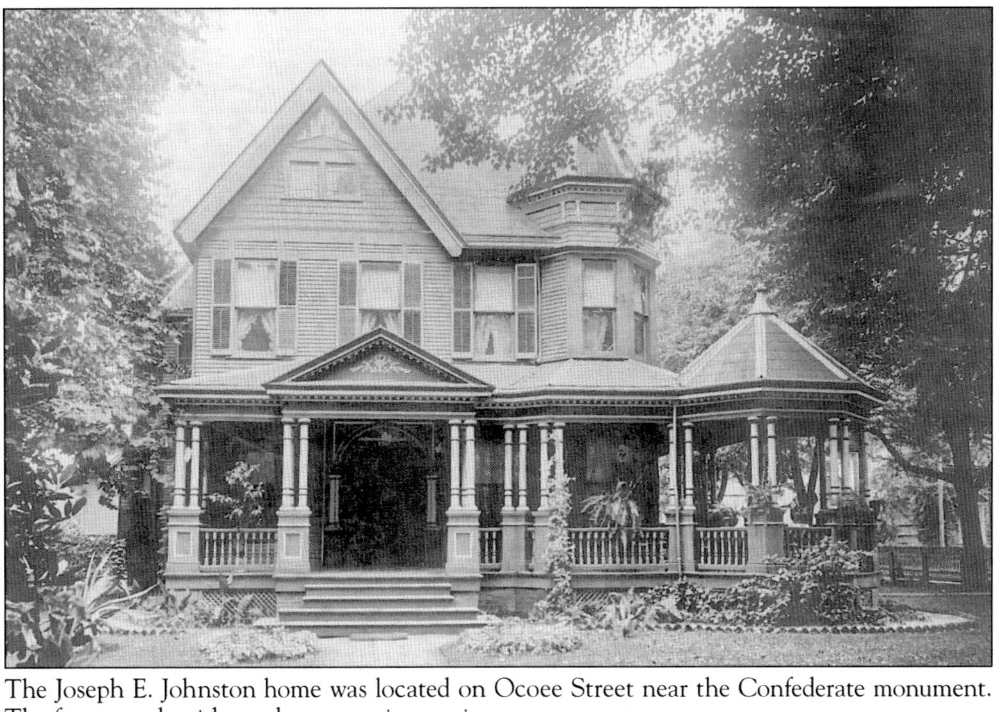

The Joseph E. Johnston home was located on Ocoee Street near the Confederate monument. The front porch with gazebo was an impressive arrangement.

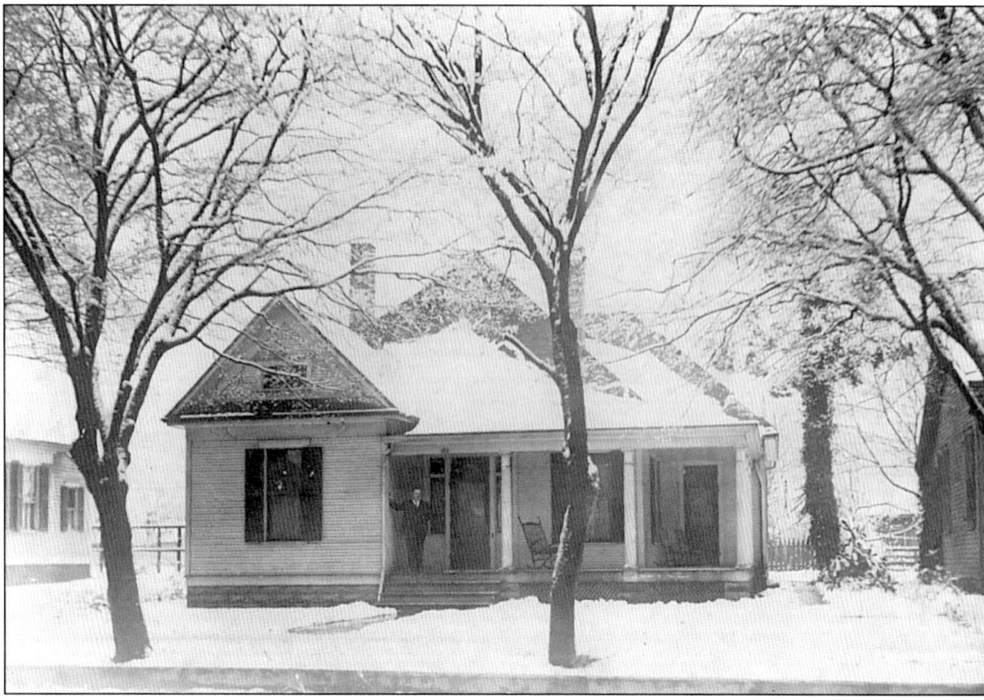

Seen here on January 3, 1914, the W.A. Lillard cottage was located on Ocoee Street.

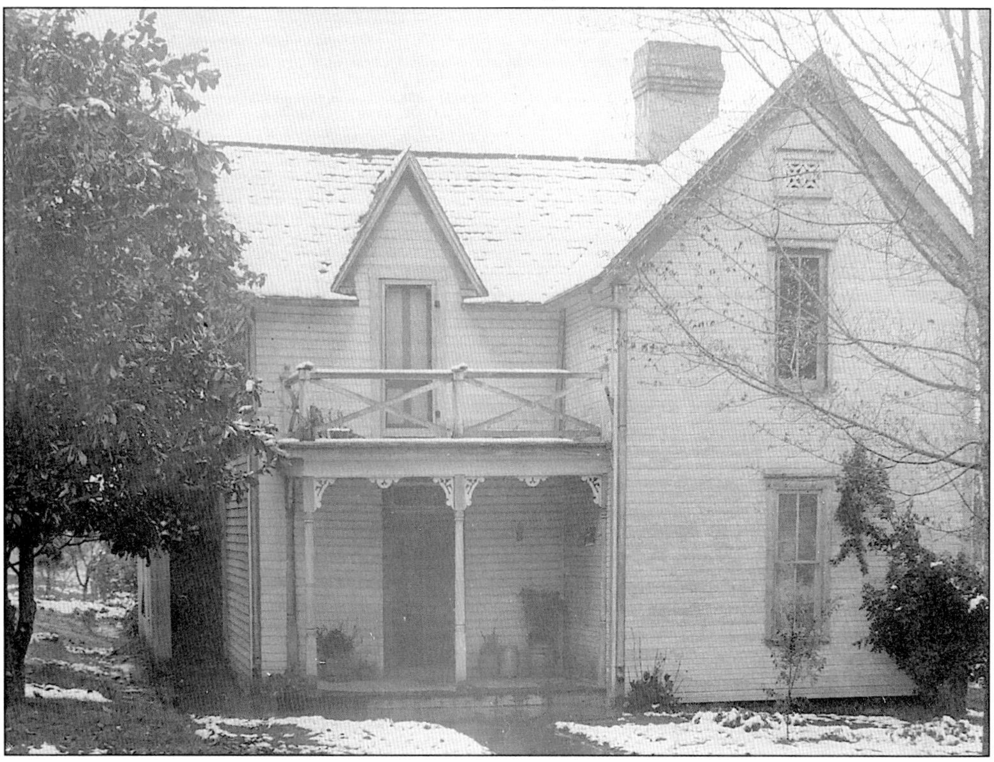

The A.J. Tomlinson house was located at 851 Gaut Street. This residence served as both home and office of the General Overseer of the Church of God.

Three

BUSINESSES

It is an active business place, and contains the county building, four churches, one Masonic Female Institute, one Masonic Lodge, one weekly newspaper . . . one bank . . . [and] about twenty stores of various kinds, one steam flouring and one saw mill, with diversified trades and professions.

—John L. Mitchell, 1860–62
Tennessee State Gazetteer and Business Directory (p. 42)

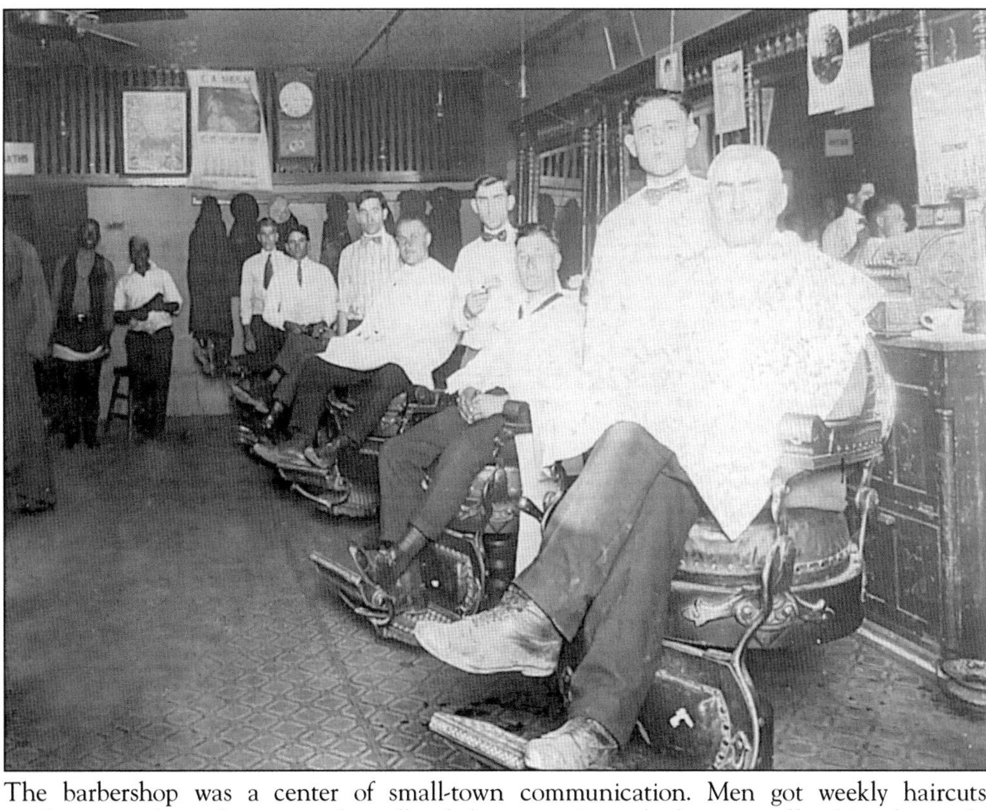

The barbershop was a center of small-town communication. Men got weekly haircuts, or shaves, and caught up on the talk of the town. Even baths were offered in this early-1900s photograph.

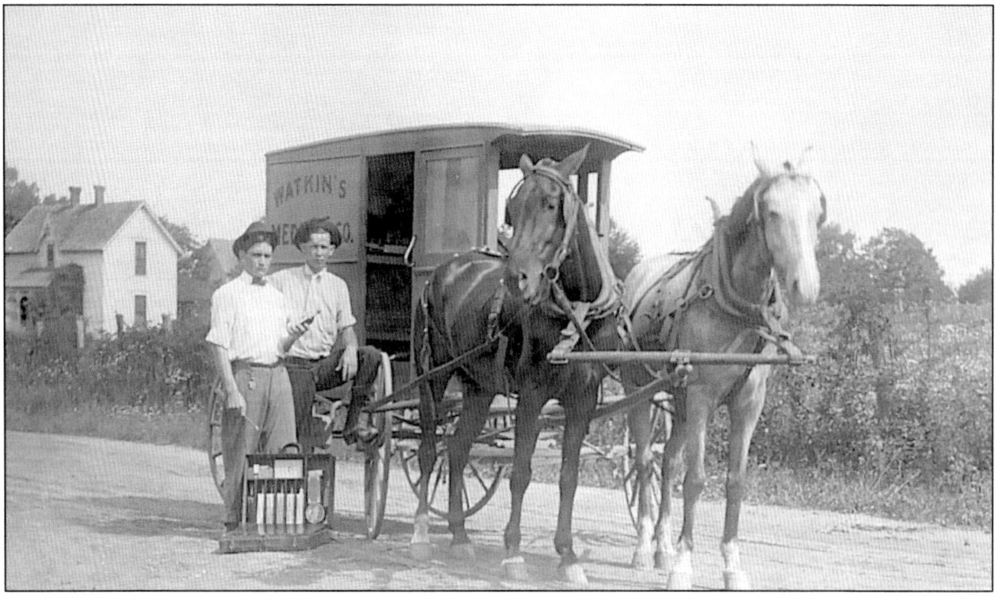

The Watkins Medicine Company used horses and wagons to deliver their products to homes in Cleveland. Victor McKamy Pirkle is standing on right.

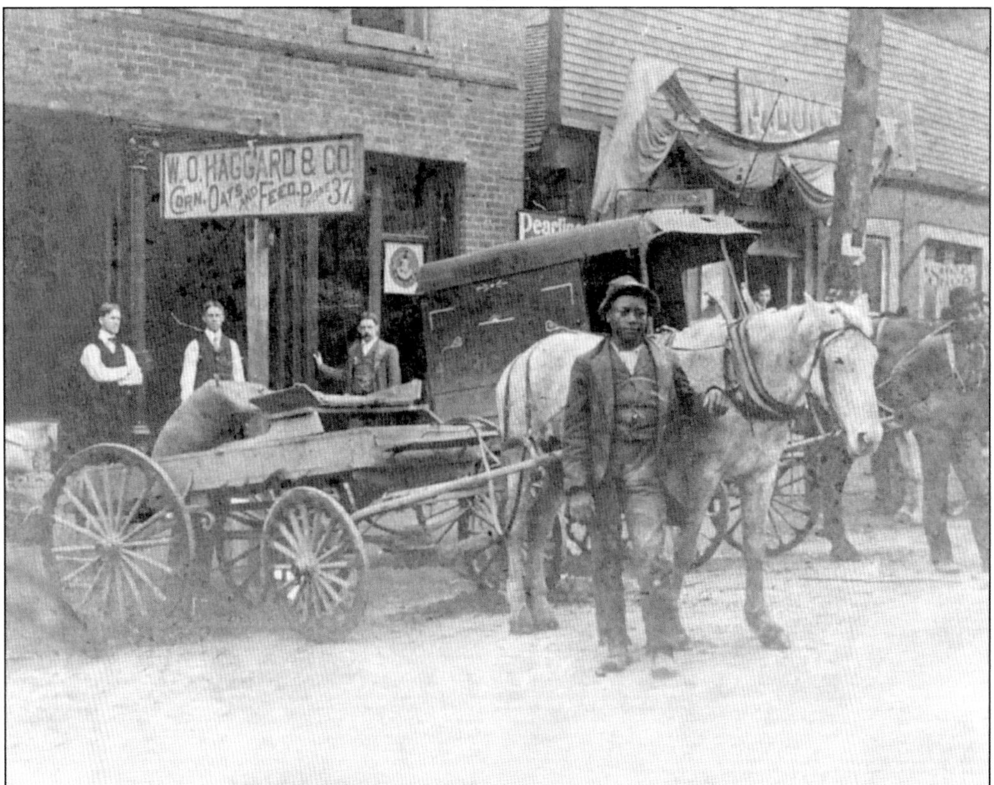

W.O. Haggard & Co. started in the grocery business in January 1892. The store supplied corn, oats, and feed, being in the wholesale as well as the retail business. Notice their phone number had only two digits—37.

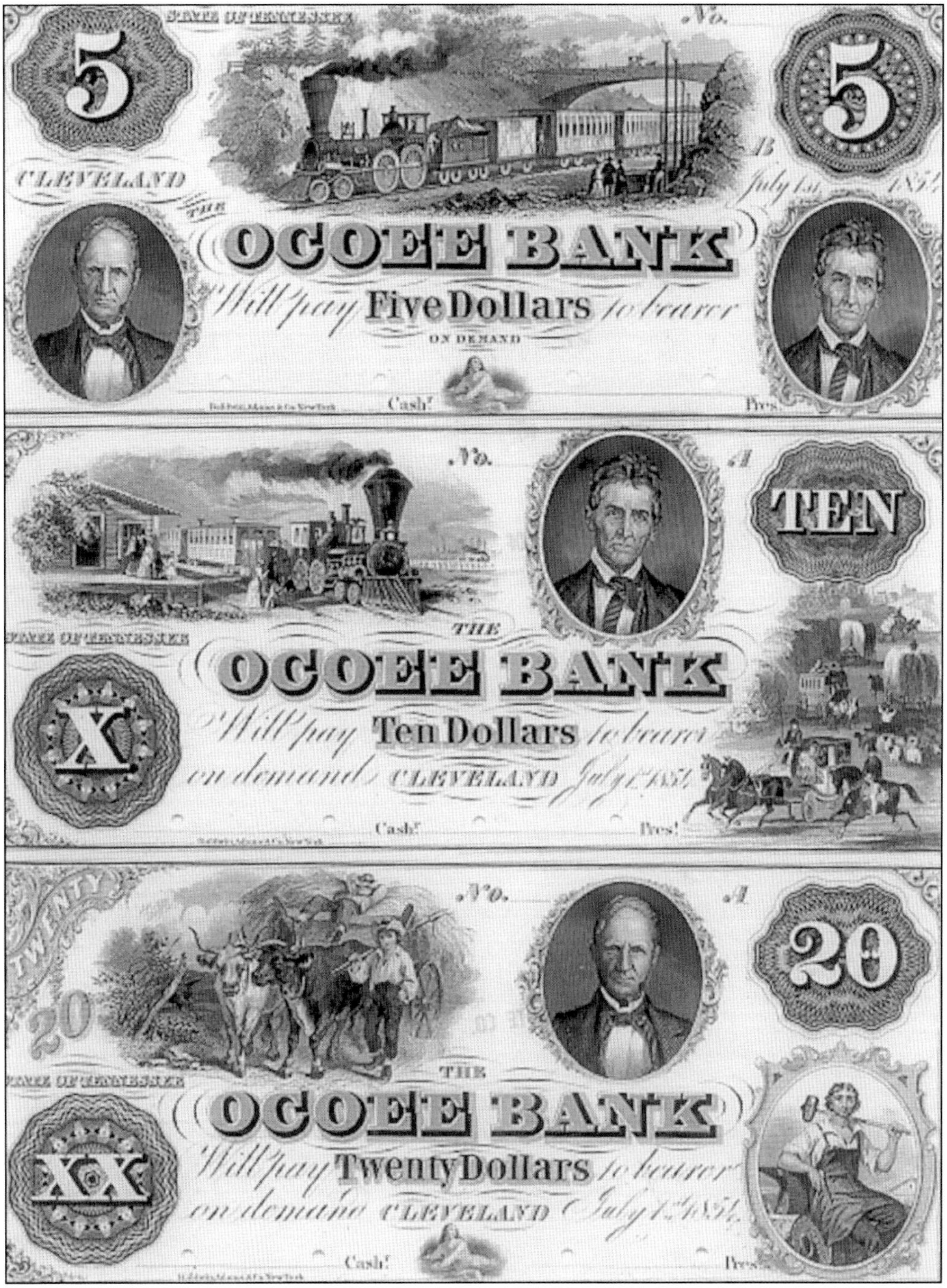

The first bank in Cleveland was the Ocoee Bank, chartered in 1854 and in business through the Civil War. Thomas H. Calloway and Euclid Waterhouse were the owners of the Ocoee Bank. Thomas J. Campbell was the cashier. The bank was located in the southeast room of the Ocoee House, on the west side of Ocoee Street between Inman Street and First Street Northwest.

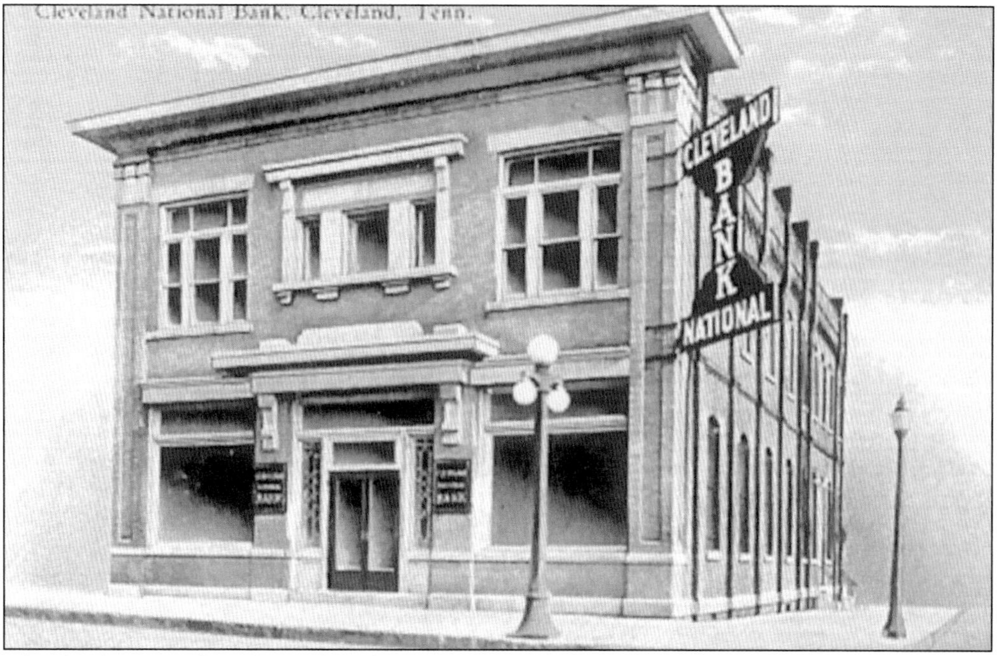

Cleveland National Bank was founded on December 26, 1866, after the War between the States left Cleveland without a bank. Julius E. Raht, D.C. McMillan, and several other businessmen pooled $100,000 and secured the charter. The first president was W.B. Reynolds, 1866–1877.

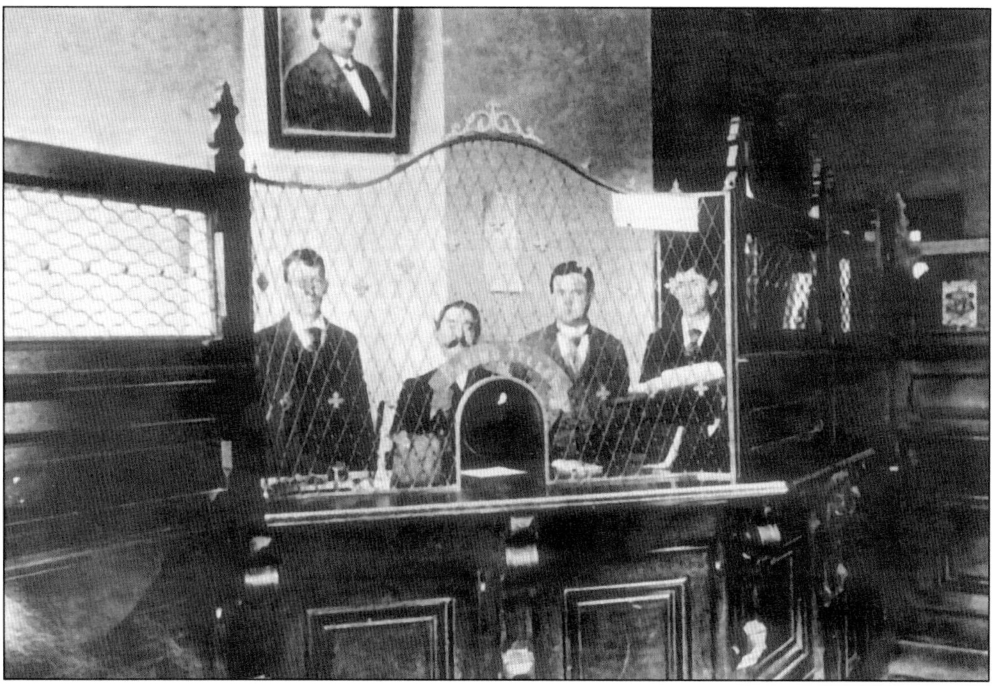

Pictured is the staff of the Cleveland National Bank in 1895; from left to right are W.P. Lang, J.H. Craigmiles, J.E. Johnston, and F.J. Harle. The picture on the wall is of J.E. Raht, second president of Cleveland National Bank.

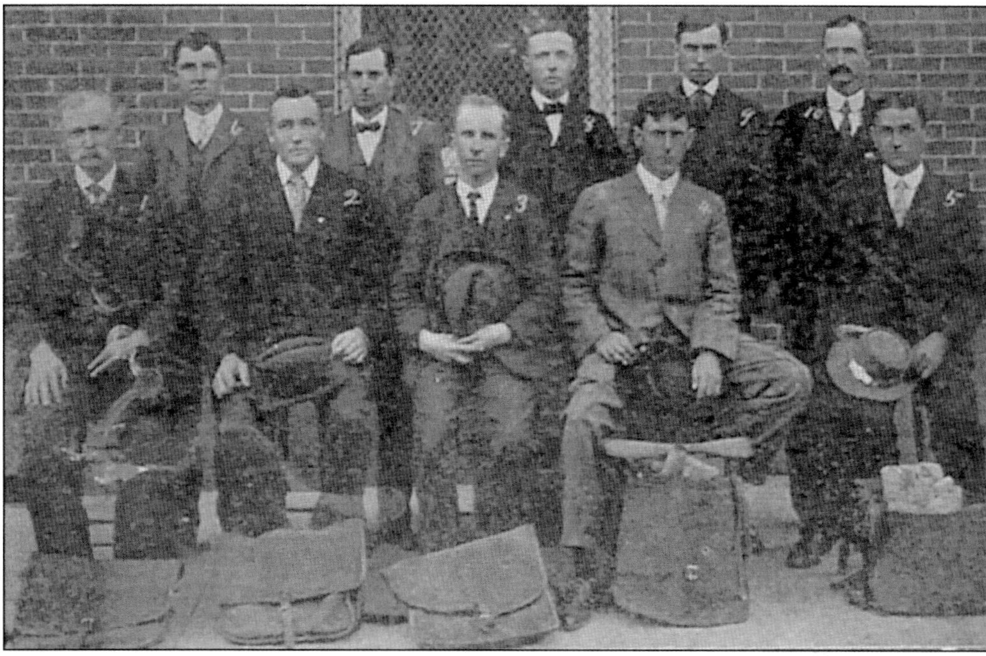

Bradley County mail carriers are shown in this real photo postcard. From left to right are I.C. Wooten, Carl Grigsby, Arthur Vest, Fred Simbro, Jerre Chambers, Frank Lawson, Myers Chittenden, Z. Butcher, Walter Lawson, and Sam E. Lee.

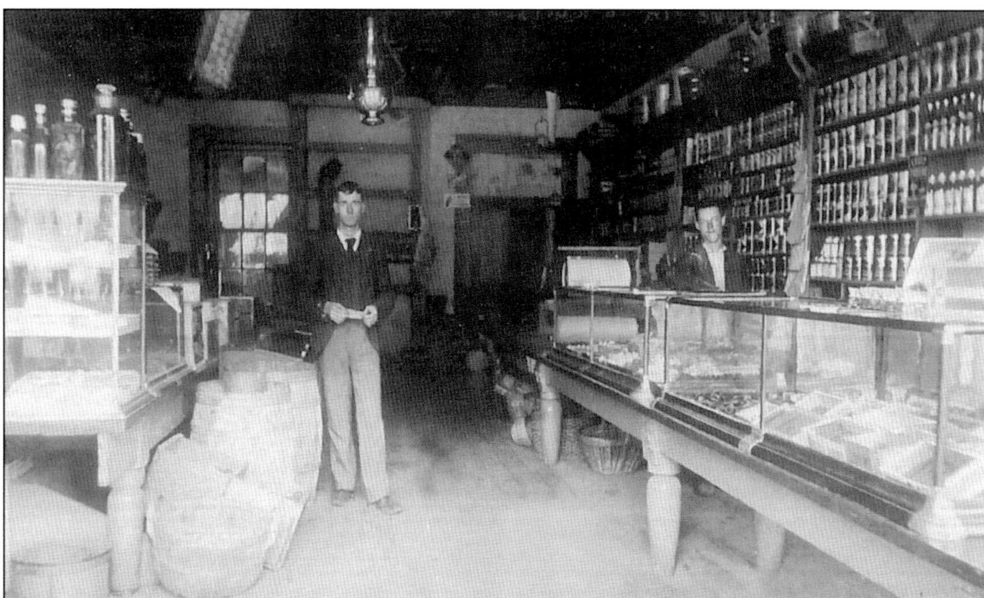

Bob Russell and Luke Hancock are shown in 1888 at Charley Neals' grocery store, considered the largest grocery store in Cleveland at that time. The store was in the northwest corner of the Ocoee House.

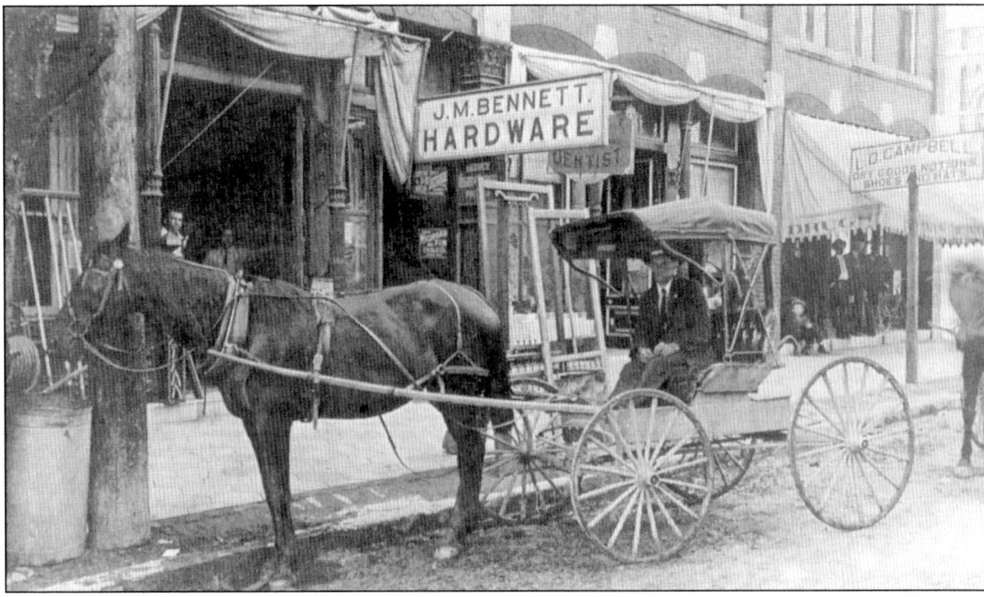

J.M. Bennett Hardware was on Ocoee Street on the east side of the square. Rural mail carrier Myers Chittenden is shown in his horse and buggy.

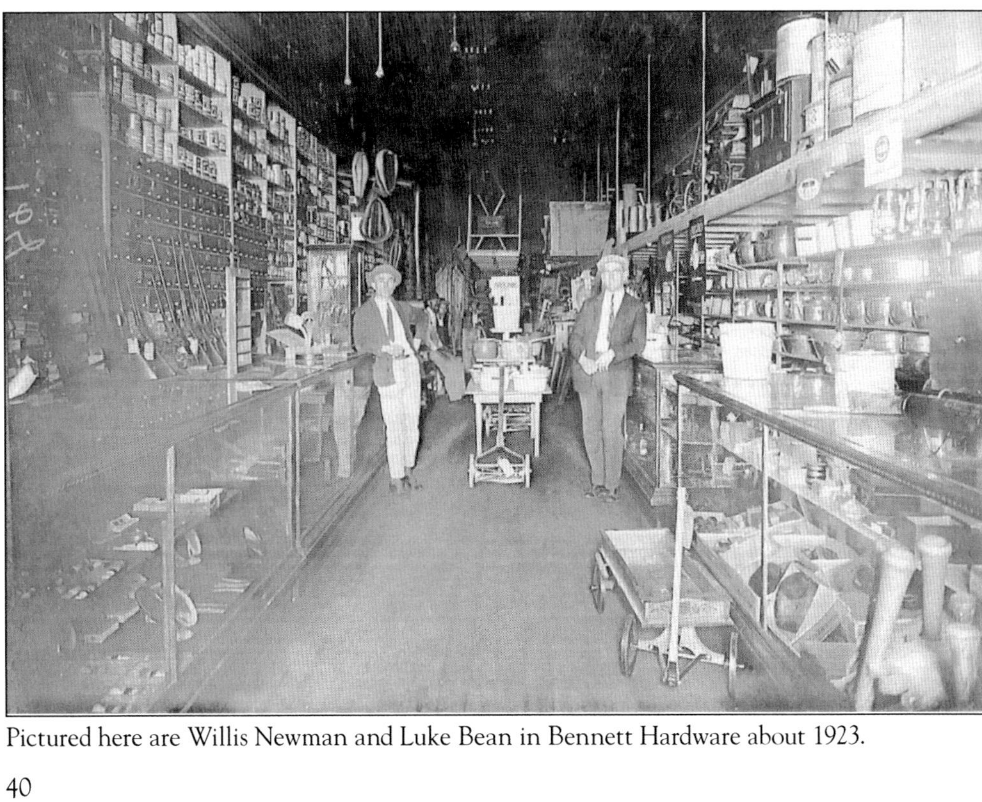

Pictured here are Willis Newman and Luke Bean in Bennett Hardware about 1923.

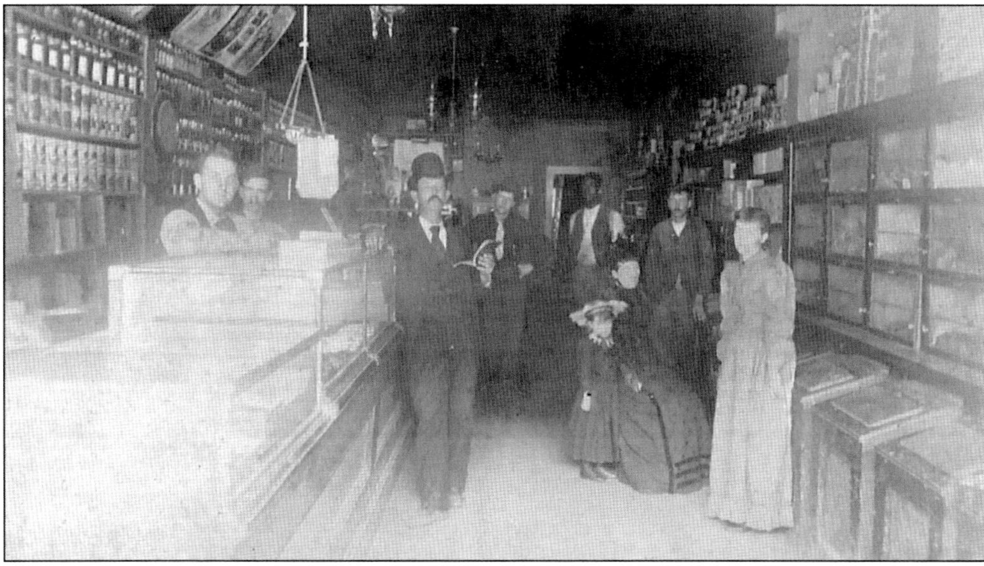

An advertisement in 1916 for George Hain Grocer states, "When you are in need of sweet, sour and mixed Pickles, Olives, Raisins, Figs, Dates, Apples, Oranges, Bananas, Peanut Butter, Swiss & Cream Cheese. I am also agent for Littlefield & Steere's fine candies which I receive weekly. I am also agent for George K. Brown & Co.'s ice cream. I can have it moulded in all kinds of figures. Ask for prices when you have banquets and entertainments." George Hain Sr. is in the center wearing a hat. George Hain Jr. is the first person on the left behind the counter.

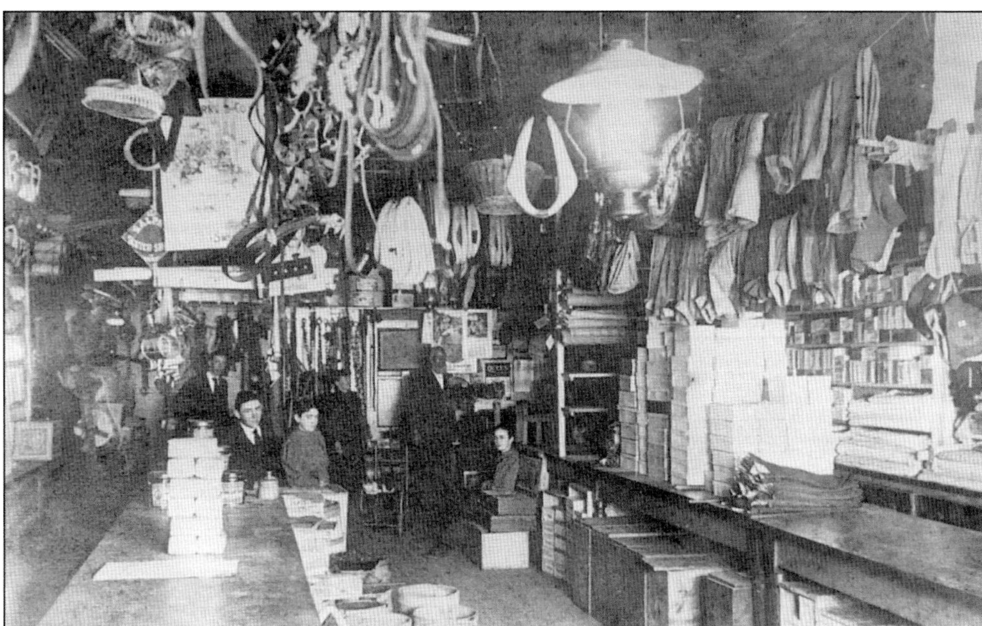

This scene is of the interior of the original store of J.H. Harle & Brothers, built in 1866. Frank J. Harle is the third person from the left, with Mary Sheddan next to him.

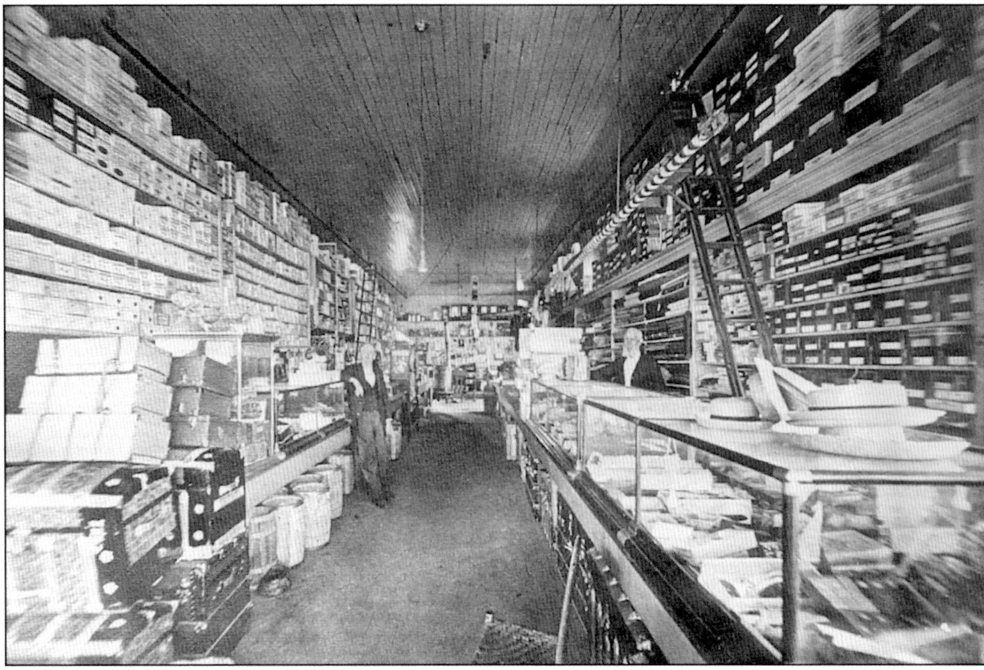

This is the interior of J.H. Harle & Bros. store rebuilt in 1905–1906, after a fire in November 1905 destroyed the original store constructed in 1866.

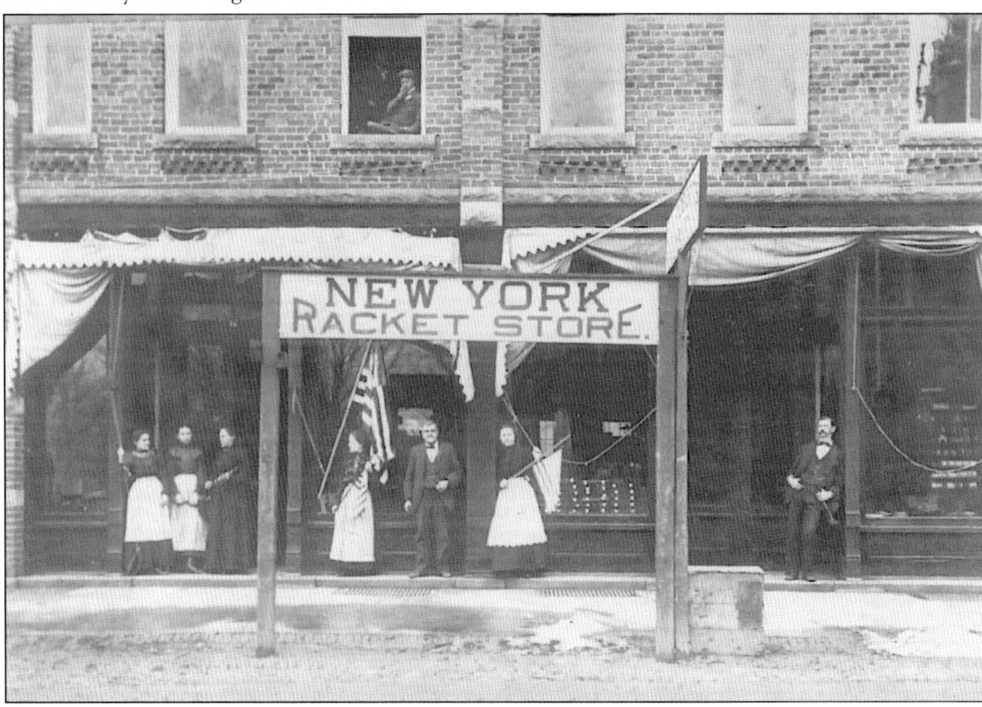

The "Racket Store," owned and operated by J.S. Roberts, was located on the north side of the courthouse square. According to legend, when darkness came, instead of lighting the kerosene lamps in the store, the owner closed the store and went home. This gave the store the name "Daylight Store."

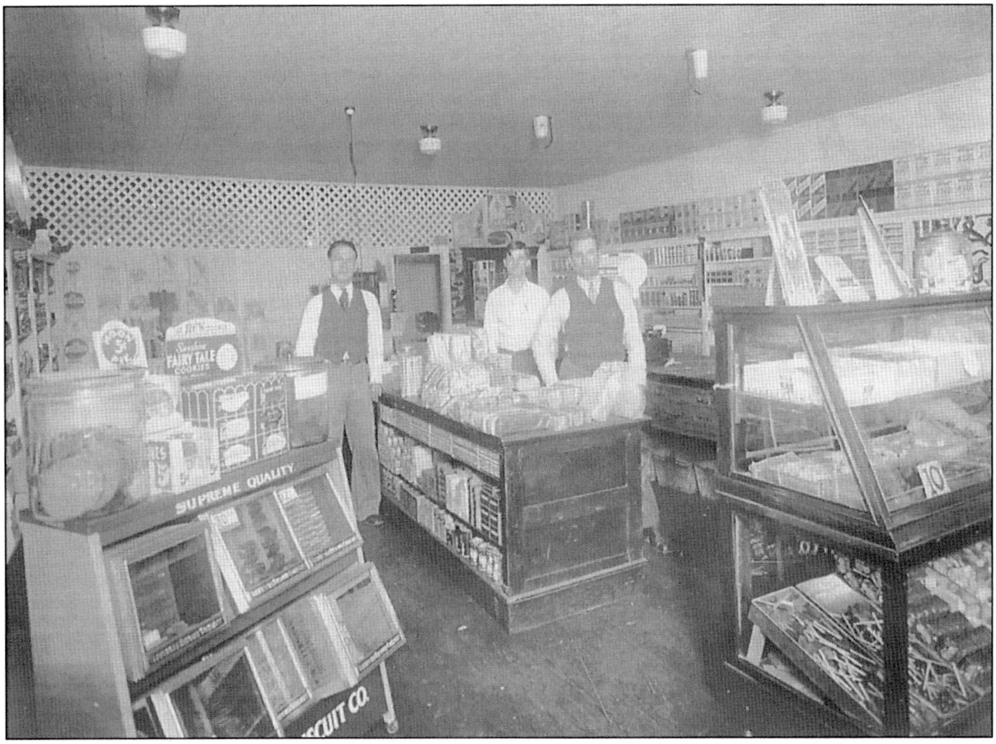

This grocery store is neat as a pin! Notice the Moon Pies, which sold for a nickel.

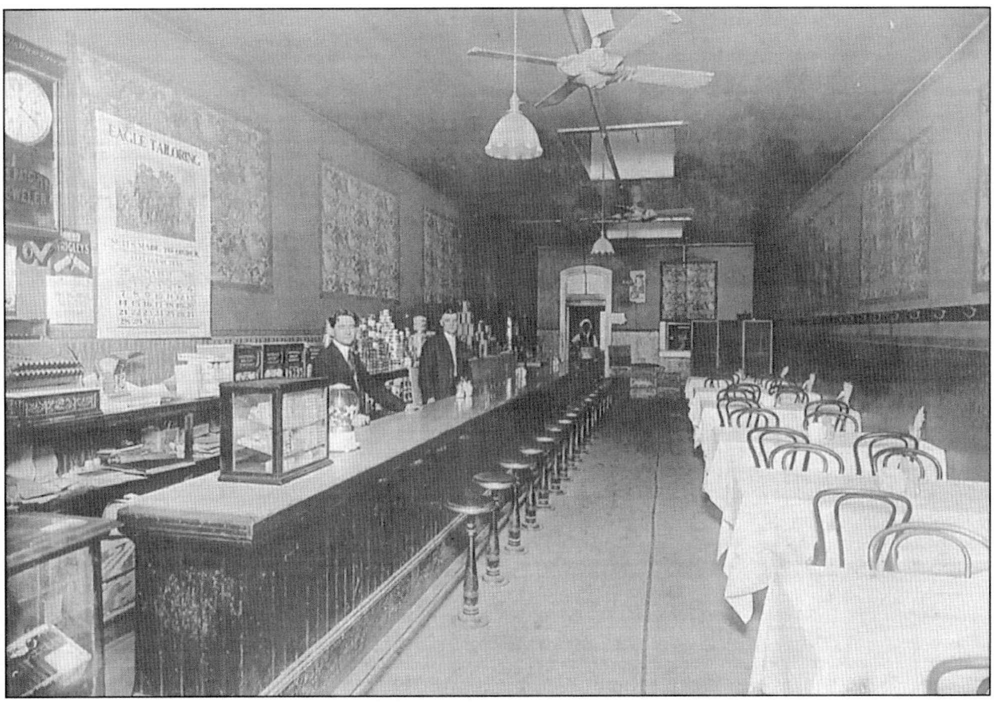

This restaurant has a calendar showing the month of March 1920. Typical for its day, diners were served at the counter or tables.

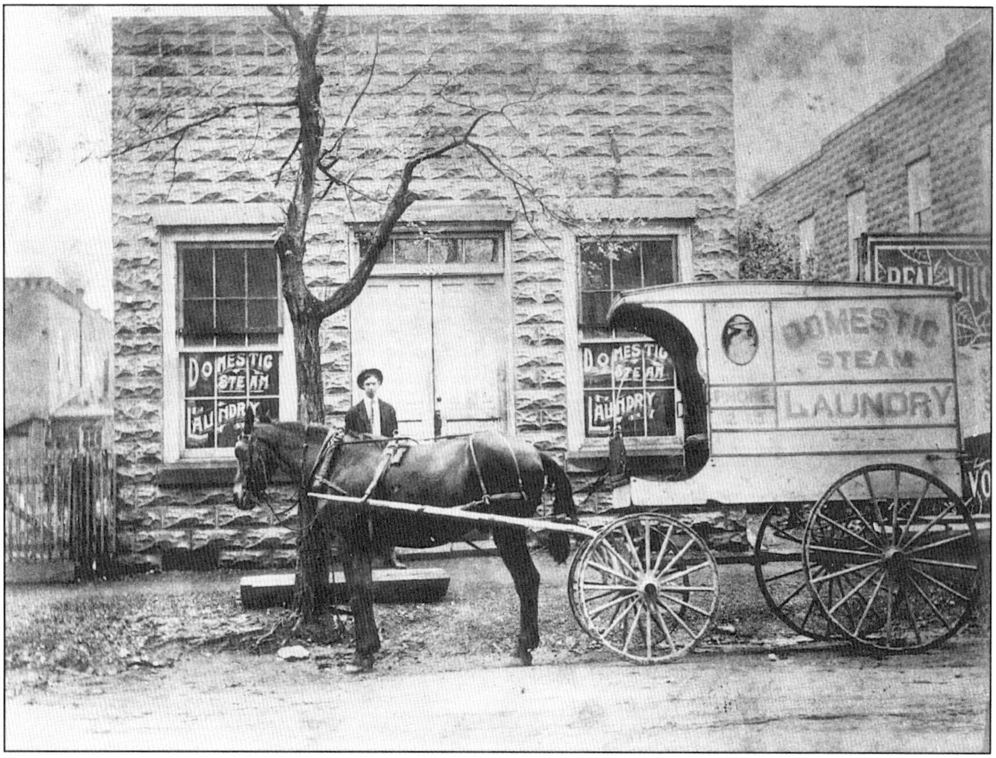

Cleveland's first laundry, Domestic Steam Laundry, owned by John Dethero, picked up and sent the clothing by rail to Chattanooga to be processed. Sam Ward is shown behind "Tip," the horse, on March 10, 1909. In 1913, the Tarpley brothers, H.F. Sr. and Charles, opened the first dry-cleaning plant in Cleveland. The building was north of and adjacent to the building formerly occupied by Domestic Laundry.

ABEL HARDWARE CO. "Established 1916"

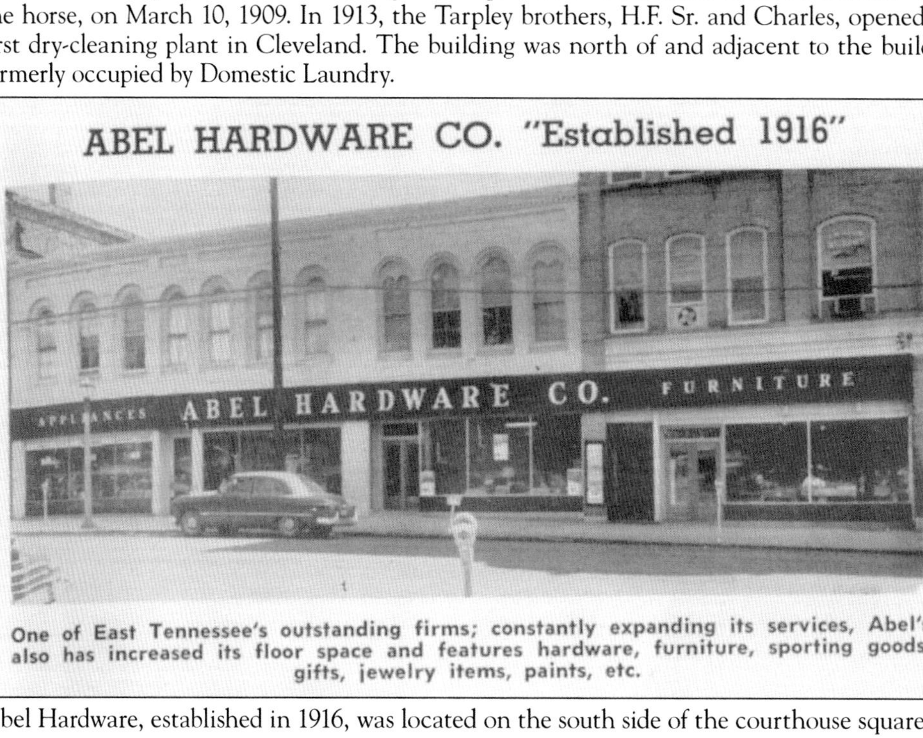

One of East Tennessee's outstanding firms; constantly expanding its services, Abel's also has increased its floor space and features hardware, furniture, sporting goods, gifts, jewelry items, paints, etc.

Abel Hardware, established in 1916, was located on the south side of the courthouse square.

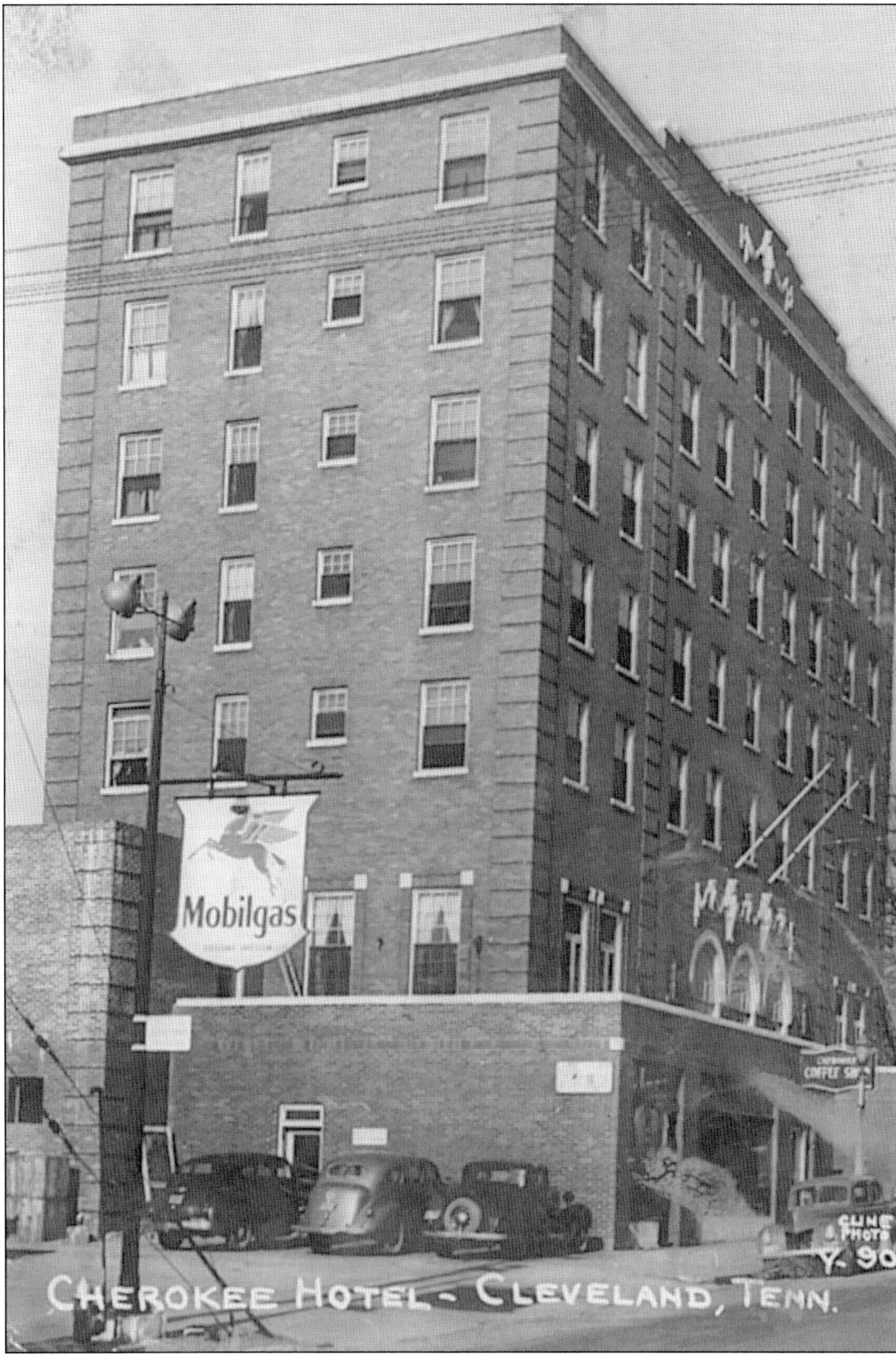

This postcard shows the Cherokee Hotel, the tallest building in Cleveland. At the groundbreaking in 1927, Rev. George W. Coleman shoveled the first spade of dirt.

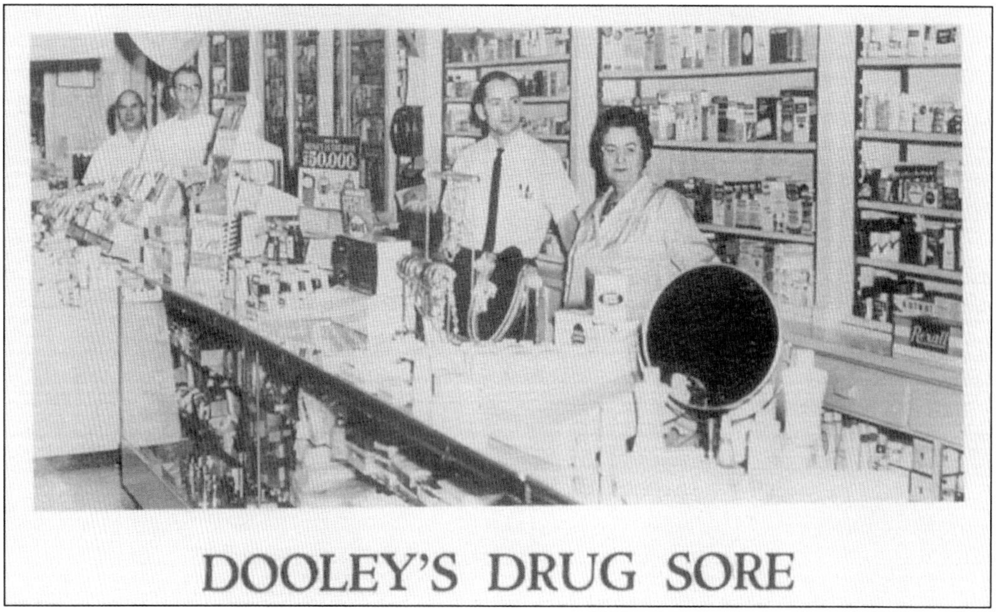

Dooley's Drug Store, formerly the Lusk Drugstore, was located in the Masonic Building. Bob Johnson is the person third from the left.

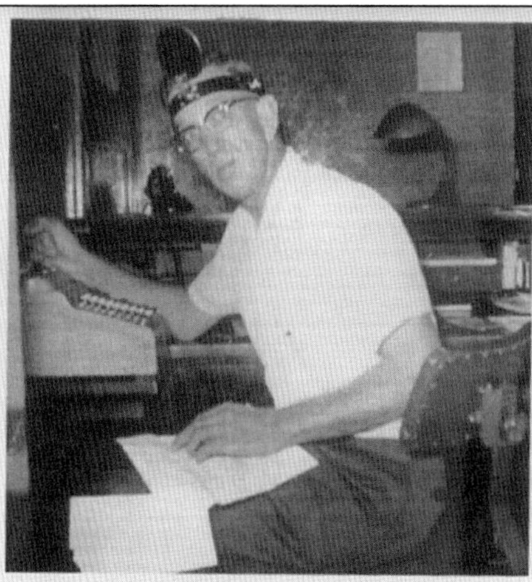

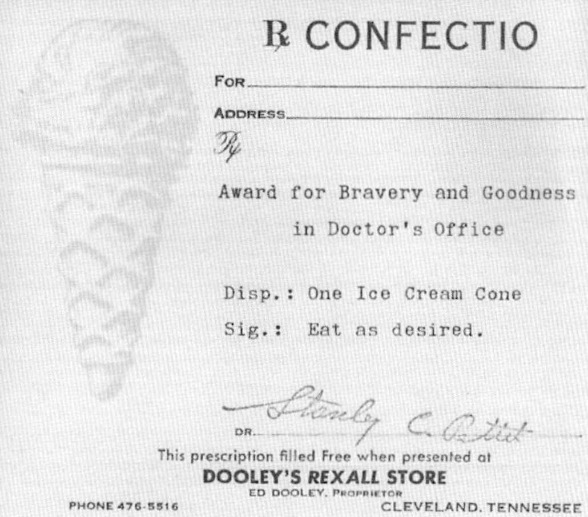

℞ CONFECTIO

FOR ____

ADDRESS ____

℞

Award for Bravery and Goodness
in Doctor's Office

Disp.: One Ice Cream Cone

Sig.: Eat as desired.

DR. Stanley C. Pettit

This prescription filled Free when presented at
DOOLEY'S *REXALL* STORE
ED DOOLEY, PROPRIETOR
PHONE 476-5516 CLEVELAND, TENNESSEE

Dr. Stanley C. Pettit came to Cleveland in 1931 and opened an osteopathic physician office. He is shown here operating a manual calculator in the 1950s. Dr. Pettit and Dooley's Drug Store offered an incentive prescription for children who were well-behaved at the doctor's office.

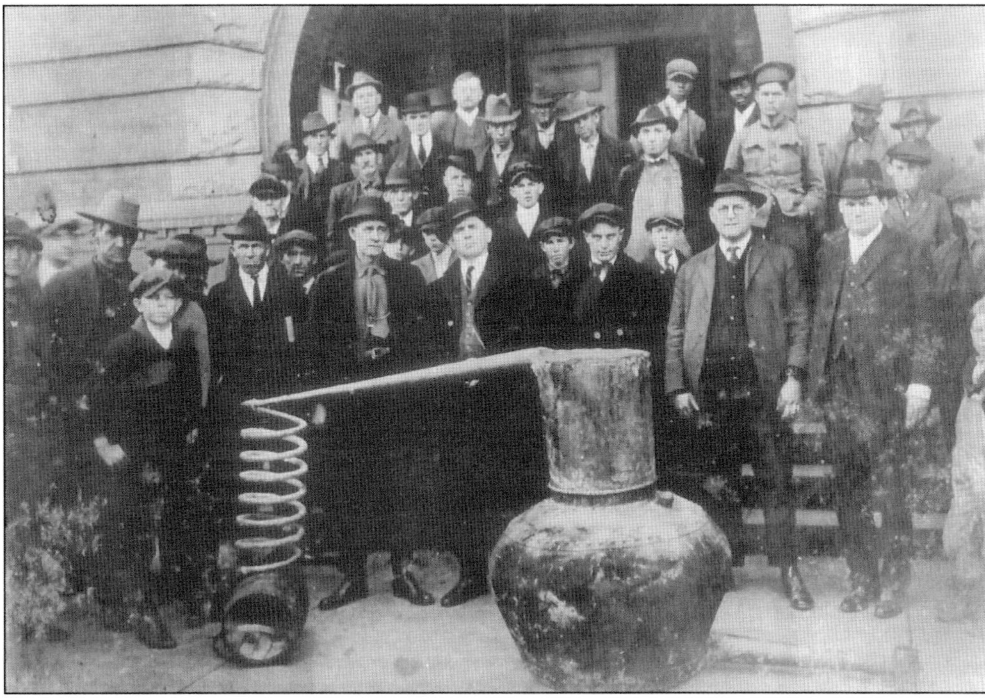

Illegal moonshine was known to be made in the hills around Cleveland. Shown here is a still confiscated and taken to the courthouse.

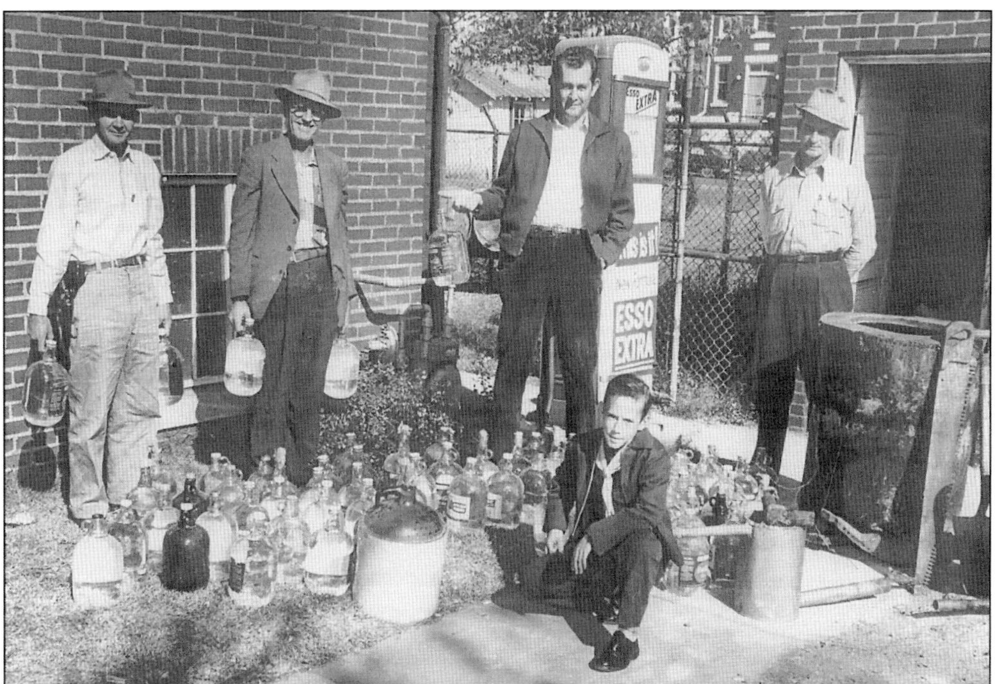

This 1959 photograph shows deputies of the Bradley County Sheriff's Office with some moonshine that had been captured. From left to right are Lee Brown, Leonard Elliot, Quin Neely, and Leroy Pippinger (chief deputy). Sitting in front is ten-year-old David Neely.

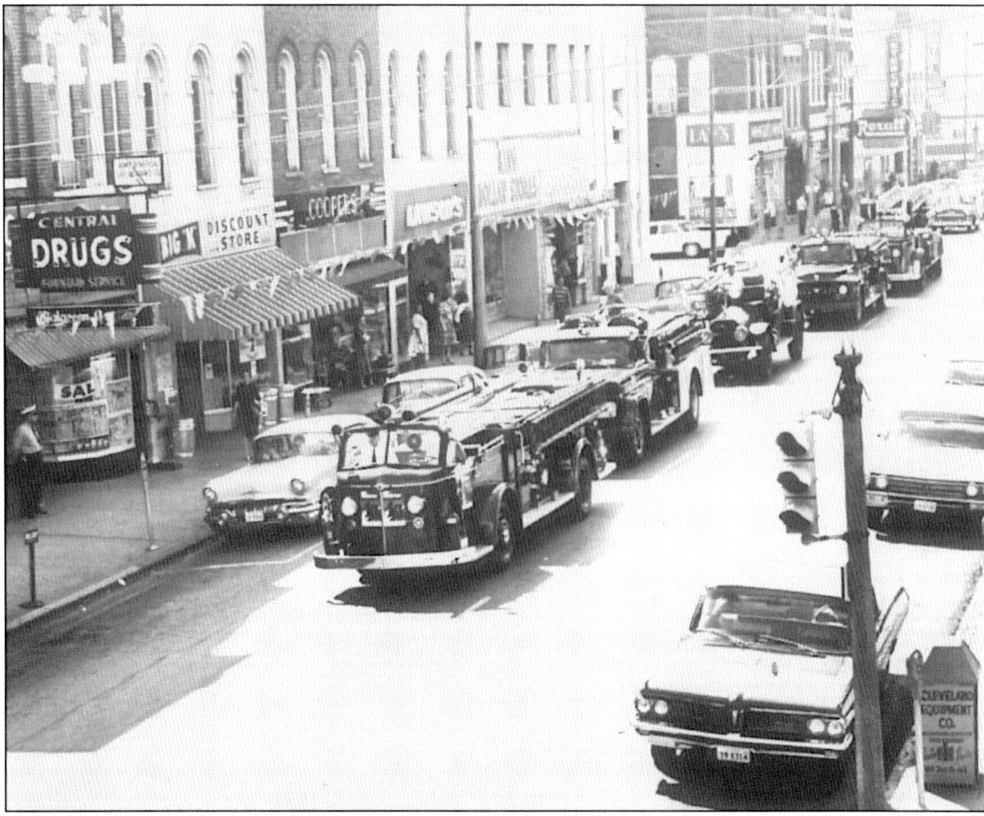

The fire department is proudly displaying its equipment in this early-1960s parade.

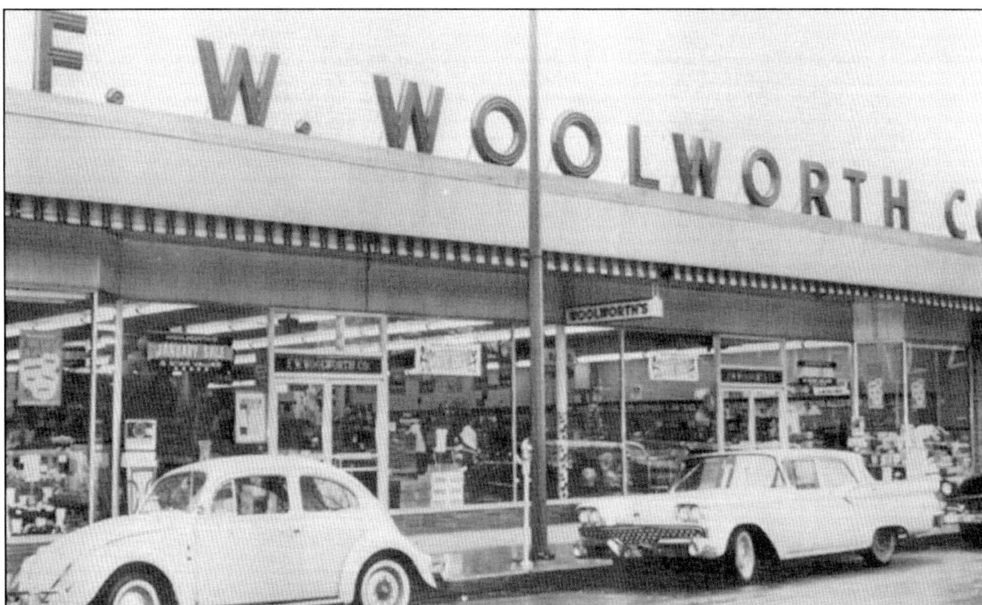

The F.W. Woolworth Company, a popular dime store, was located across from St. Luke's Episcopal Church.

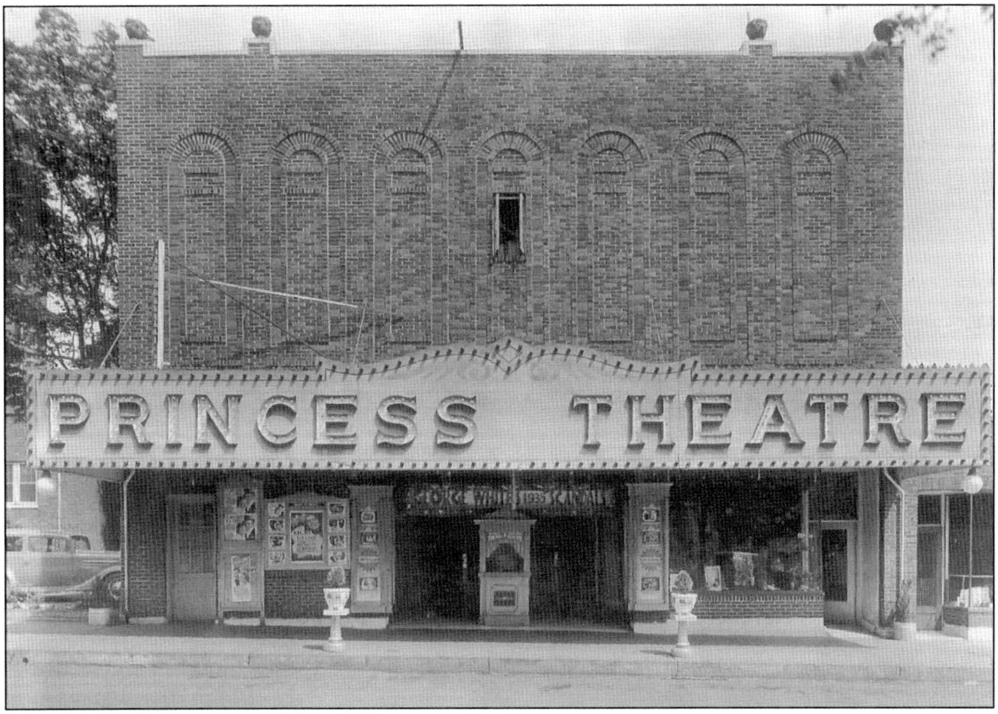

The Princess Theater is pictured here in 1935. It had a magnificent facade and was a great place to watch a movie.

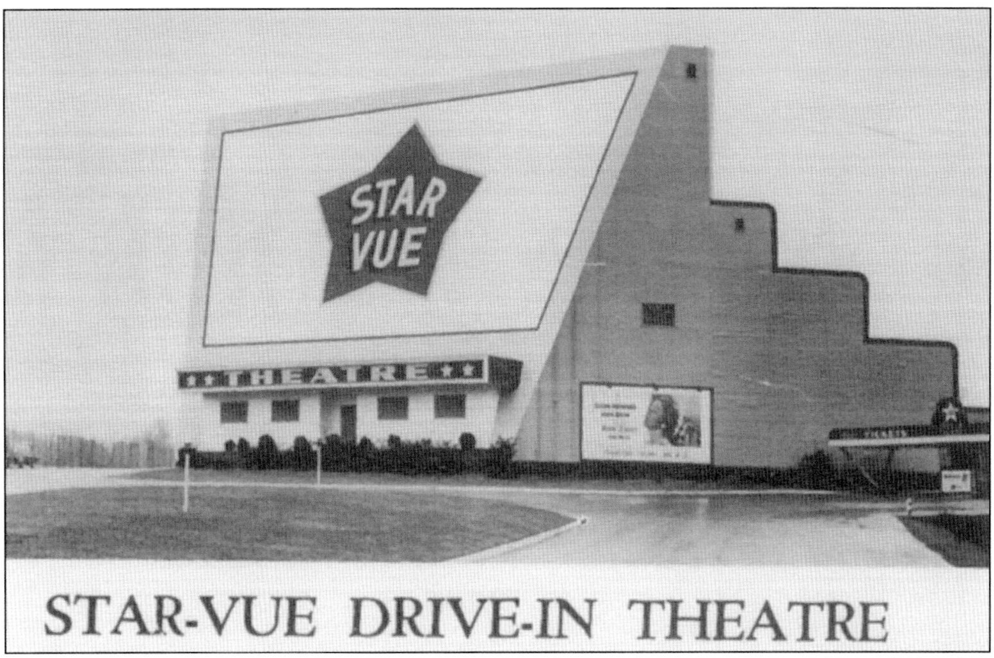

With more automobiles on the road, drive-in movie theaters became very popular with families and young people. Shown here is the Star Vue Theatre. For young children the Star Vue had swings, a merry-go-round, seesaws, and even pony rides. Other drive-in theaters were the Cherokee and the Colonial.

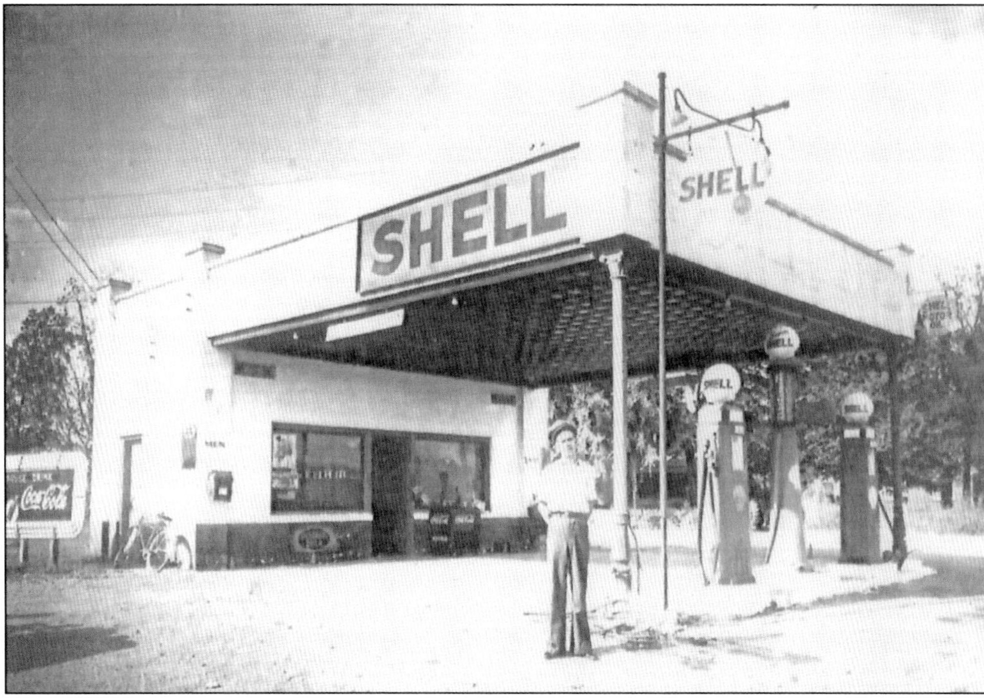

This is one of three Shell gasoline service stations in Cleveland where drivers took their automobiles to be serviced. Seventeen-year-old Elmer Cartwright proudly stands in front of the station on North Ocoee Street.

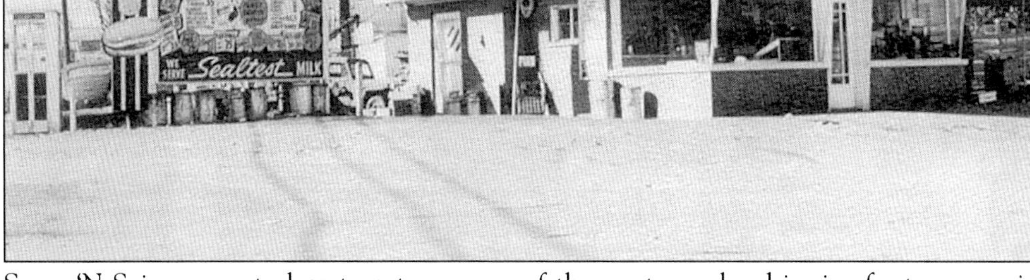

Sugar 'N Spice, a great place to eat, was one of the most popular drive-ins for teenagers in the 1960s.

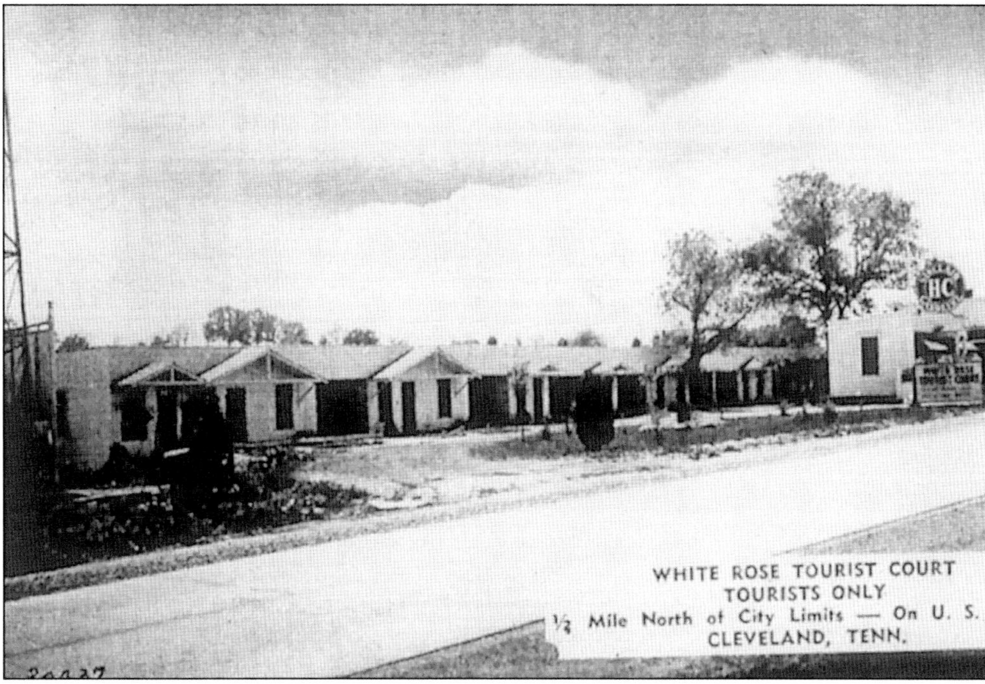

This postcard is of the White Rose Tourist Court, located on North Ocoee Street.

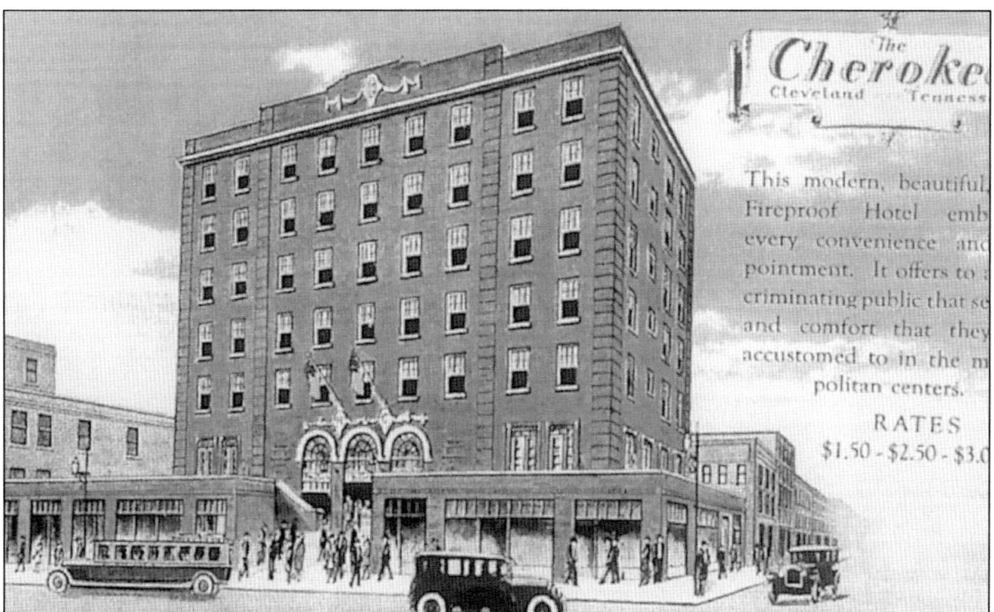

The Cherokee Hotel, built in 1928, was a seven-story building that had a large ballroom for banquets, parties, and civic club meetings.

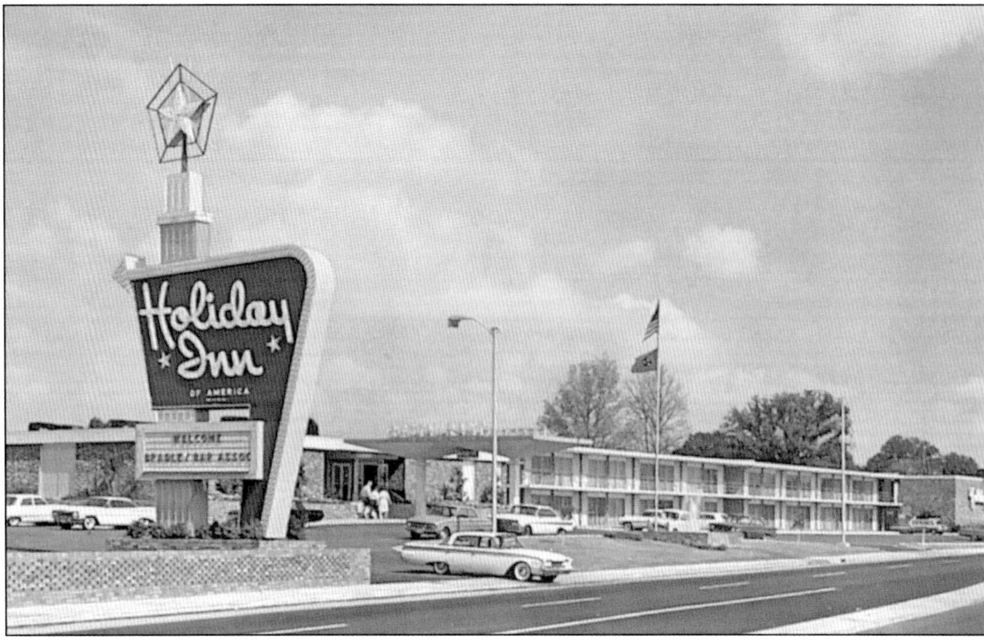

Cletus Benton built the Holiday Inn across from the Village Shopping Center. It was the site of many banquets, and the dining room was extremely popular.

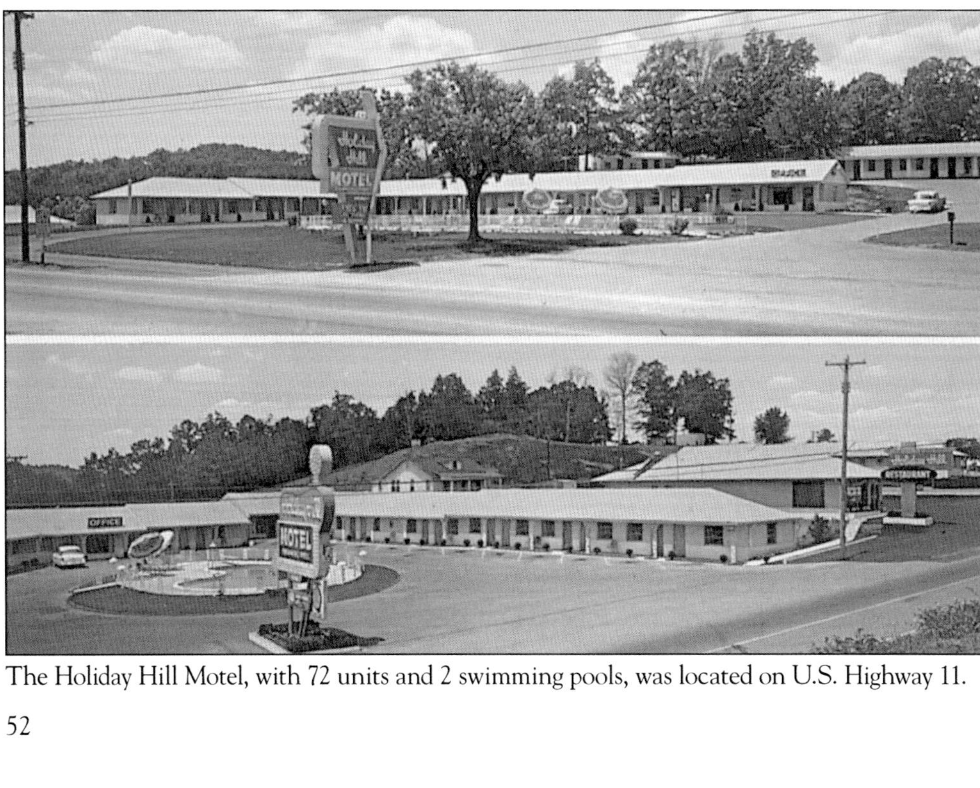

The Holiday Hill Motel, with 72 units and 2 swimming pools, was located on U.S. Highway 11.

Four

INDUSTRY

So, that is our story. We relish the past for the success it has brought us, but we look forward to the future with great anticipation. The United States will see industrial growth and economic growth and engineering achievements which will surpass the imagination of the most optimistic.

—S.B. Rymer Jr.
Chairman, president, and chief executive officer of Magic Chef, Inc.
October 18, 1979

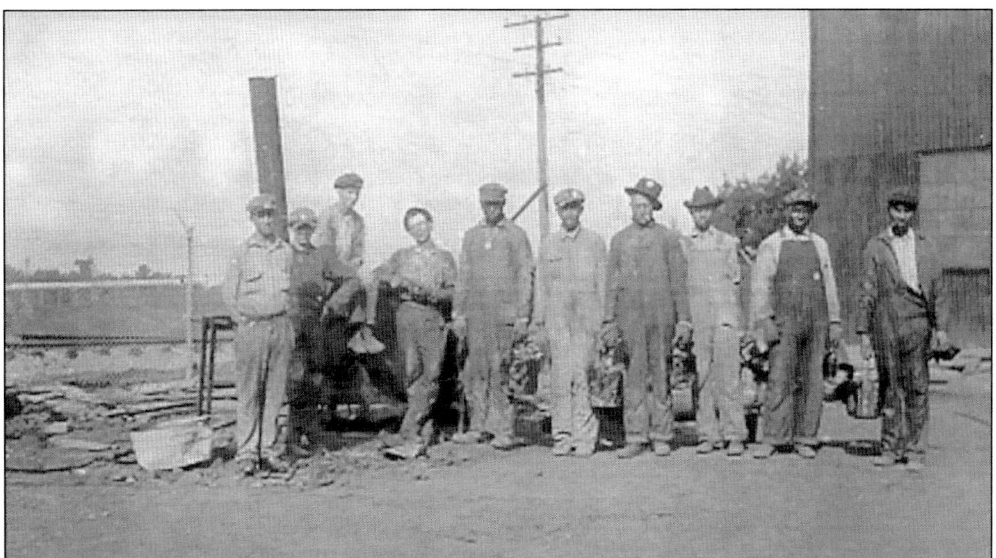

Industry has been very important to the growth of Cleveland. Shown here are ten workers. The man on the far left is John Baker; Ed Dinsmore is the person sitting.

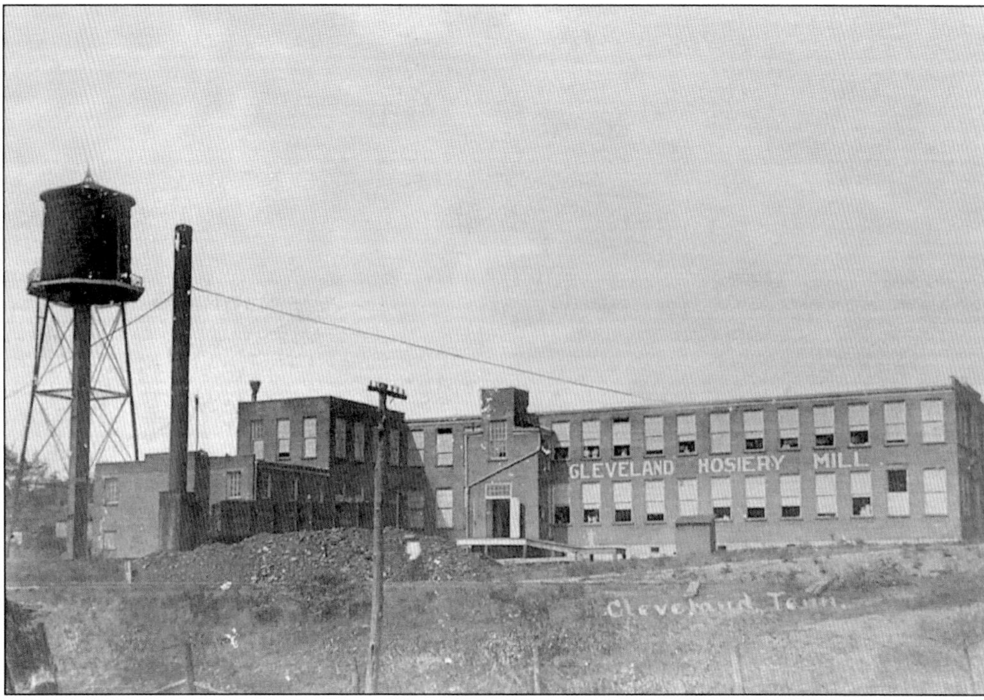

This postcard shows the Cleveland Hosiery Mill, which was located on Sixth at Church Street.

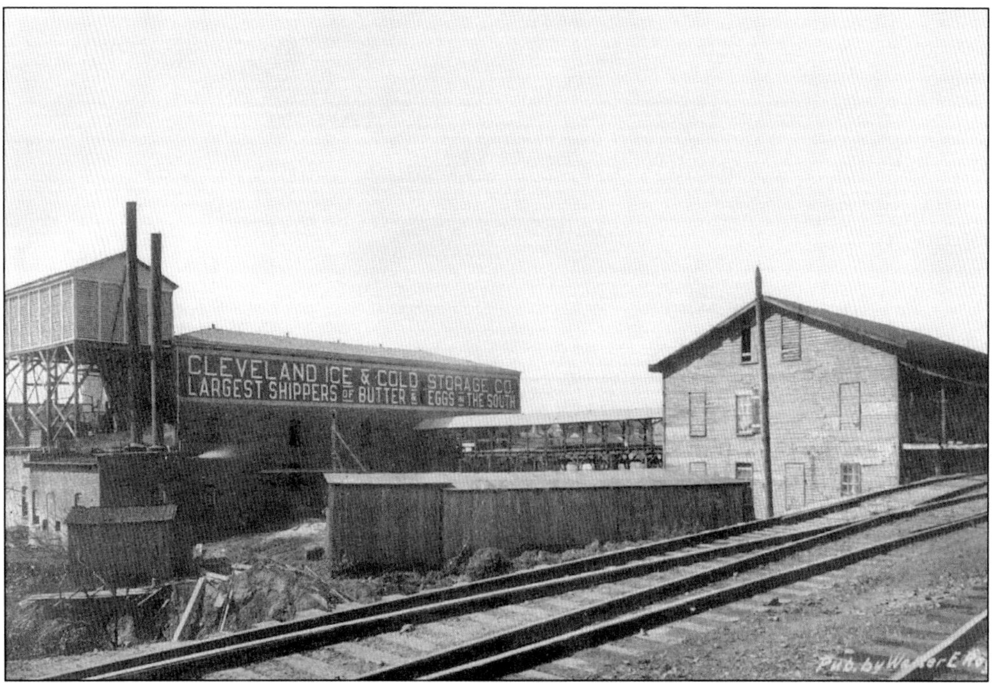

Before refrigeration, ice was extremely important for perishable foods. The Cleveland Ice & Cold Storage Company claimed to be the largest shipper of butter and eggs in the South.

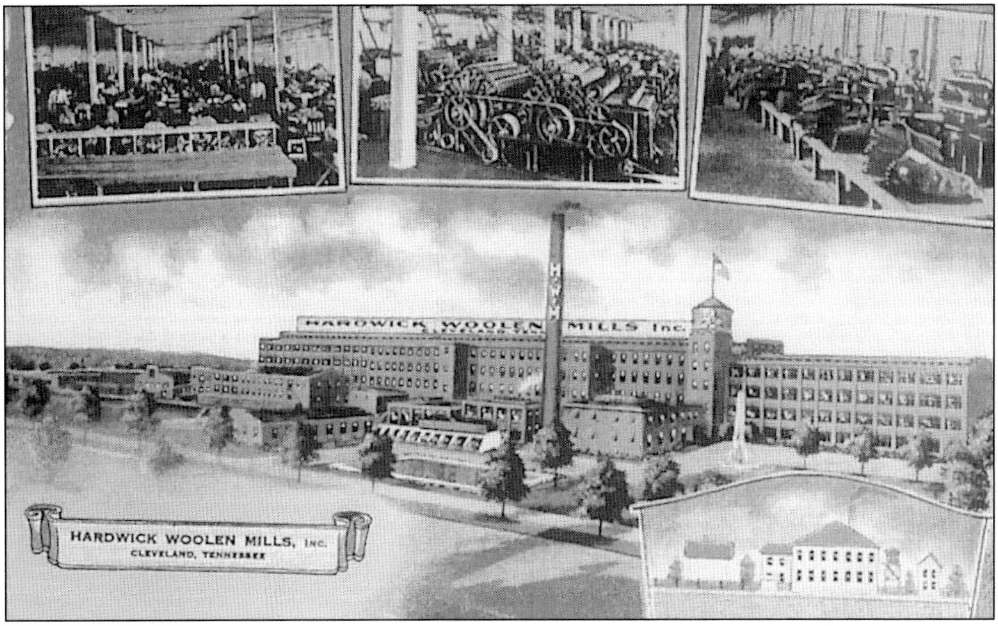

On July 28, 1880, John H. Craigmiles, John H. Parker, P.B. Mayfield, and C.L. Hardwick filed for a charter for Cleveland Woolen Mills. Then on October 1, 1880, the mill started full operation. The plant operated from 6:00 a.m. to 6:00 p.m. daily except Saturdays and Sundays. In 1929, Hardwick Woolen Mills advertised as the "World's Largest Clothing Manufacturers."

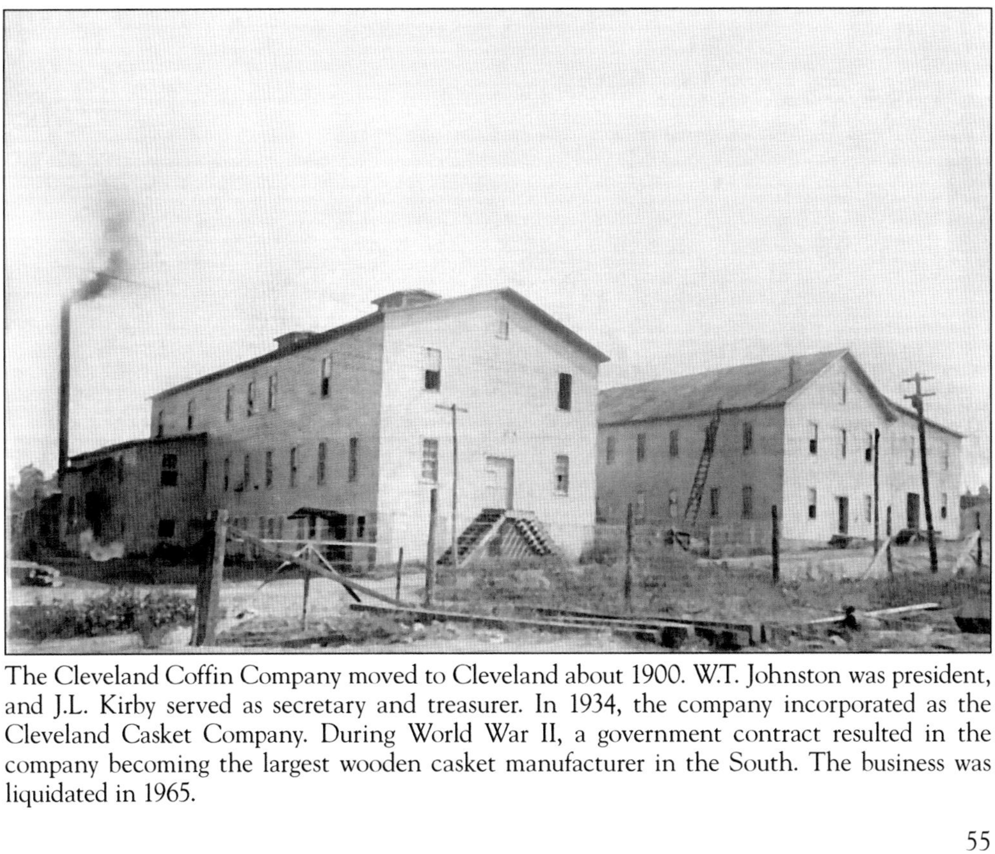

The Cleveland Coffin Company moved to Cleveland about 1900. W.T. Johnston was president, and J.L. Kirby served as secretary and treasurer. In 1934, the company incorporated as the Cleveland Casket Company. During World War II, a government contract resulted in the company becoming the largest wooden casket manufacturer in the South. The business was liquidated in 1965.

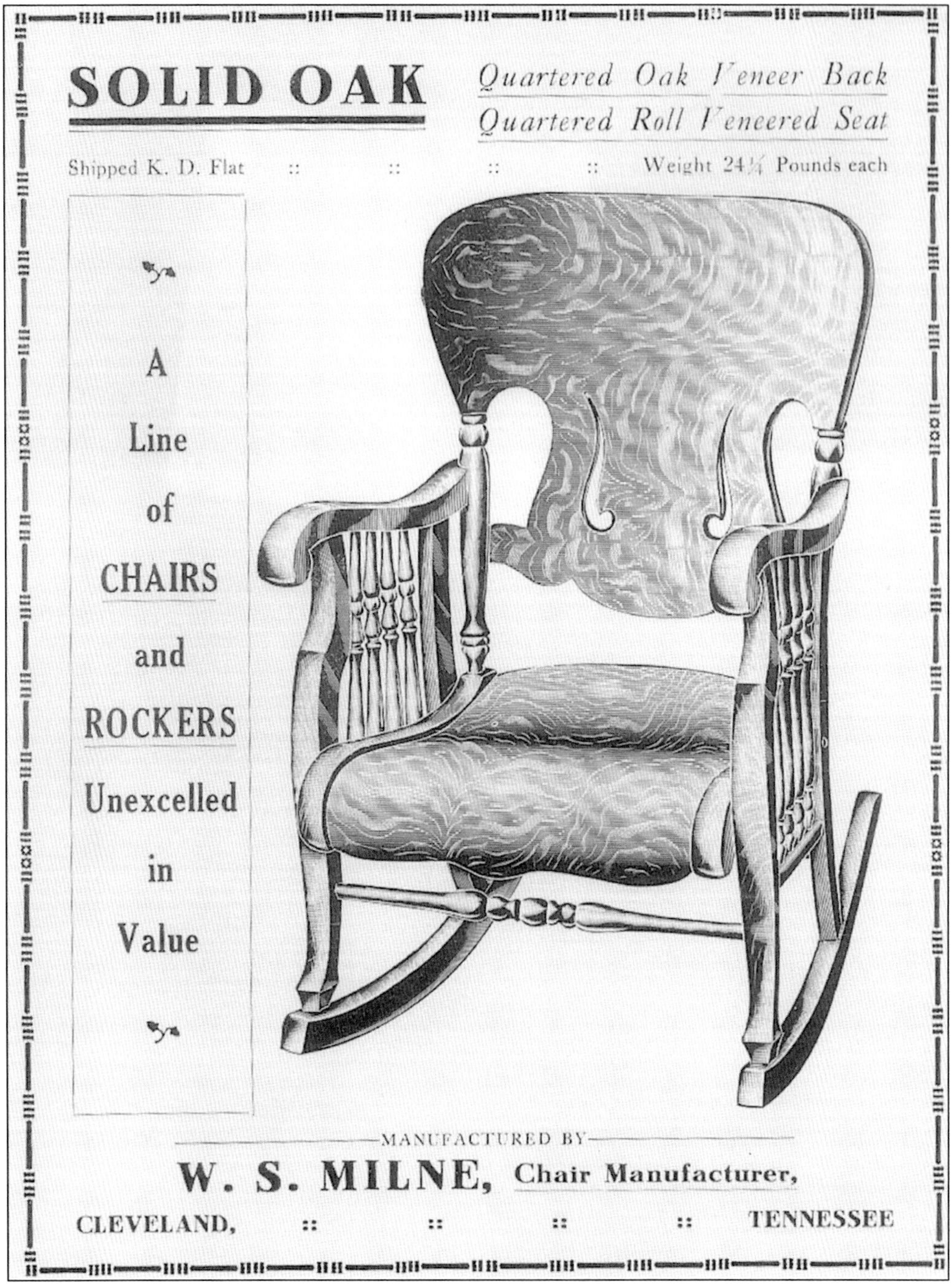

W.S. Milne manufactured wooden chairs and rockers, as shown in this 1916 advertisement.

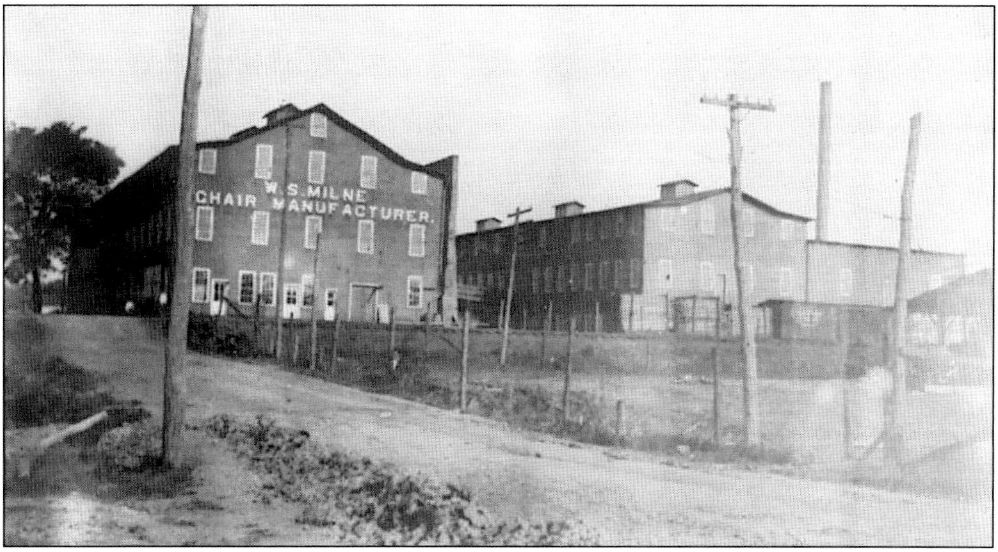

The Cleveland Chair Company was started in 1884 by C.T. Campbell, W.P. Campbell, and W.F. Miller. It was sold to W.S. Milne and Son of Canada in 1888 and became the W.S. Milne Chair Manufacturing Company.

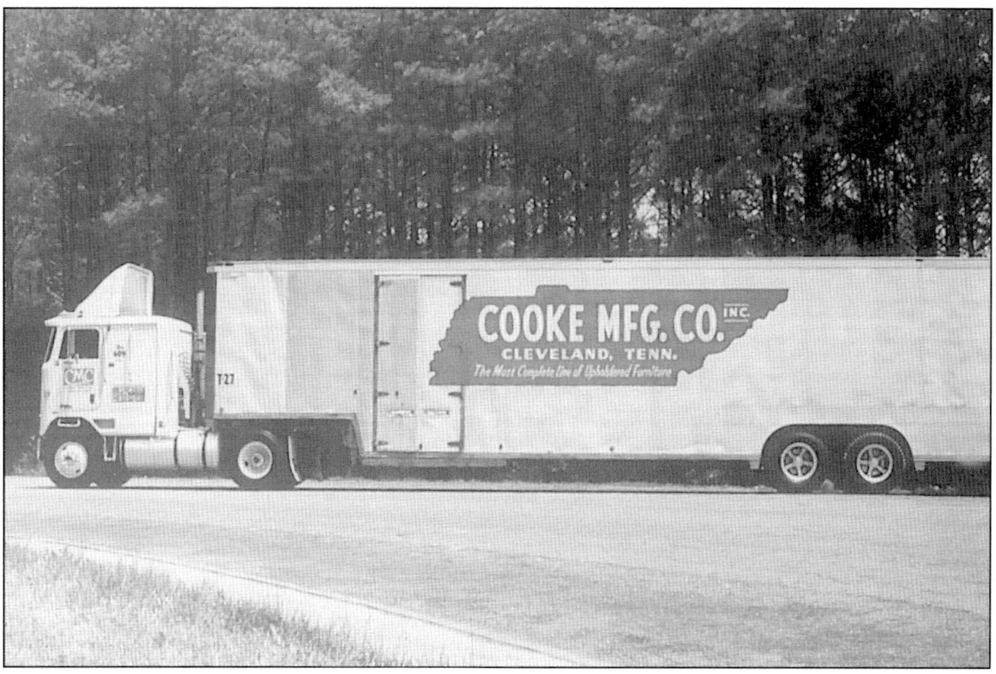

James A. Cooke started Cooke Manufacturing Company in 1958. Its slogan was "The Most Complete Line of Upholstered Furniture." Cleveland became a center of the upholstered furniture industry with plants including Cleveland Chair, Jackson Manufacturing, Collins Manufacturing, Maples Chair, Kay Line, Wilson Chair, and many others.

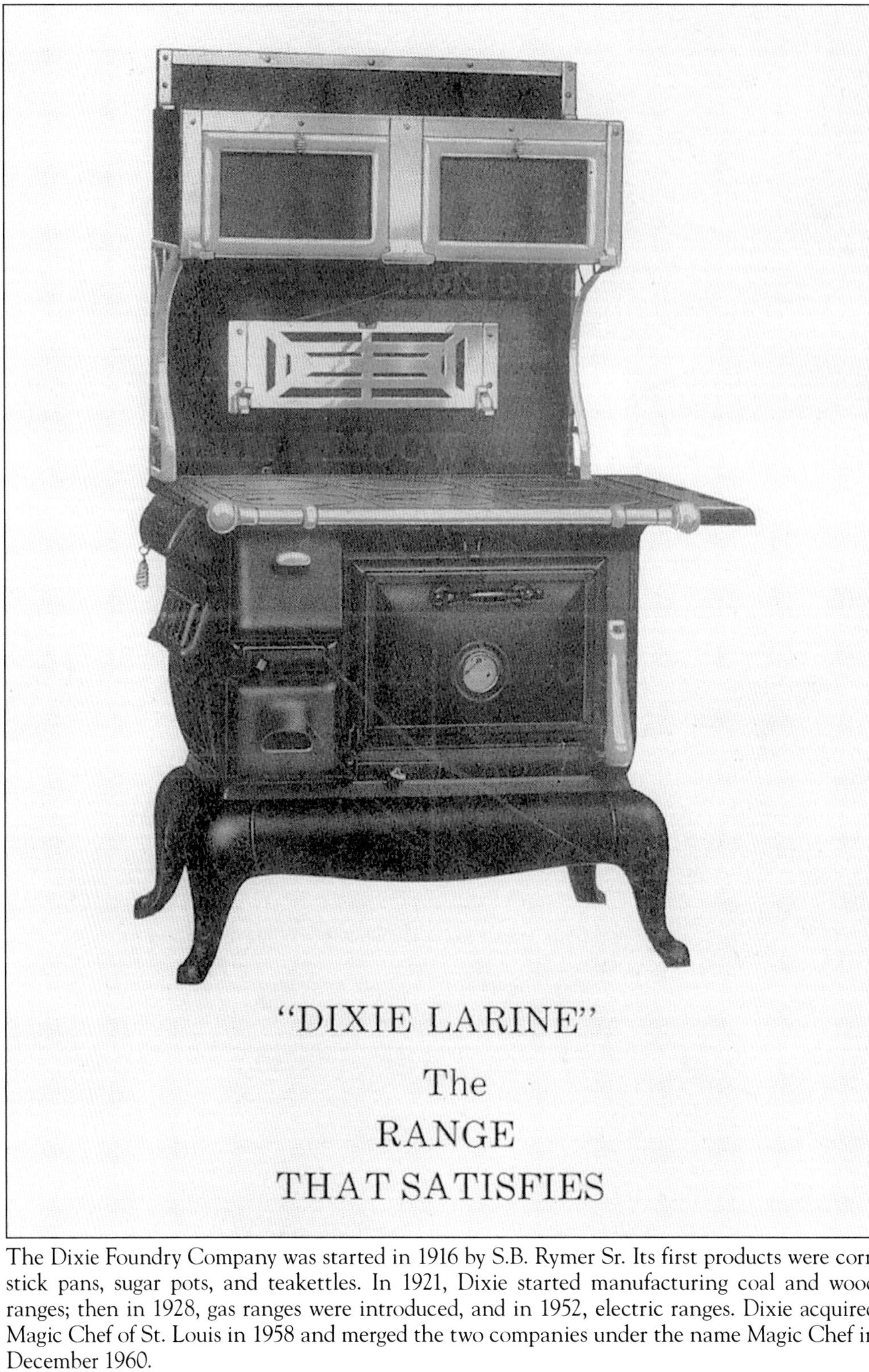

The Dixie Foundry Company was started in 1916 by S.B. Rymer Sr. Its first products were corn stick pans, sugar pots, and teakettles. In 1921, Dixie started manufacturing coal and wood ranges; then in 1928, gas ranges were introduced, and in 1952, electric ranges. Dixie acquired Magic Chef of St. Louis in 1958 and merged the two companies under the name Magic Chef in December 1960.

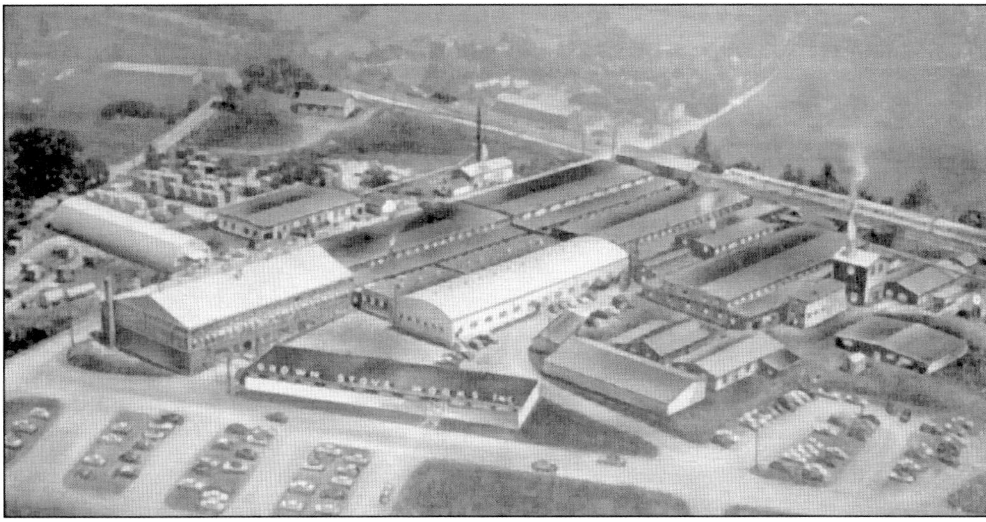

Brown Stove Works was organized in 1935 with Grover Cleveland Brown as president. The company purchased 16 acres on Carolina Avenue and constructed new buildings for the manufacture of coal and wood cook and heating stoves. Brown manufactured its first gas range in 1948.

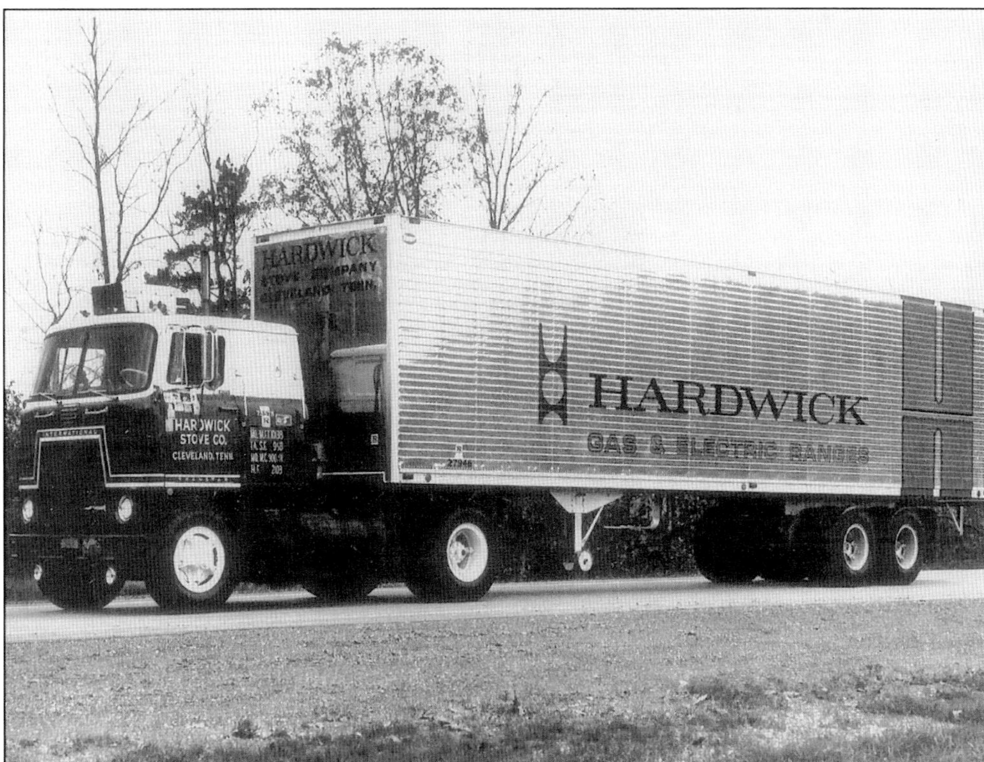

The Hardwick Stove Company was started in 1879 with Joseph H. Hardwick as the first president. Hardwick produced stoves with the names of "The Cleveland" and "The Sunny South." On January 16, 1981, the Hardwick Stove Company merged with the Maytag Corporation of Newton, IA.

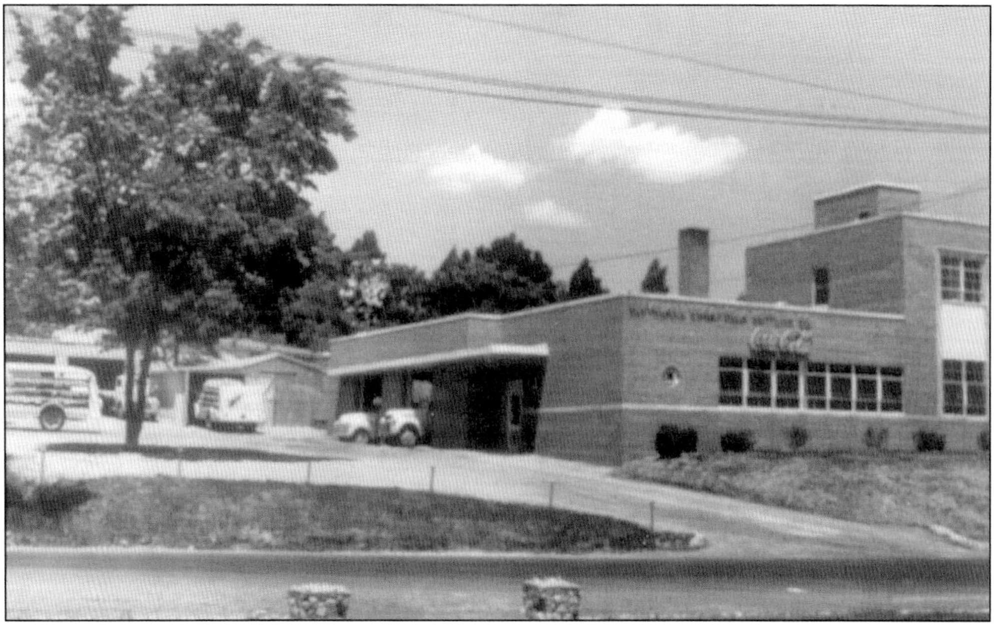

In 1904, Columbus A. Mee Jr. and J. Hardie Johnston opened a small bottling plant on Inman Street near the depot. In the beginning, they bottled only soda water. In 1907, the Cleveland Bottling Works was chartered and soon thereafter began to bottle Coca-Cola locally. The plant was relocated on South Ocoee Street and remodeled by 1929.

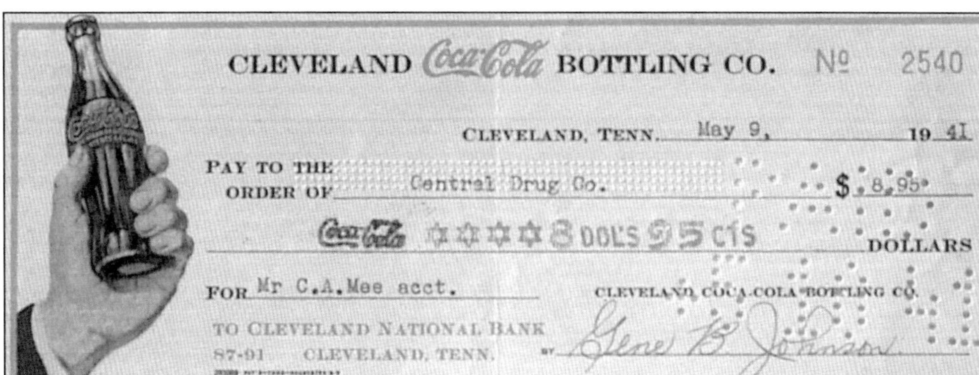

By 1929, the bottling works was turning out 600 cases of cold drinks daily. C.A. Mee Jr. and Mrs. Cora Johnston were partners with Gene Johnson in charge of sales. When Mee retired, Gene Johnson became president and served in that capacity for many years.

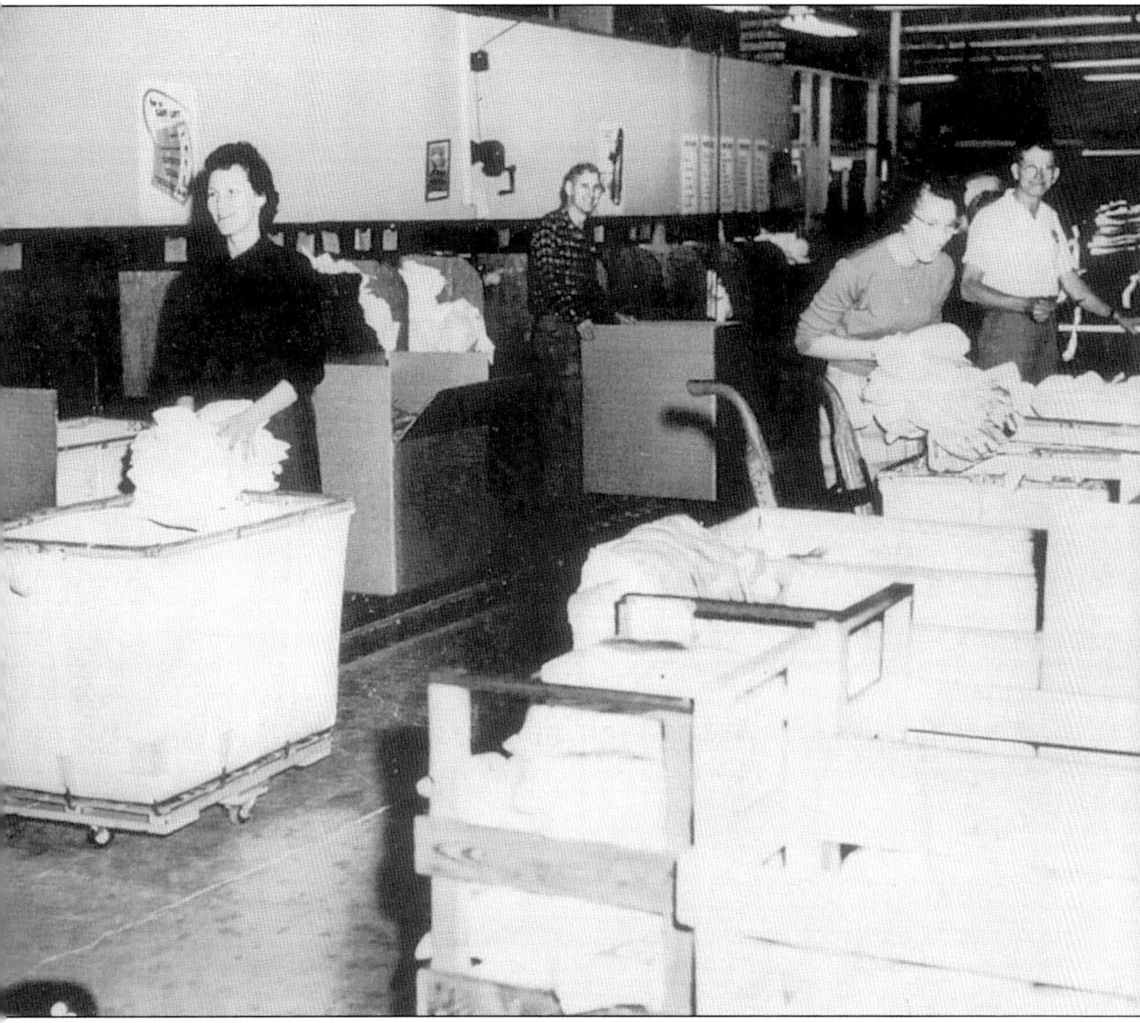

The American Uniform Company moved from Minneapolis, MN, to Cleveland in 1949. Frank Miles was the president. It was the first major industry to relocate from the North to Cleveland.

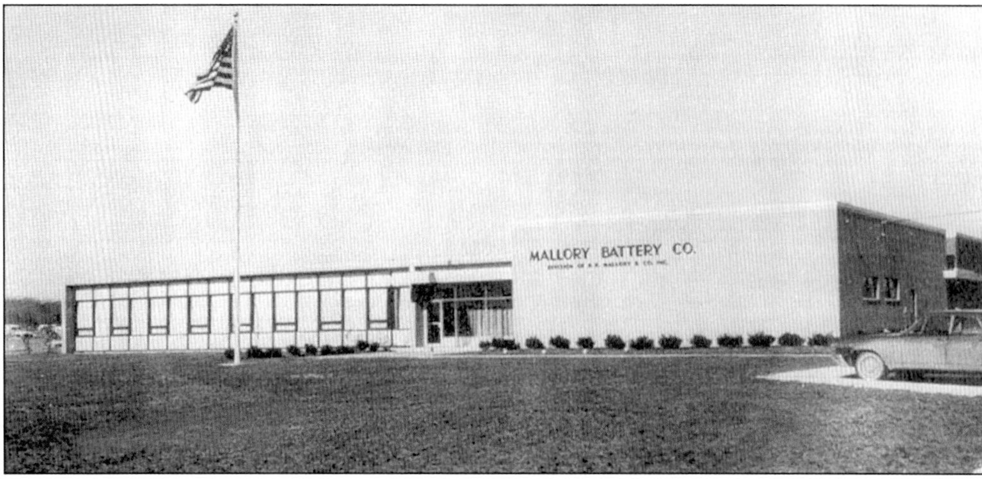

In 1960, the Mallory Battery Company moved to Cleveland and opened its plant on Mouse Creek Road. Since 1966 the company has operated under the name Duracell.

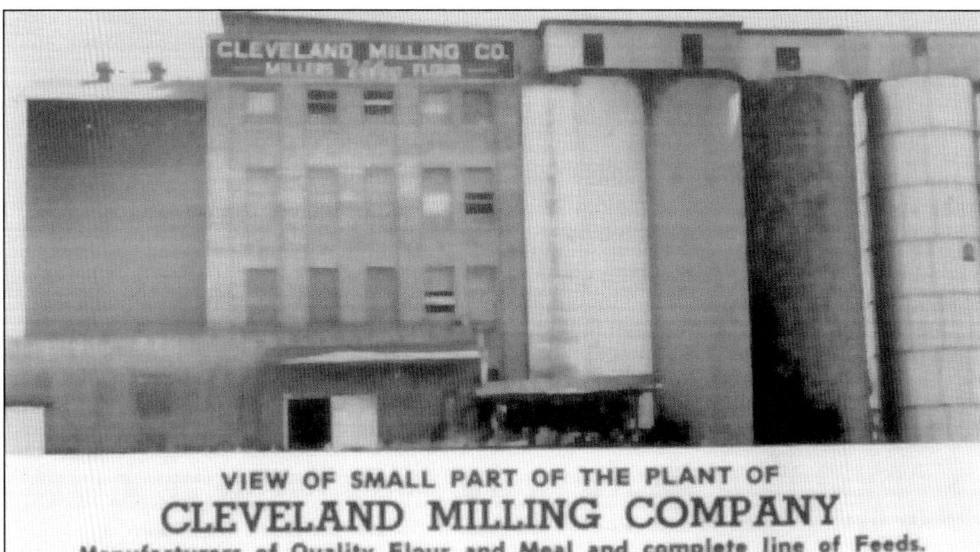

Located on Central Avenue, the Cleveland Milling Company was formed in 1901 by George Hain, W.T. Johnson, J.H. Milne, and J.F. Johnston. Hugh M. Knox became secretary of the company in 1906. His son, T.J. Knox, joined the company in 1927 and later became president, serving until 1972.

Five

RELIGION

Man, it is said, is a religious animal; he has a religion of some kind. He may be ignorant and superstitious, or he may on the other hand be intelligent, educated and cultivated; he is religious all the same.

—The Reverend George W. Coleman
Retired clergyman and resident of Cleveland in 1927

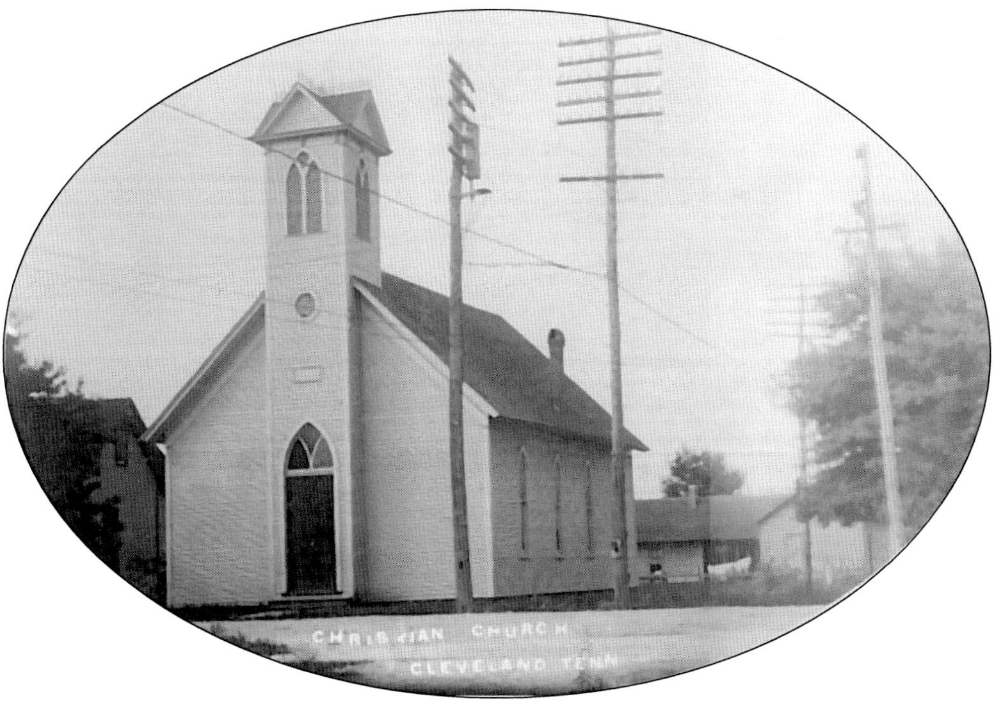

The Christian Church (Disciples of Christ) bought this wooden structure in 1898. The Evangelical Association, a German pietistic sect formed by Jacob Albright in Pennsylvania in 1800, had built this structure in 1887 as a mission church of the Indiana Conference. It was the only building constructed by this denomination in Tennessee.

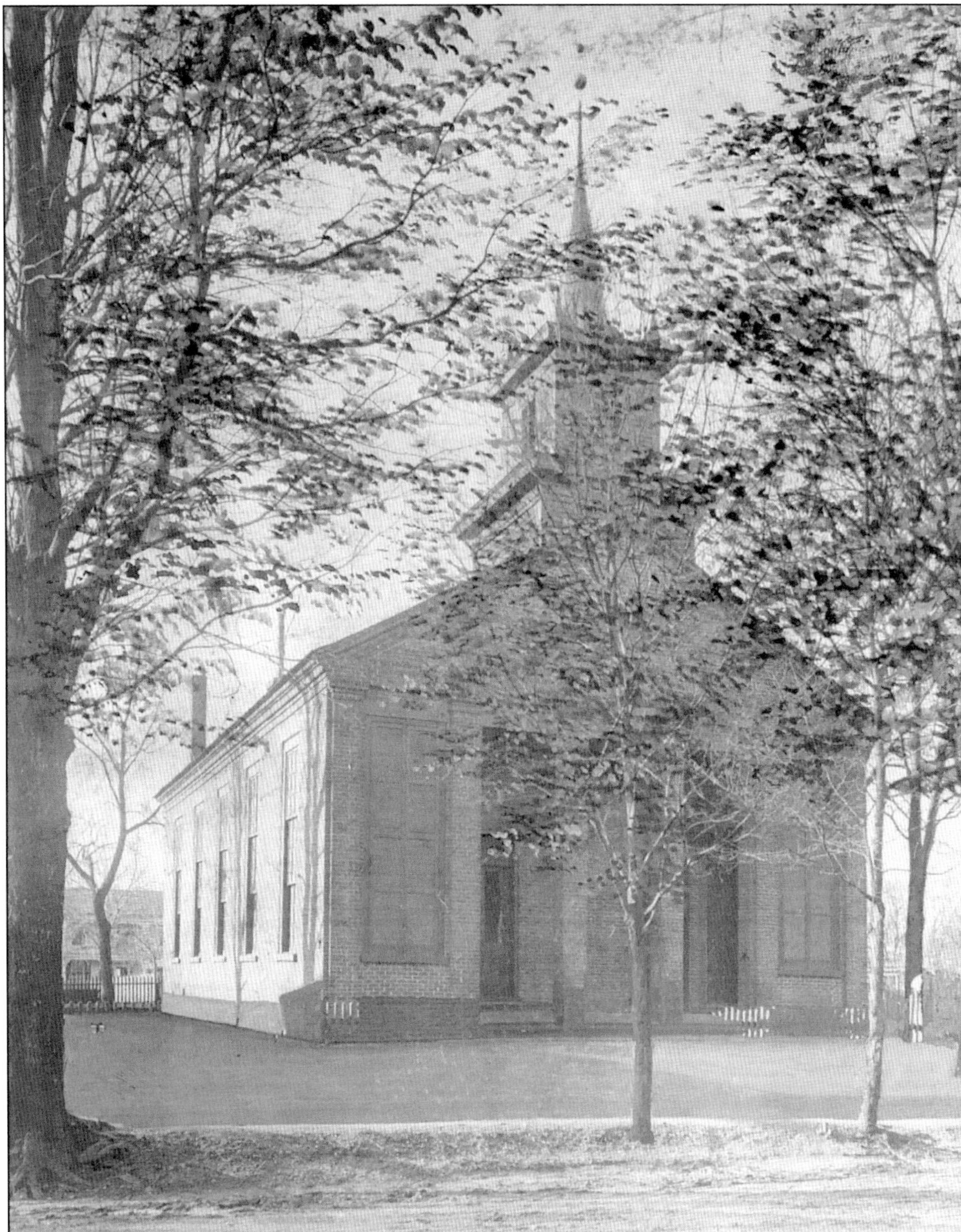

On October 22, 1858, Rev. James N. Bradshaw dedicated the present sanctuary of First Presbyterian Church, located on Ocoee Street. In 1957 the education building was constructed, and in 1999, a narthex connecting the sanctuary to the education wing and a new fellowship hall were added.

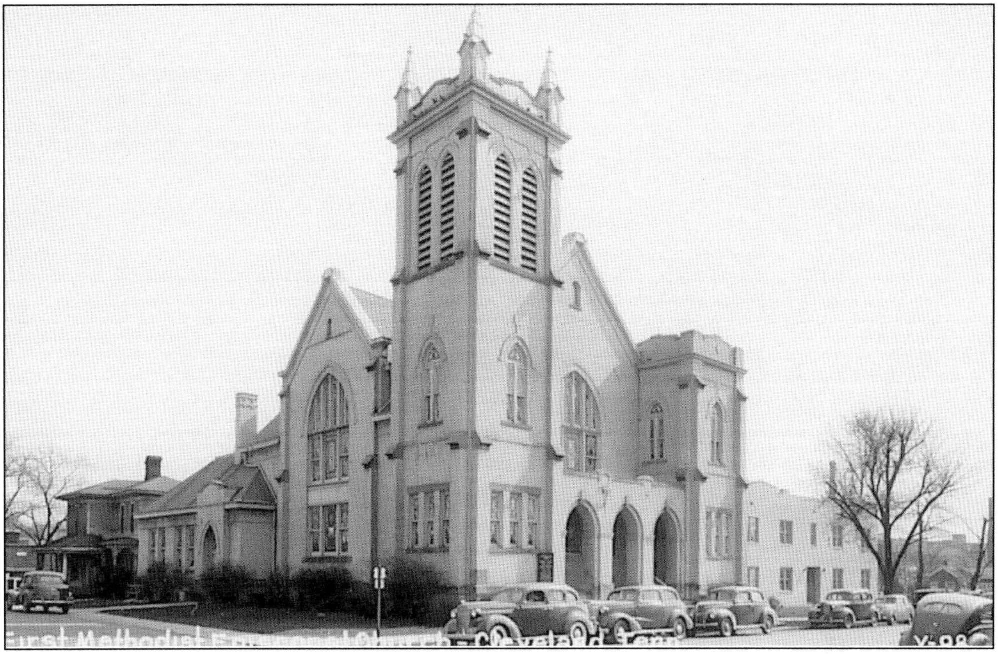

The First Methodist Episcopal Church, built in 1912 on South Ocoee Street, is shown in this postcard. This congregation and Broad Street Methodist Church have a common beginning in the Methodist Church, which first met in 1837 in the log cabin courthouse. In 1979, First Methodist relocated to North Ocoee Street.

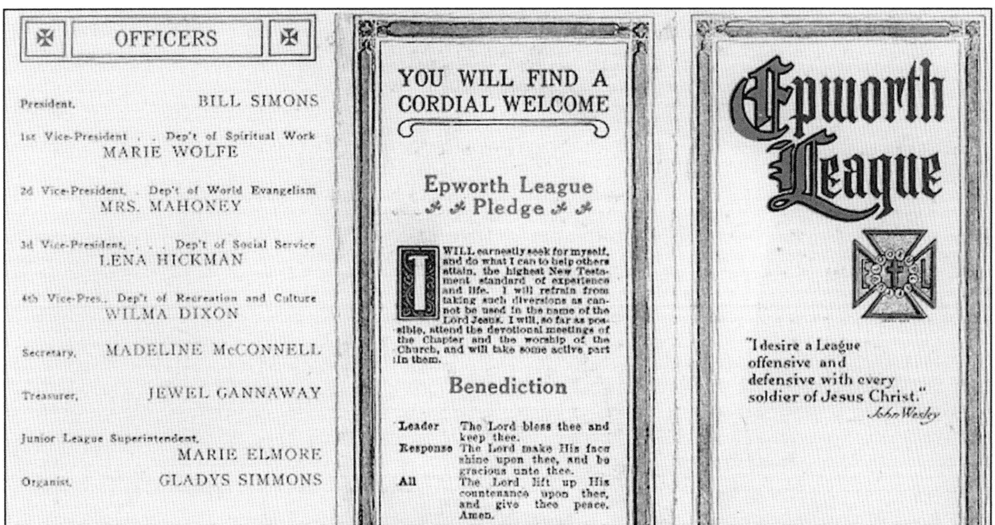

OFFICERS

President, BILL SIMONS

1st Vice-President . . Dep't of Spiritual Work
MARIE WOLFE

2d Vice-President, . Dep't of World Evangelism
MRS. MAHONEY

3d Vice-President, . . . Dep't of Social Service
LENA HICKMAN

4th Vice-Pres., Dep't of Recreation and Culture
WILMA DIXON

Secretary, MADELINE McCONNELL

Treasurer, JEWEL GANNAWAY

Junior League Superintendent,
MARIE ELMORE

Organist, GLADYS SIMMONS

THE METHODIST BOOK CONCERN
740 RUSH STREET, CHICAGO

YOU WILL FIND A CORDIAL WELCOME

Epworth League Pledge

I WILL earnestly seek for myself, and do what I can to help others attain, the highest New Testament standard of experience and life. I will refrain from taking such diversions as cannot be used in the name of the Lord Jesus. I will, so far as possible, attend the devotional meetings of the Chapter and the worship of the Church, and will take some active part in them.

Benediction

Leader — The Lord bless thee and keep thee.
Response — The Lord make His face shine upon thee, and be gracious unto thee.
All — The Lord lift up His countenance upon thee, and give thee peace. Amen.

Epworth League

"I desire a League offensive and defensive with every soldier of Jesus Christ."
John Wesley

From 1888 to 1939, the society for young people in the Methodist Episcopal Church and the Methodist Episcopal Church, South, was the Epworth League. Pictured is a tri-fold card with the list of officers, pledge, and benediction of the league.

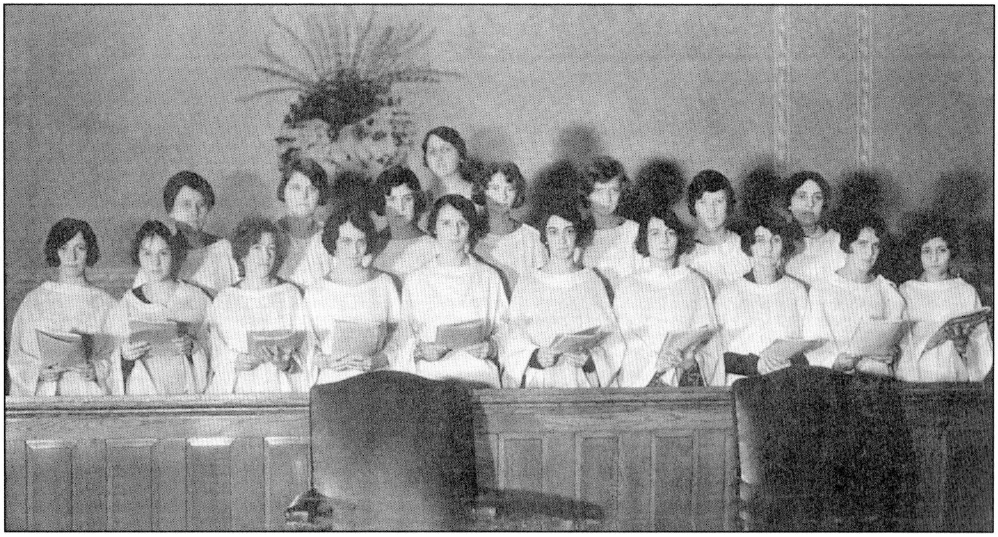

Pictured is the All Girls Choir of the First Cumberland Presbyterian Church in 1927. The church is a direct descendant of the Cumberland Presbyterians organized in the Cleveland log courthouse on July 16, 1837. Choir members are, from left to right, as follows: (front row) Gladys McIntire, Edith Bunch, Bessie Baker, Hazel Cooper, Ruth McKenzie, Jessie Cooper, Edna White, Mrs. LaVon Weeks, and Emily Swartz; (middle row) Mrs. L.R. Johns, Hazel Renner, Evelyn Pack, Bonnie Gay Wilson, Dorothy Swartz, Pearl Gray, and Louise Harle; (back row) Mrs. Edna Harle.

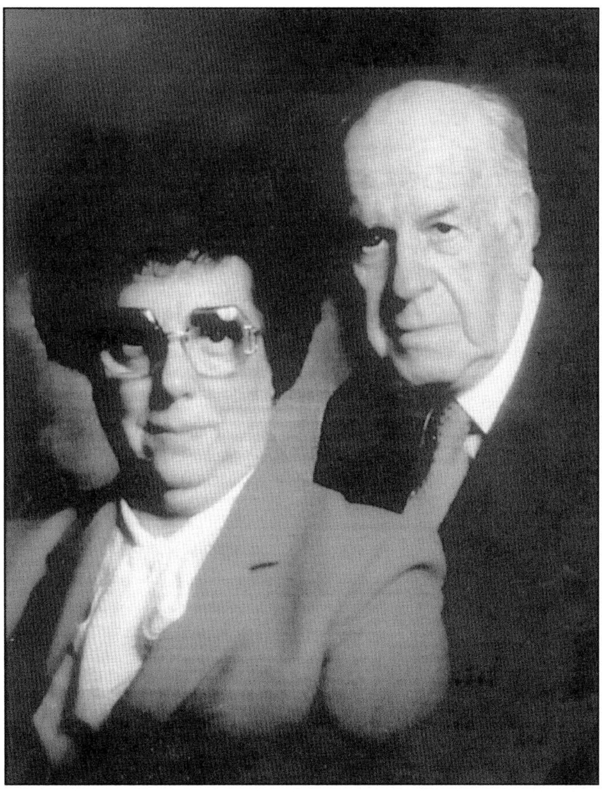

The Reverend and Mrs. M.E. Littlefield, both ordained ministers, came to Cleveland in 1945 and began ministering to the physical as well as spiritual needs of people. Their ministry led to the establishment of the non-denominational Faith Memorial Church. Their major focus was ministry to children, such as the annual Christmas "Toys for Tots" program. In addition, the couple began the first bus ministry in the community as well as a weekly radio program, "The Sunshine Broadcast." Brother Littlefield was born in Maine (November 9, 1908–January 18, 1996) and his wife, Gladys, was born in Pennsylvania.

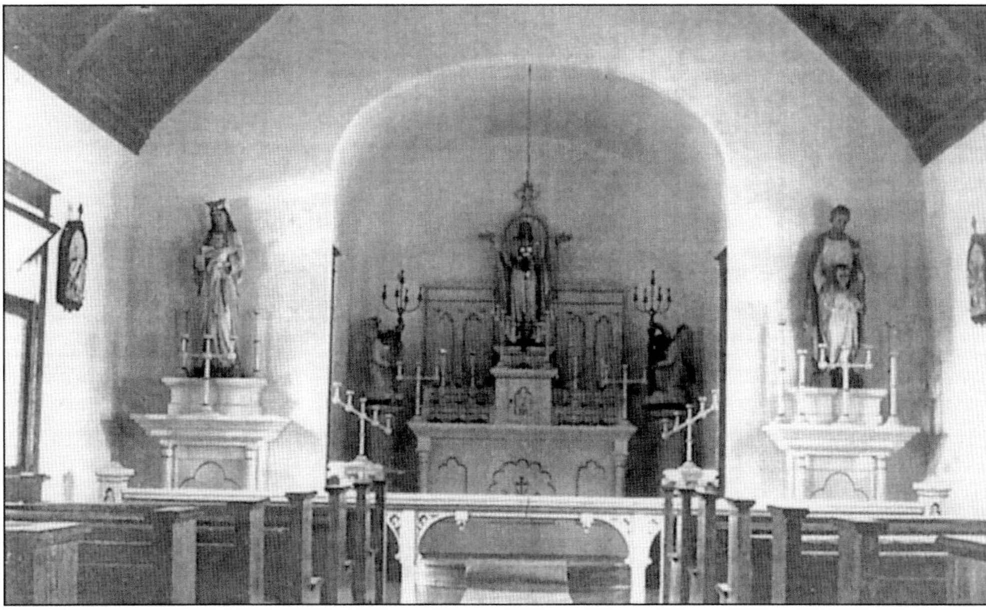

This interior view of the Church of the Resurrection shows a magnificent altar and nave. The church was used until Saint Therese de Lisieux was built in 1961.

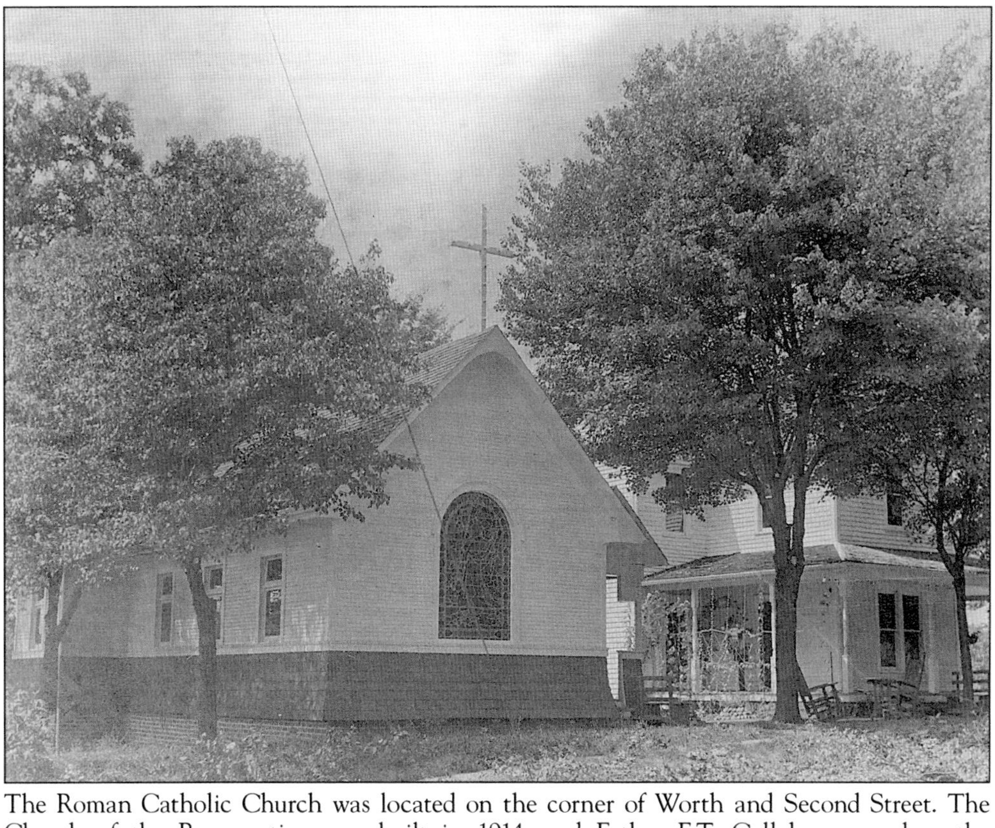

The Roman Catholic Church was located on the corner of Worth and Second Street. The Church of the Resurrection was built in 1914, and Father E.T. Callahan served as the first priest.

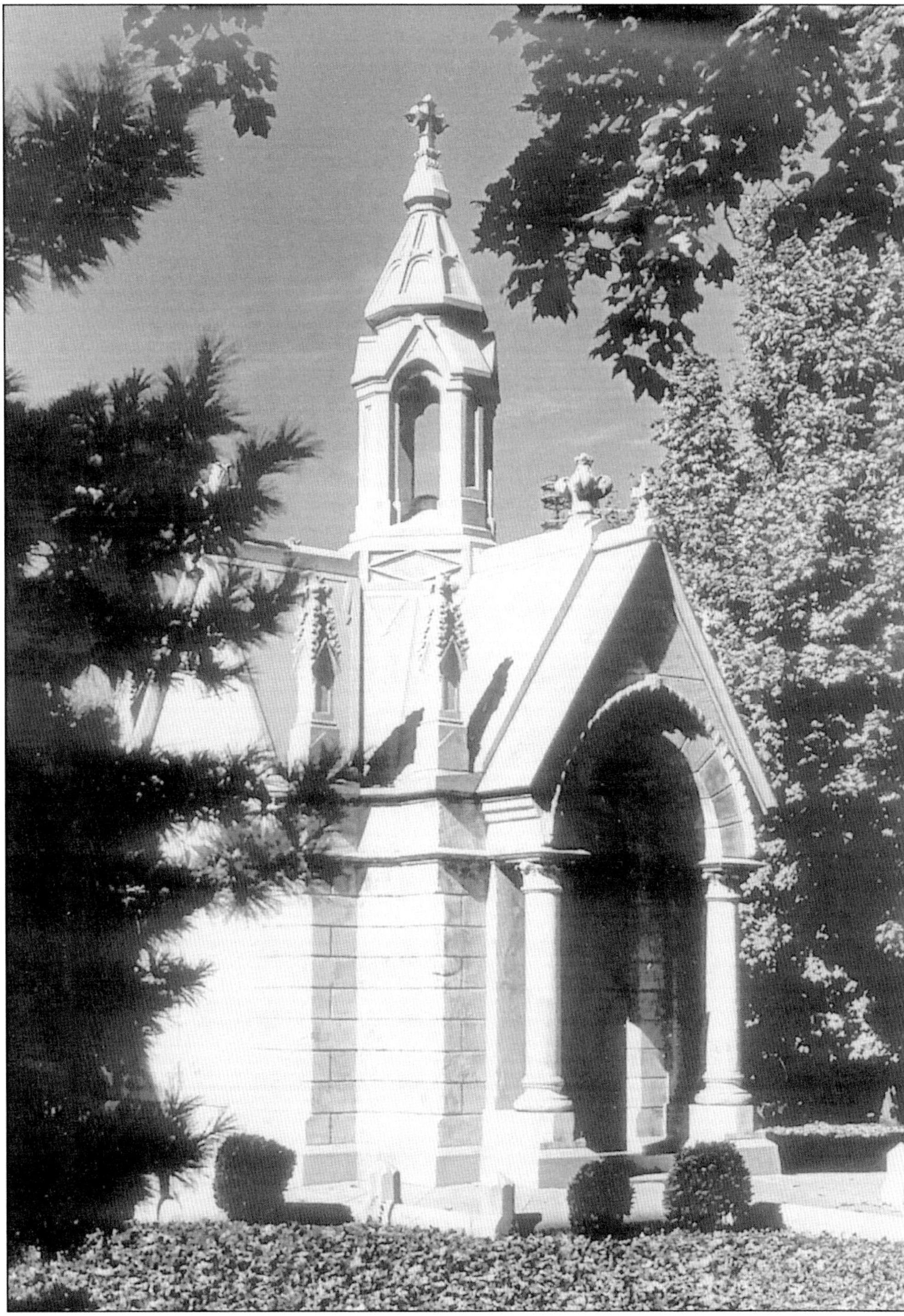

Nina Craigmiles died tragically after being struck by a train on October 11, 1871. Her father, John H. Craigmiles, built a new church building (St. Luke's) in her memory. This mausoleum, where Nina and other family members are interred, is constructed of Carrara marble with walls 4 feet thick.

St. Alban's was the original name of the Episcopal parish in Cleveland. After Nina Craigmiles was killed on October 11, St. Luke's Day, the communicants of St. Alban's voted to rename their church in her memory. The church became Saint Luke's Episcopal Church.

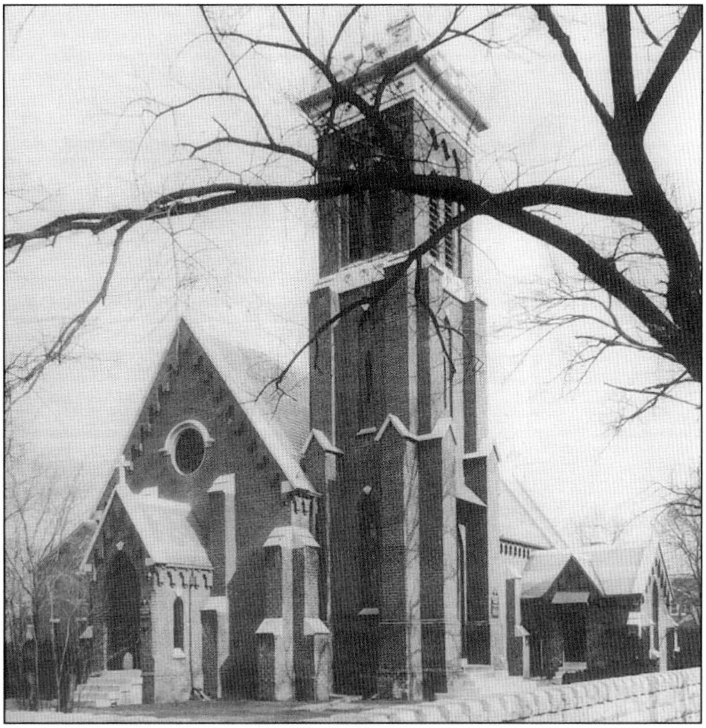

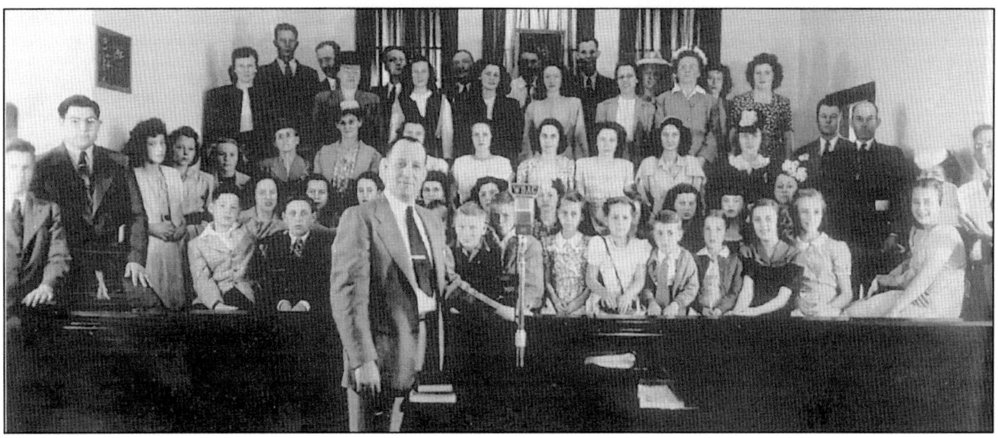

This is the choir of Big Springs Methodist Church about 1944. Standing at the WBAC microphone is Pastor Pete Gentry. Pictured from left to right are the following: (two ladies standing) Jimmie Gentry and Roberta Berry Lyle; (two men standing) Kenneth Johnson and unidentified; (first row) Kenneth Berry, two unidentified, James Lake Kimsey, unidentified, Juanita Goins, two unidentified, Polly Wooden, Itzelteen Beaty Matthews, Elizabeth Wooden, Wanda Headrick Harvey Jesse, and Charlie Woods (choir director); (second row) Mary Gentry, Doris Goins Geren, Margaret Hicks, Daisy Walker, unidentified, Billie Berry, unidentified, Wilma Kelly Ratcliff, and four unidentified; (third row) Jayleen Haney Elrod, Hattie Byrd, Eva Clark, Nan Pettit Wilson, Nada Wilson, Louise Pettit Jenkins, Irene Duncan Geren, Edna Humberd Parkinson, Bob Parkinson, and Pryor Johnson; (fourth row) Mable Byrd Haney, Ollie Millaway, unidentified, Pearl Odom Howard, Tomilene Duncan, Davis Sorg, Leola Headrick, Mrs. Burl Moss, and unidentified; (last row) three unidentified, Alva Byrd, unidentified, Leonard Beaty, Marie Kimsey Wrinkle, and unidentified.

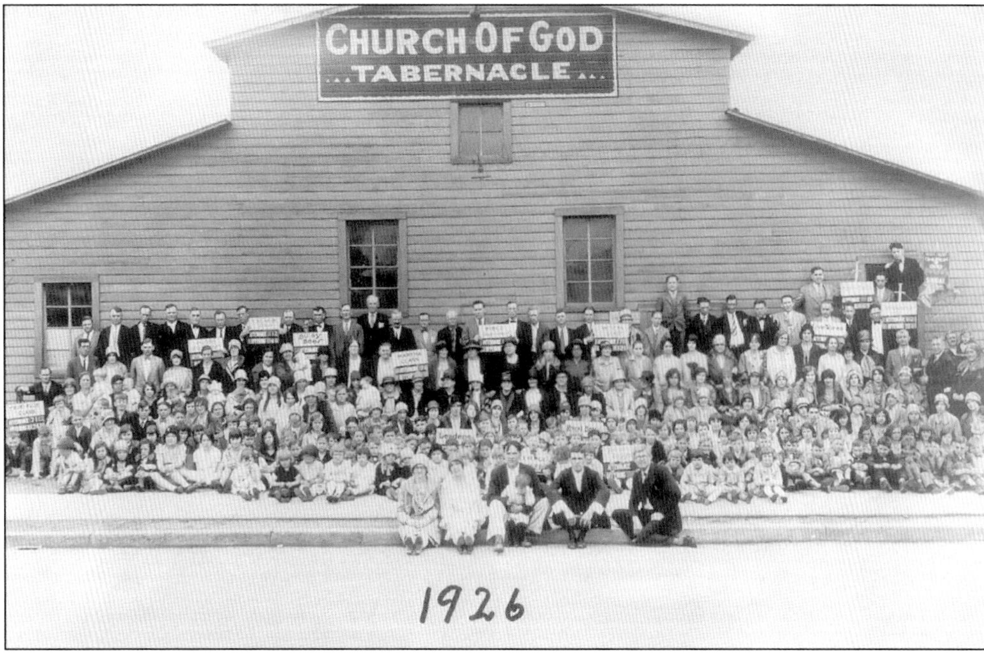

The Church of God Tabernacle had an attendance rally day in 1926. Each class holds a banner with attendance and offering for the day. Classes include Beacon Light, Martha Class, Busy Bees, True-Blue Class, Merry Maids, and Live Wires.

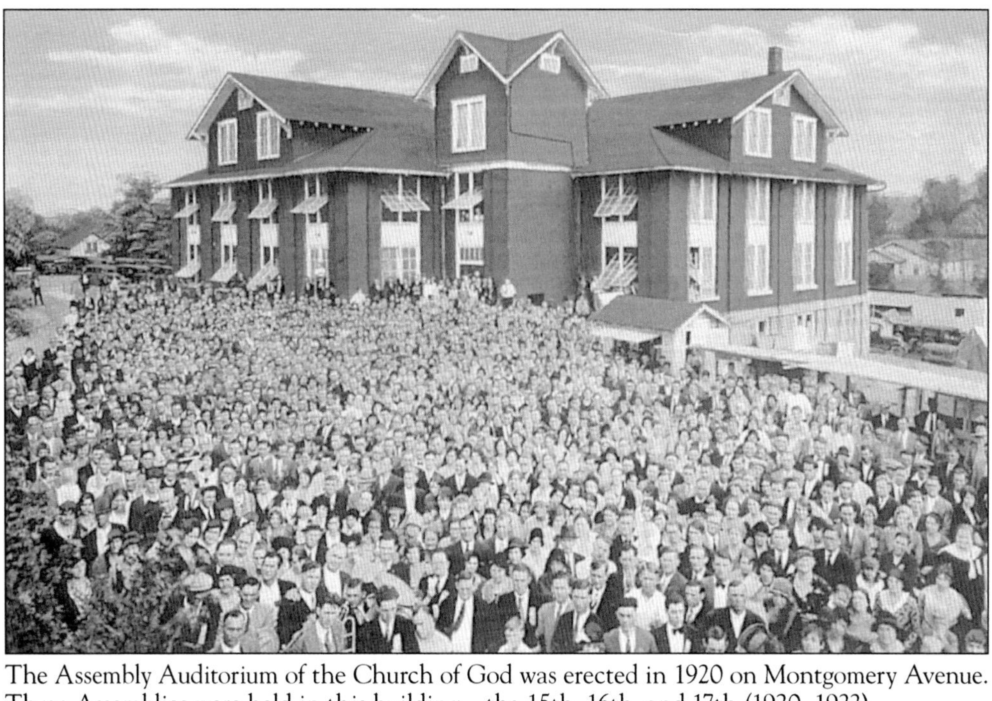

The Assembly Auditorium of the Church of God was erected in 1920 on Montgomery Avenue. Three Assemblies were held in this building—the 15th, 16th, and 17th (1920–1922).

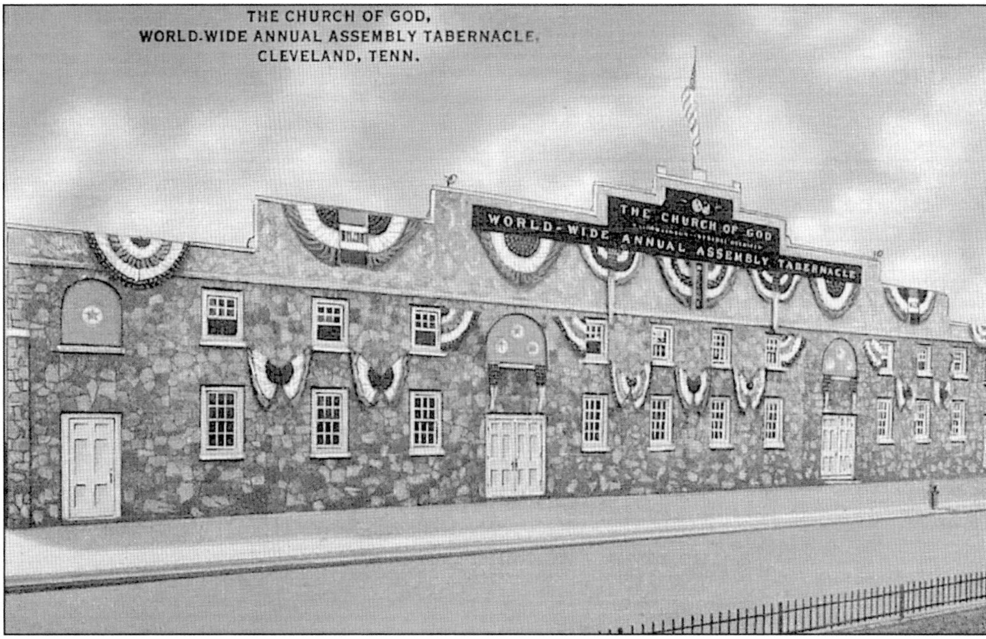

The World-Wide Assembly Tabernacle of the Church of God of Prophecy was located at Bible Place on Central Avenue. It burned in the 1980s.

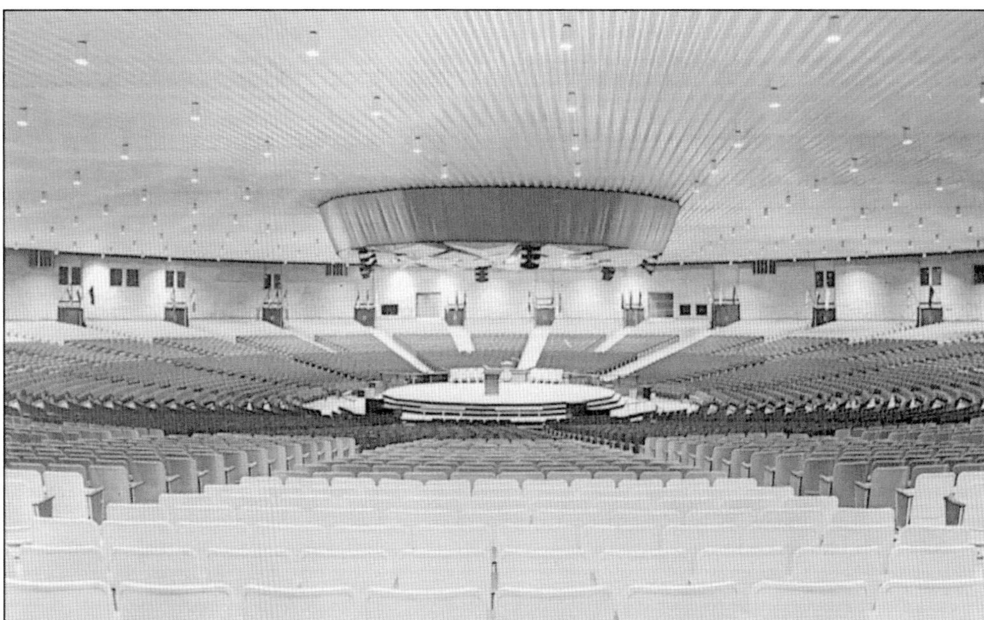

This postcard shows an interior view of Assembly Tabernacle at International Headquarters of the Church of God of Prophecy. This building was demolished in 1999.

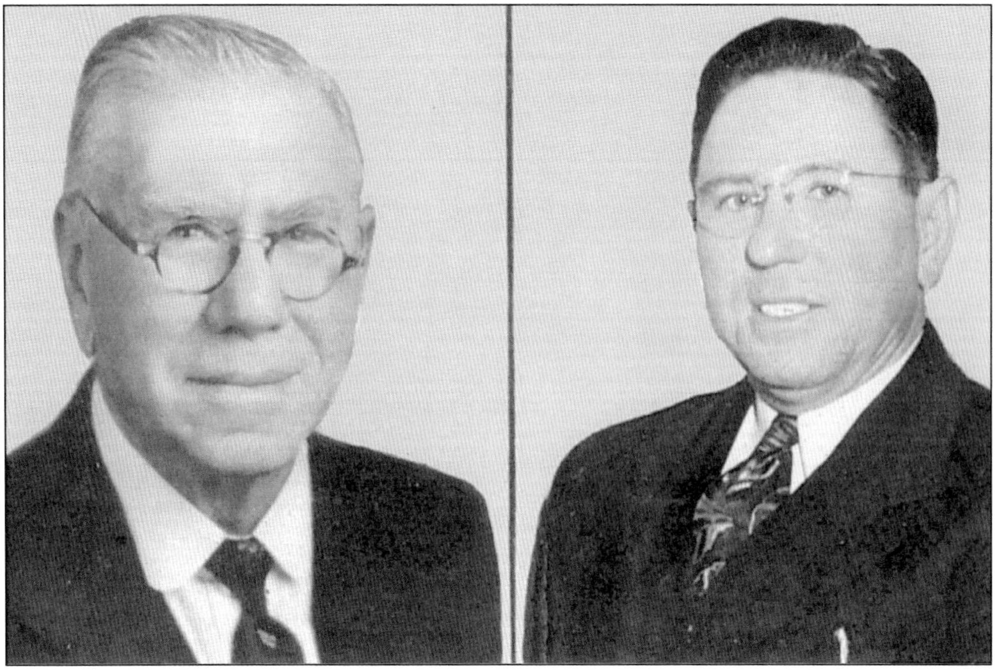

A.J. Tomlinson was the General Overseer of the Church of God. A major schism occurred in 1923, and he became Overseer of the Church of God of Prophecy. His son, Milton A. Tomlinson, succeeded him in 1943.

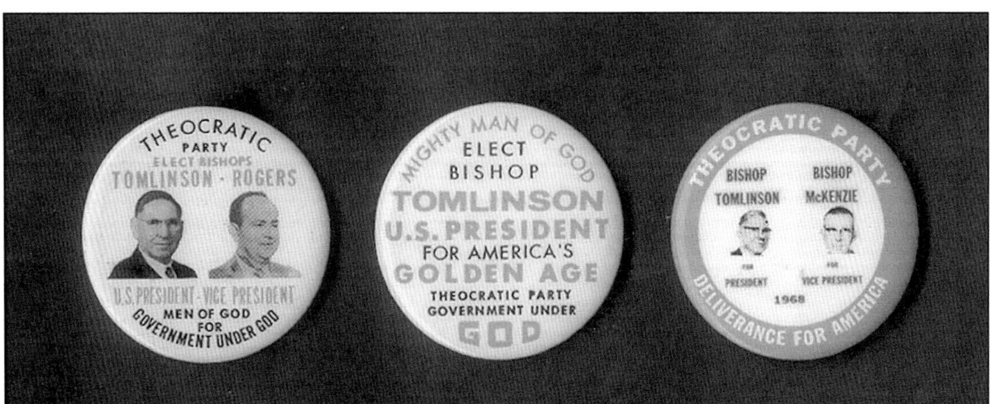

Homer Tomlinson was the eldest son of A.J. Tomlinson and the only person from Bradley County to ever run for president of the United States. He led the Theocratic Party ticket in 1960, 1964, and 1968.

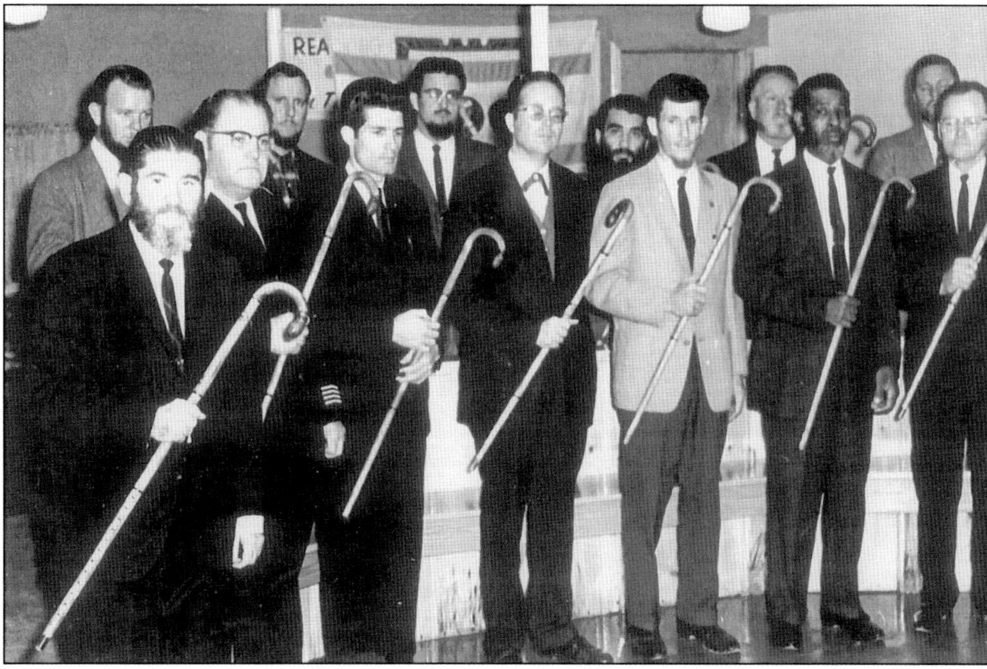

Grady Kent was chief bishop of the Church of God—Jerusalem Acres. The Council of Elders in 1959 included, from left to right, the following: (front row) Grady Kent, R.L. Simons, Bob McGlimery, Elford Collins, Eldon McNabb, Johnny Williams, and D.E. Garr; (back row) Marion W. Hall, W.J. Fox, Earl Stewart, David Williams, John H. Looper, and Floyd Burton.

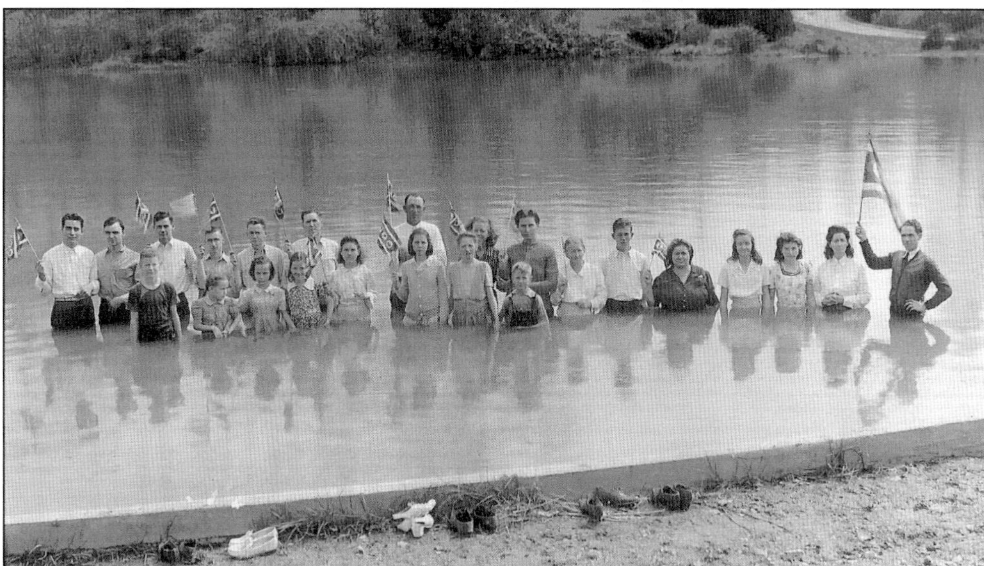

The Church of God conducted a baptism in 1943 in Sikes Lake on Harrison Pike. Notice the shoes at the edge of the water. Pictured from left to right are the following: (front row) James Pentcost, two unidentified, Exess Calfee, Ruth Calfee, Alberta Bird, Melba Phillips, and Ruth Pentcost; (back row) Harper Hunter, unidentified, Everett Atnip, Carl Lawson, T.W. Goins, William Phillips, Fain F. Gibbons, Alineen Cannon, unidentified, Mrs. Roy Cannon, unidentified, Inez Kinser, two unidentified, Brownie Fulbright, and Charles Batson.

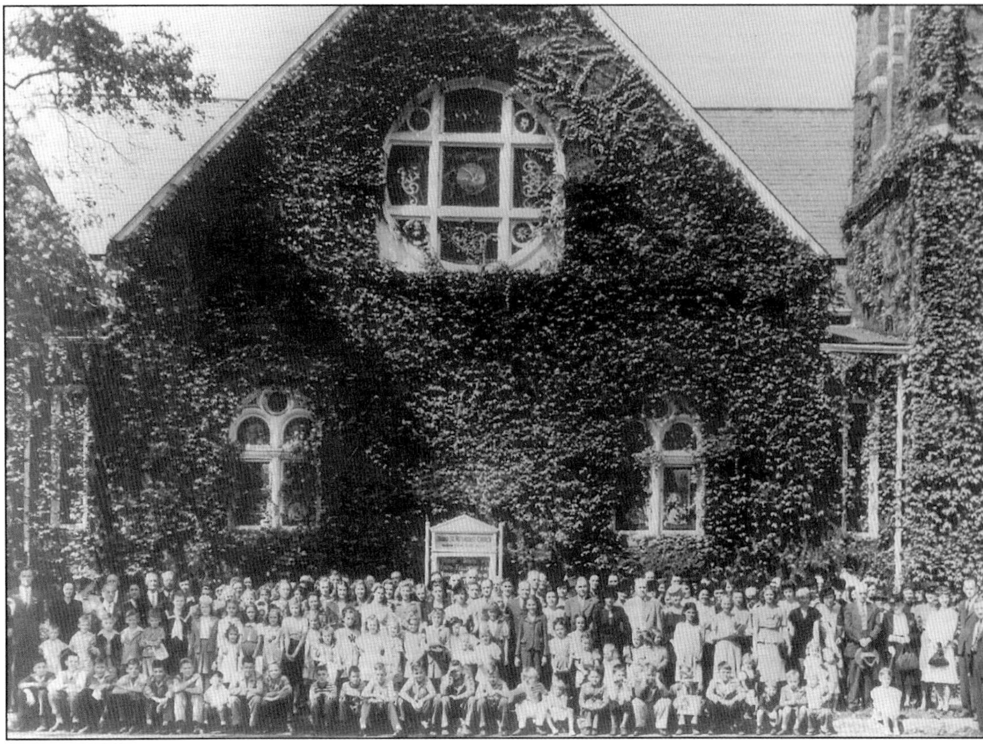

In 1837, Rev. Charles K. Lewis was sent by the Holston Conference to pastor the Methodist Episcopal Church in Cleveland. This building of Broad Street United Methodist Church, formerly known as Lea Street Methodist Episcopal Church, South, is shown on a Sunday School Rally Day in 1942. The church sanctuary was approved for inclusion on the National Register of Historic Places on April 5, 1984.

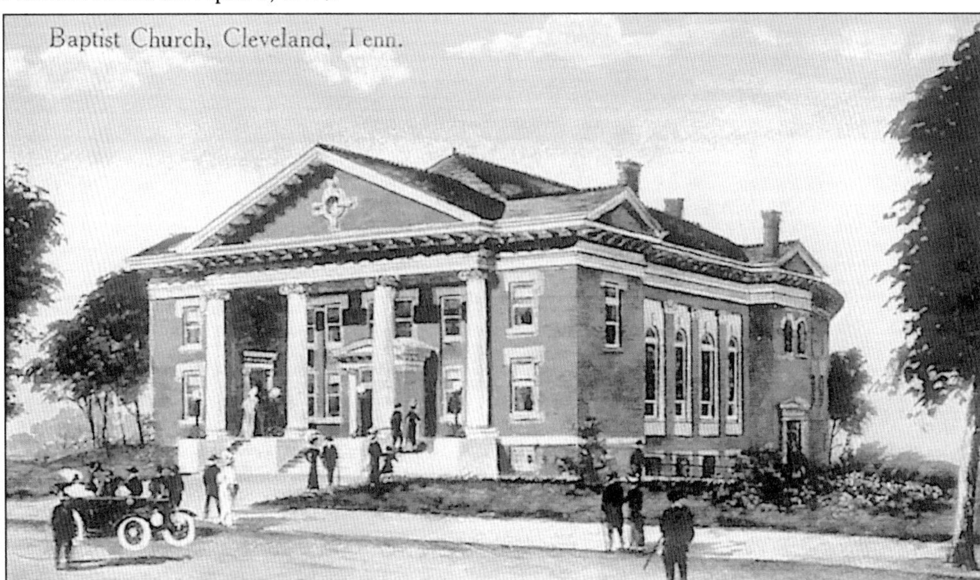

This postcard of the Baptist church was mailed in 1915. An interesting aspect about this card is that the artist's rendering was not accepted by the church.

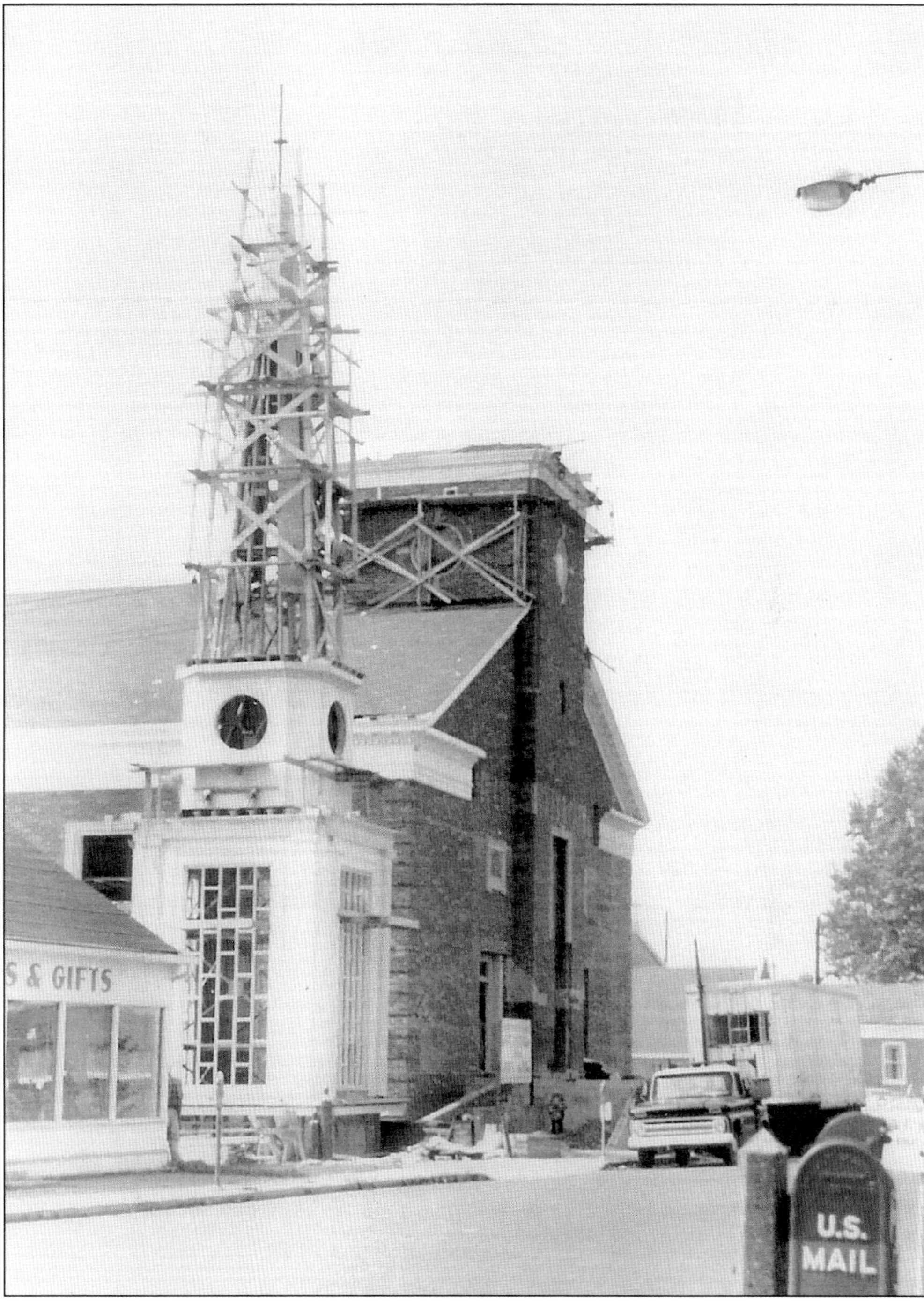

First Baptist Church is the largest church in Cleveland with almost 4,000 members. The sanctuary was remodeled in 1966, and here the new steeple is ready to be raised. Another expansion of this sanctuary was completed in 1998.

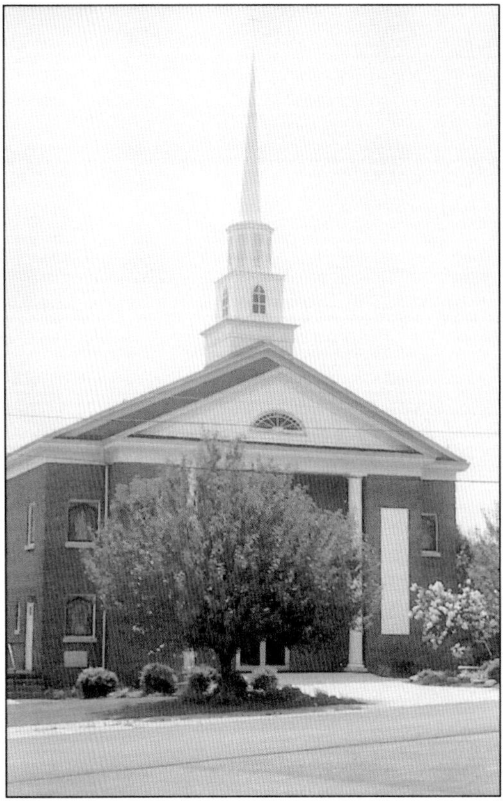

Big Springs Baptist Church was organized on April 6, 1913, at the Inman Street Baptist Church. Rev. Sam Melton was pastor of this church for 29 years.

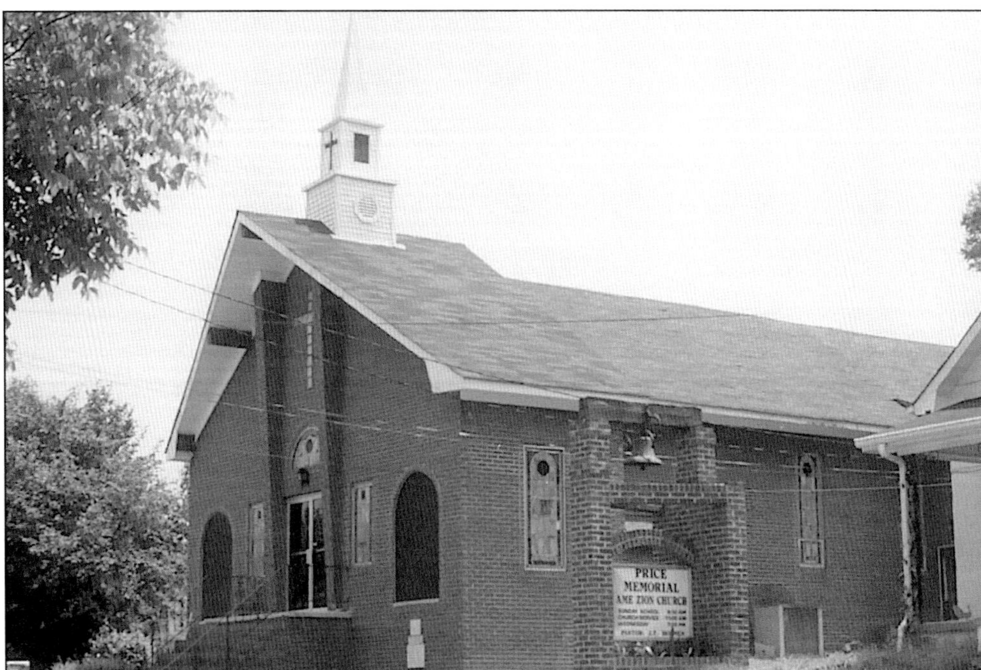

Price Memorial African Methodist Episcopal Zion Church is located on Dooley Street. The church was named for Dr. Joseph Charles Price, pastor from 1875 to 1880.

Six

Education

The location of the school [Centenary College] at Cleveland has always seemed to me fortunate. True, the town was small, say, twenty-five hundred or three thousand people there, but while the war had devastated the town and country around, still the principal business men there were of the old stock of citizens who had struggled through the war together, and were like old neighbors ready to go hand in hand together to rebuild the waste places, a united citizenship.

—David Sullins
Recollections of an Old Man, 70 Years in Dixie 1827–1897 (pp. 381–382)

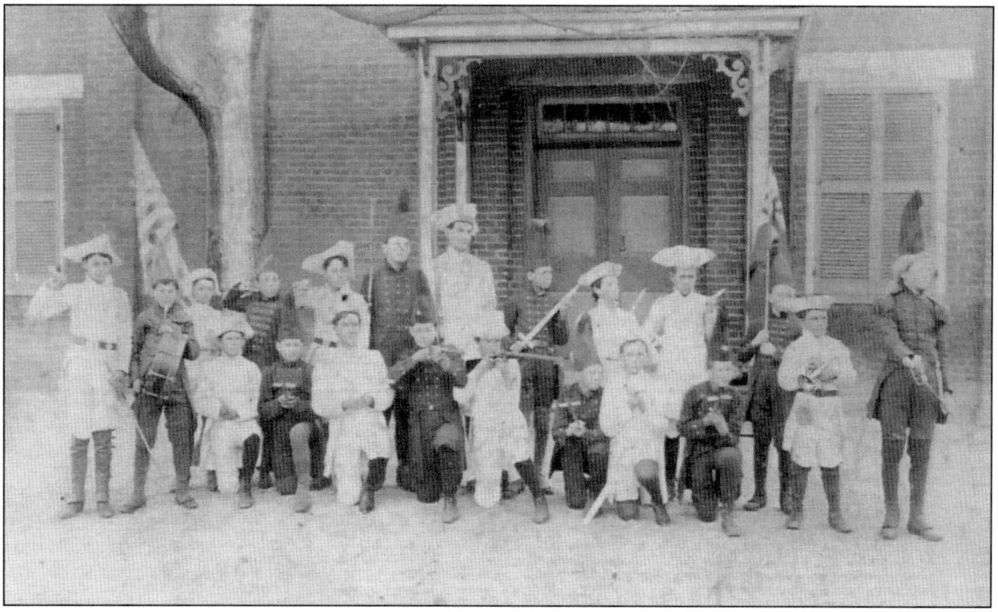

Shown on December 23, 1896, the members of a local drill team are, from left to right, as follows: (kneeling) Oscar McLain, Will Fillauer, Loyd Cate, Charlie Shugart, Marvin McNeer, Will Rogers, Paul Thomas, and Harry Shugart; (standing) Paul Russell, David Cate, Maynard Ramsey, Euclid Paul, Henry Paul, Ron Shugart, Will Kirby, Walter Wilson, Guy Dickie, Wallace Lillard, Willie Dethero, Kimsey Geren, and Karl Hearsk.

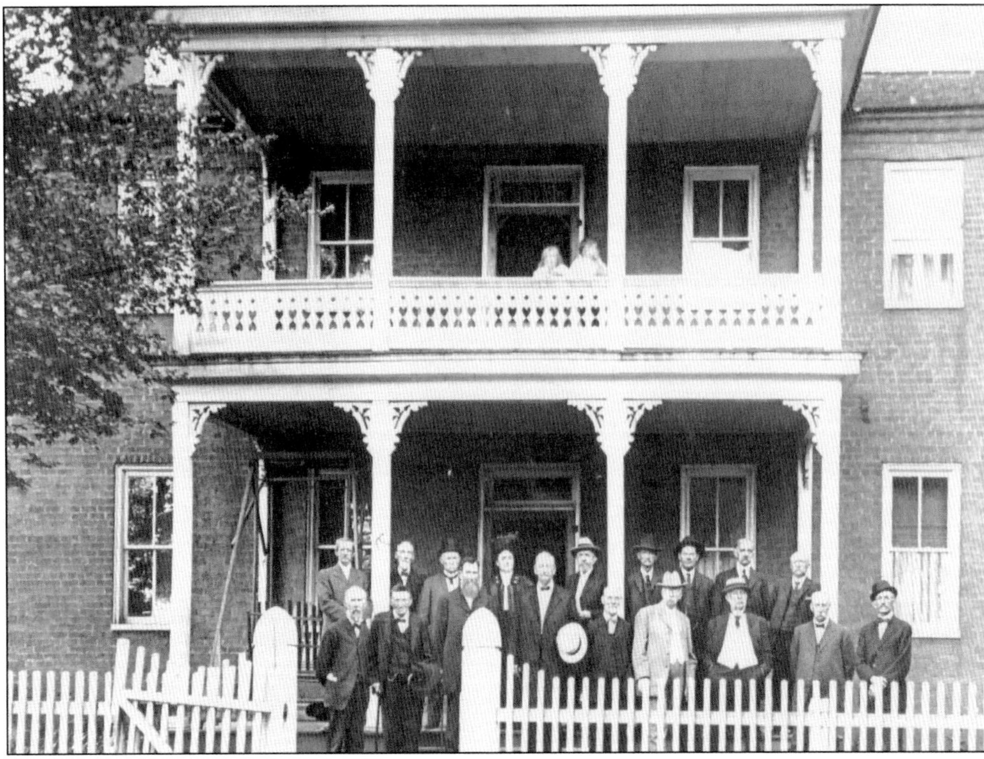

Oak Grove Academy, a boys school, was granted a charter in 1837. "The little red brick school" was erected in 1840. James Tedford was employed to take charge of the academy in 1840. After two years he was succeeded by Henry W. von Aldehoff, a Prussian. Shown here is a reunion in 1902 of students from 1861. Professor T.M. Burkett, who operated the school until the Civil War, is the man in the center holding his hat with his wife beside him.

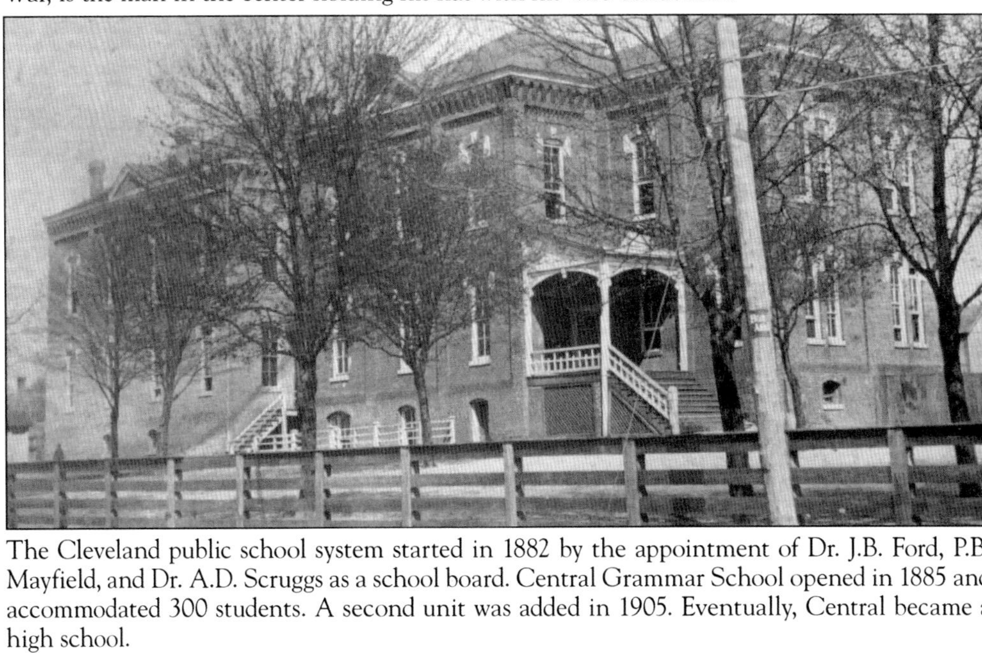

The Cleveland public school system started in 1882 by the appointment of Dr. J.B. Ford, P.B. Mayfield, and Dr. A.D. Scruggs as a school board. Central Grammar School opened in 1885 and accommodated 300 students. A second unit was added in 1905. Eventually, Central became a high school.

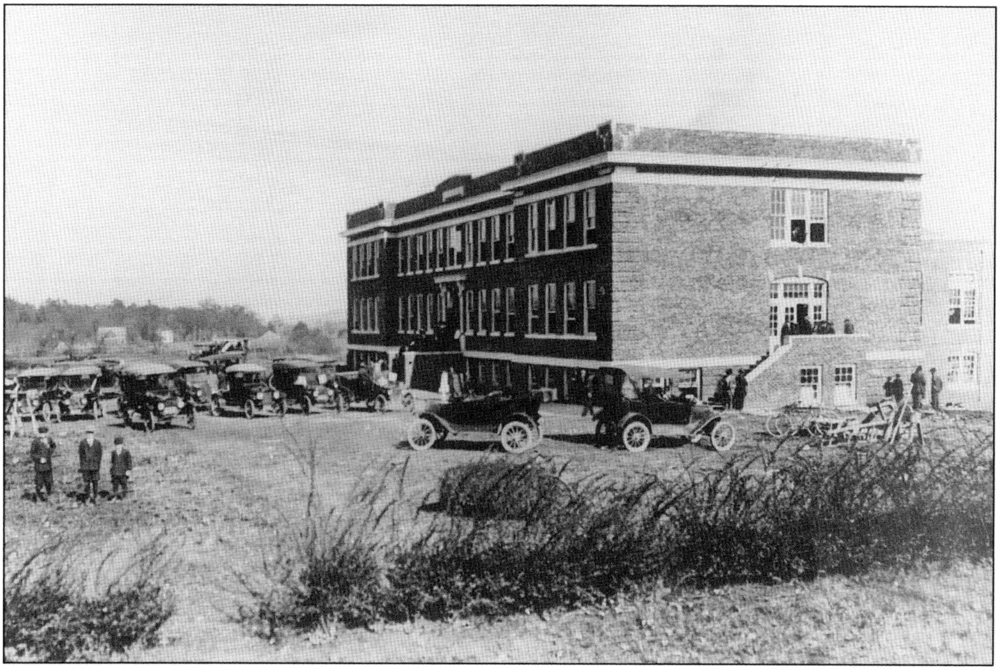

Bradley Central High School was opened in 1916 as the result of a merger of Bradley High School in Charleston and Central High School in Cleveland.

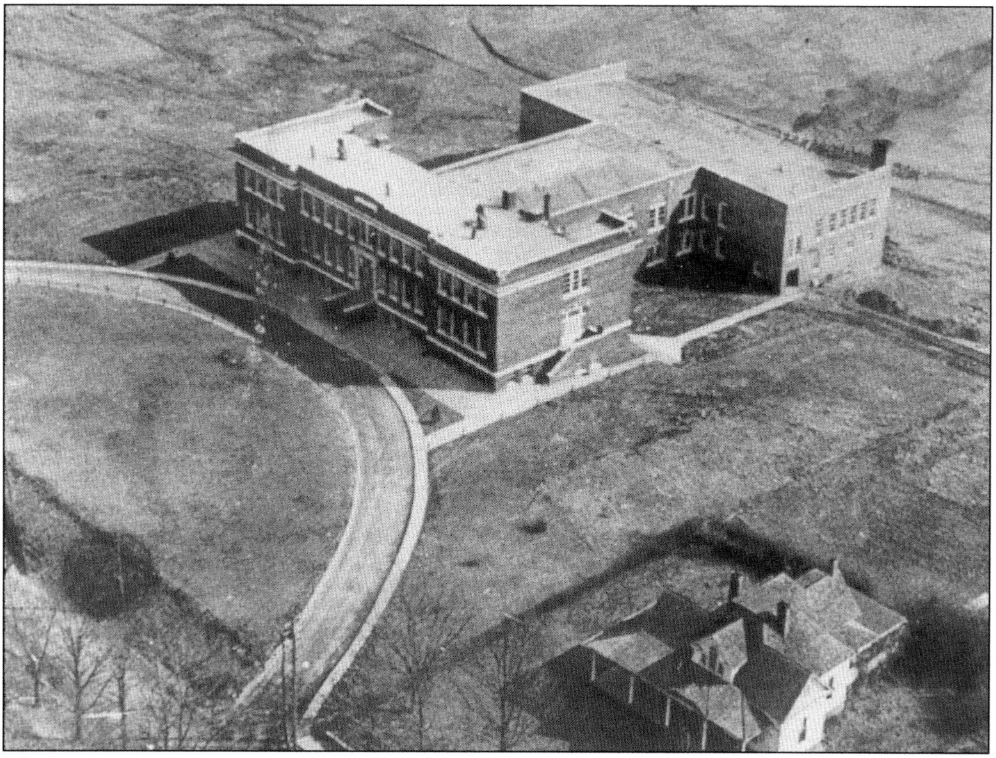

This is an aerial view of Bradley Central High School showing the new addition on the rear. The school was built just outside of the city limits on North Ocoee Street.

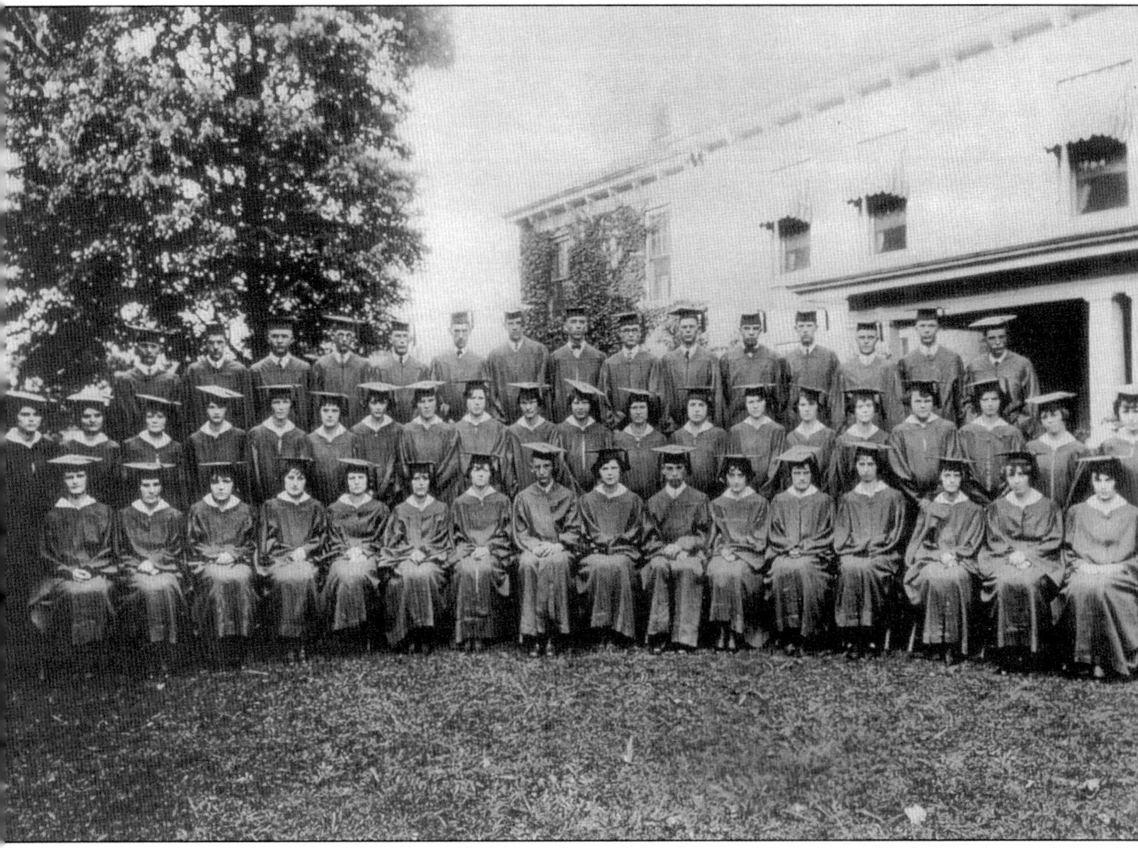

The 1925 graduating class of Bradley Central High School was composed of 17 males and 34 females. This picture was made on the lawn at the C.C. Card home on Church Street.

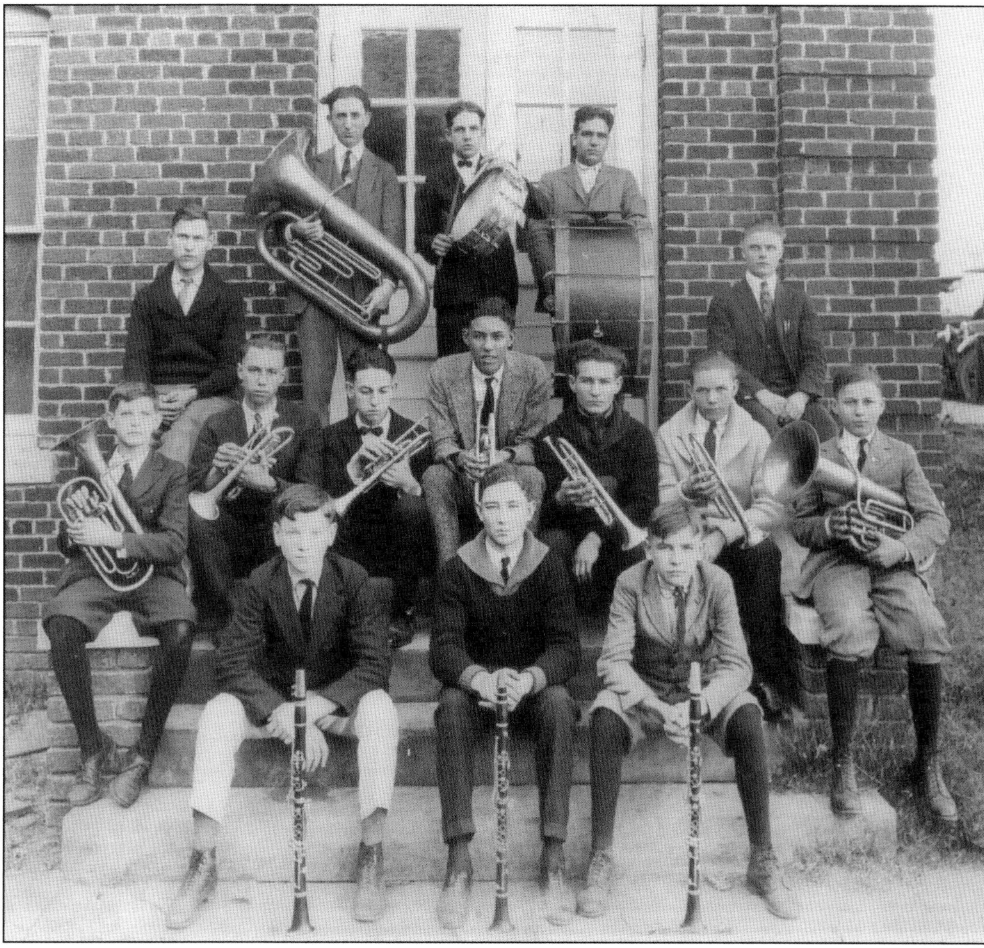

These are the members of the Bradley High School band in 1924. Notice that some of the young men are wearing knickers.

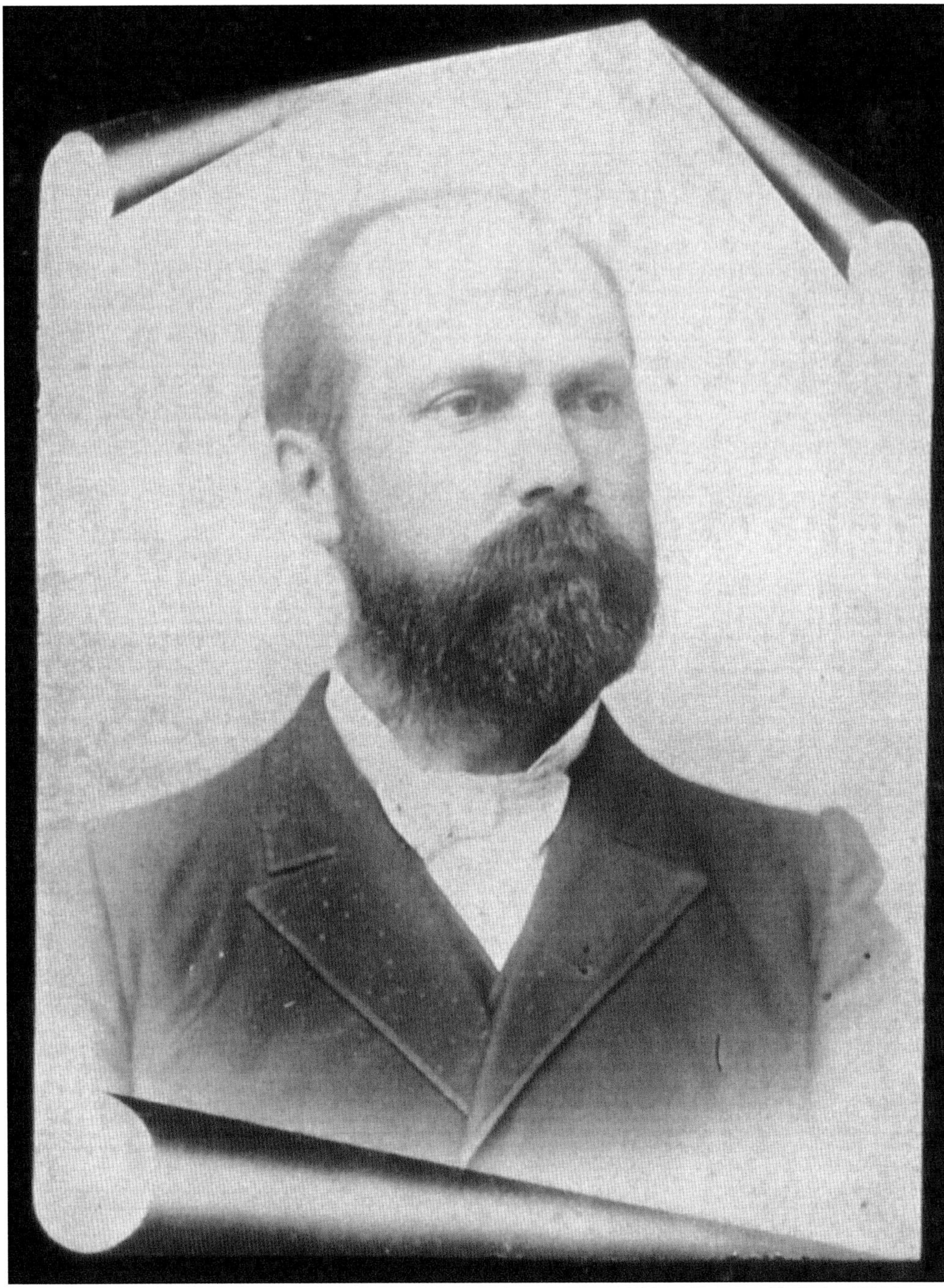

Much admired and respected, Professor DeWitt Clinton Arnold has been called the "Father of the graded school system of Cleveland." He was a native of Ohio, coming to Cleveland because of ill health. He served as superintendent of the city schools from 1885 until 1921, with the exception of 1901–1903.

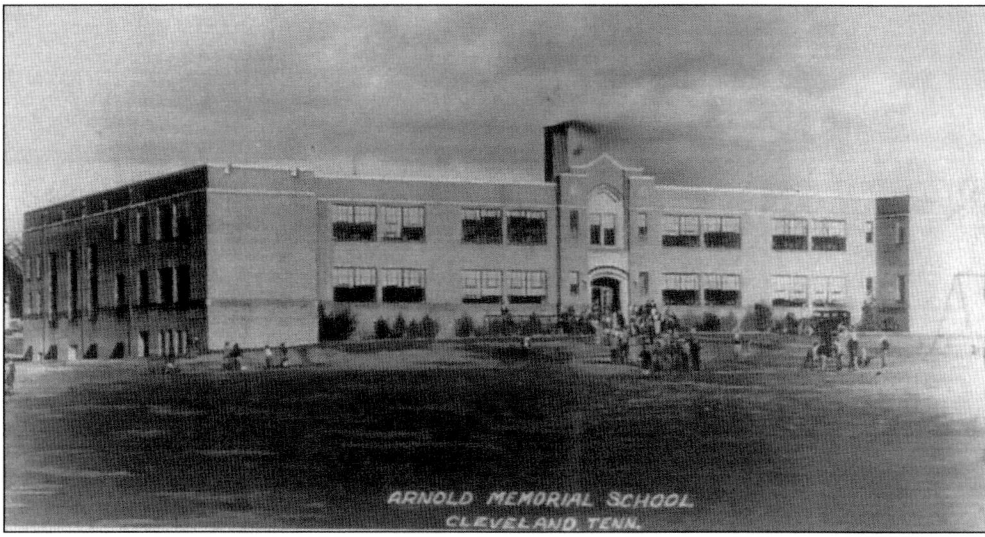

Arnold Memorial School, named for Superintendent D.C. Arnold, was completed in 1929. At that time, it contained 20 classrooms, a manual training shop, library, study hall, an auditorium with a seating capacity of 1,200, a cafeteria that could accommodate 300 at one time, and an office suite of three rooms.

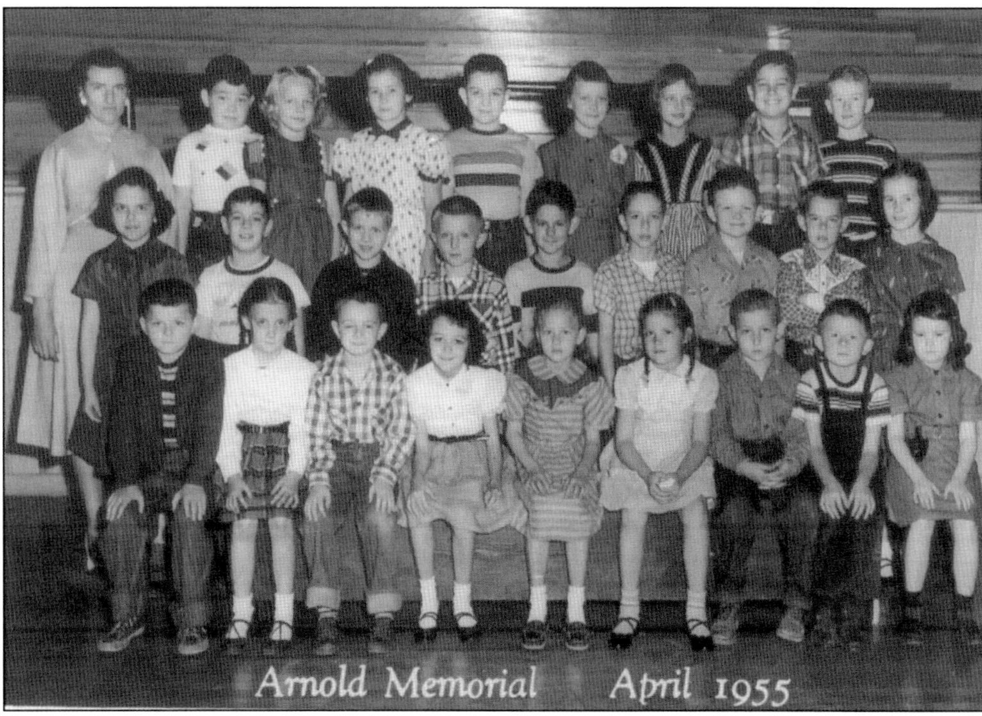

Pictured here is Ileen Rucker's second grade class at Arnold Memorial in 1955. The students are, from left to right, as follows: (front row) Terry Morrow, Sally Nevin, Eddie Finnell, Mary Lou Cooke, Patsy Coe, two unidentified, David Spencer, and Susie Wilson; (middle row) Martha Hobbs, unidentified, Guy Bevins, John Davis, Steve Owens, Gary Trimm, Tommy Gatlin, Mike Revenig, and Dionne Barger; (back row) Dennis Guffey, Patricia Burns, Harriet Lee, Dick Erwin, Etta Faye White, unidentified, Ben McClary, and Jim Hicks.

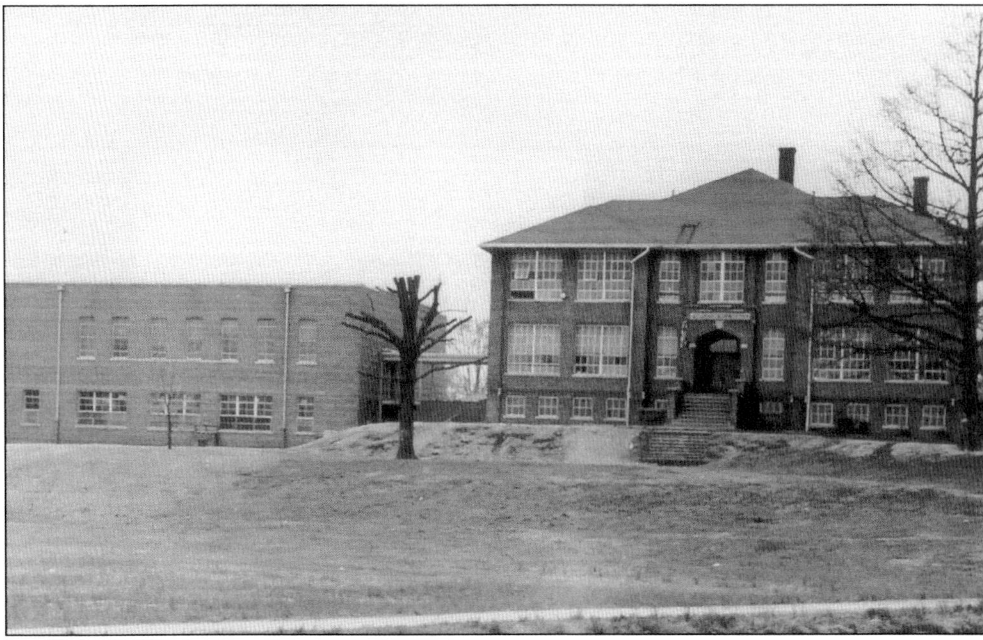

Templeton Hill School, erected in 1924 in South Cleveland, is shown here in 1956. Templeton Hill was vacated by Cleveland City Schools at the end of the 1970–71 school year, but the building continued in use in the fall by Bradley County Schools, which designated it Big Springs at Templeton Hill in order to replace Big Springs, which had burned a few days before the end of the spring semester.

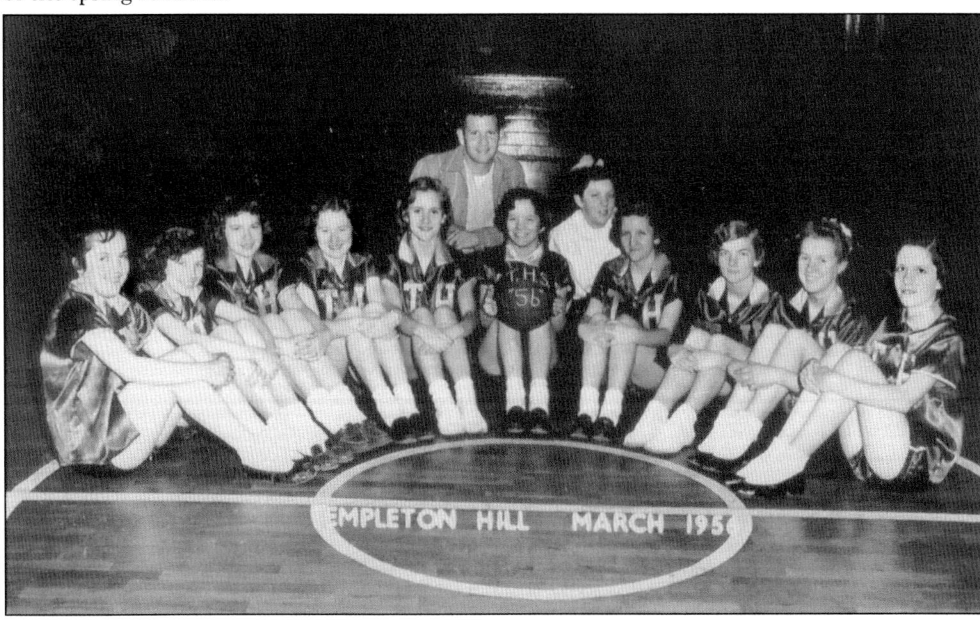

Athletics is an important facet of school life. Shown here is Coach Robert Henley with the Templeton Hill eighth grade girls basketball team in 1956; they are, from left to right, Patsy Mullinax, Juanita Tipton, Johnnie Gooch, Linda Waller, Jimmie Lou Giles, Christina Moore, Shirley Cupp, Shelby Townsend, Kathryn Wilhoit, and Linda Cupp. The girl in white is Martha Gregg, team manager.

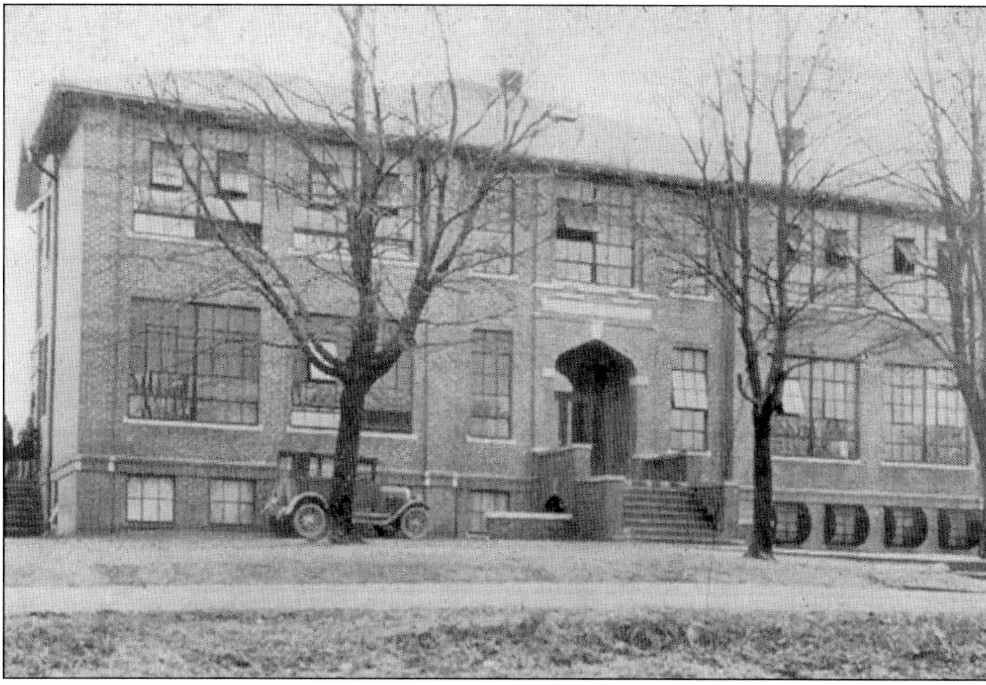

The wooden building of College Hill School for Blacks was razed, and a new brick structure was built in 1924, which included 12 grades from elementary to high school.

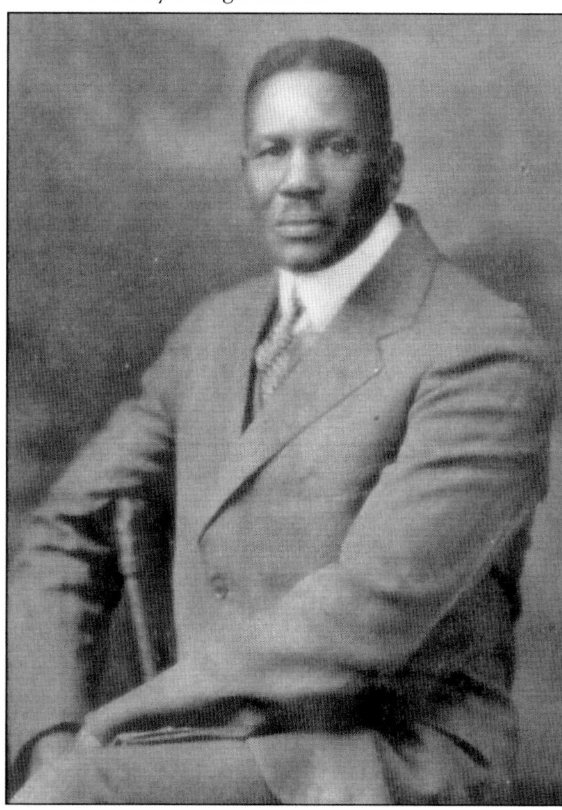

Upshur Lloyd Knox was the honored principal of College Hill School. His wife, Corrine, was the librarian. The students, who loved and respected Knox, dedicated the first issue of the school's yearbook to him. Knox was active in improving the community and served as treasurer of the Enterprise League. His son, George H. Knox, was reportedly the first African American born in Speck Hospital. The board of education erected a historical marker in loving memory of Professor and Mrs. U.L. Knox. Located on the campus of the school that he loved and served, the marker read as follows: "I have no greater joy than to hear that the children walk in truth. III John 4."

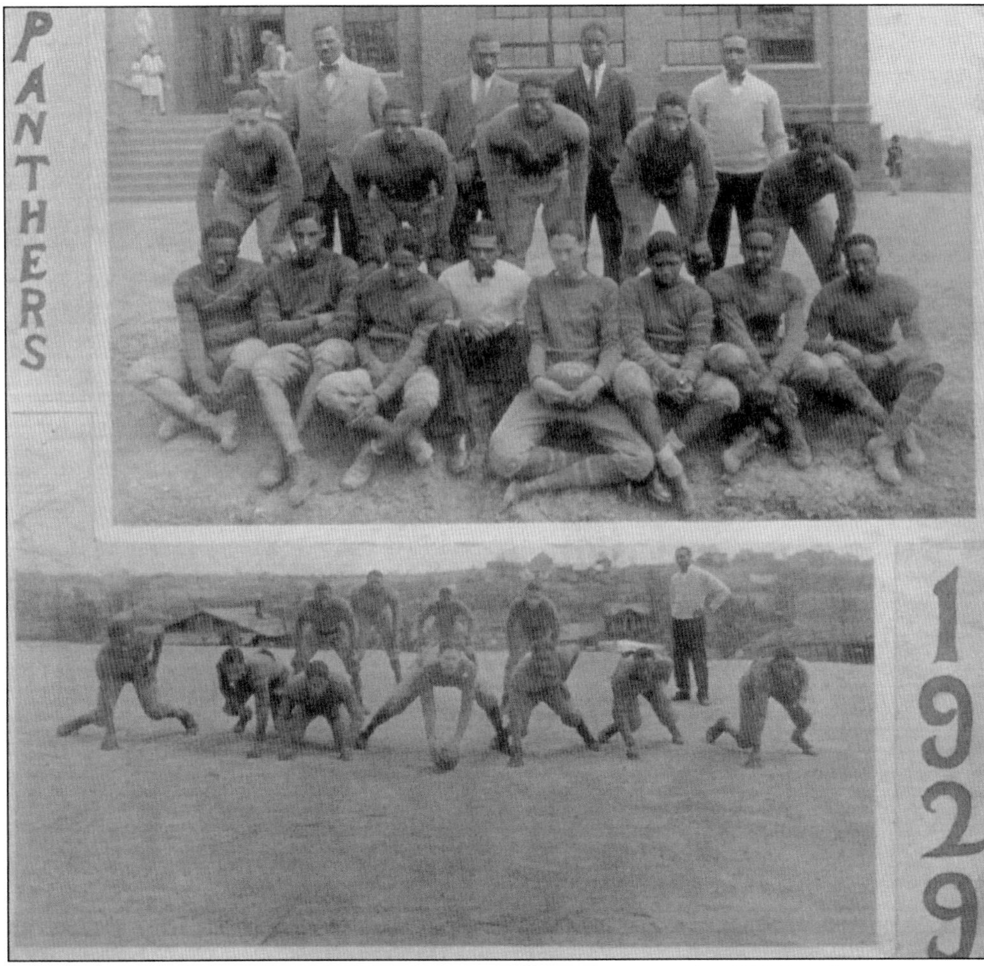

College Hill was known for its fine sports teams. Shown here are the 1929 Panthers.

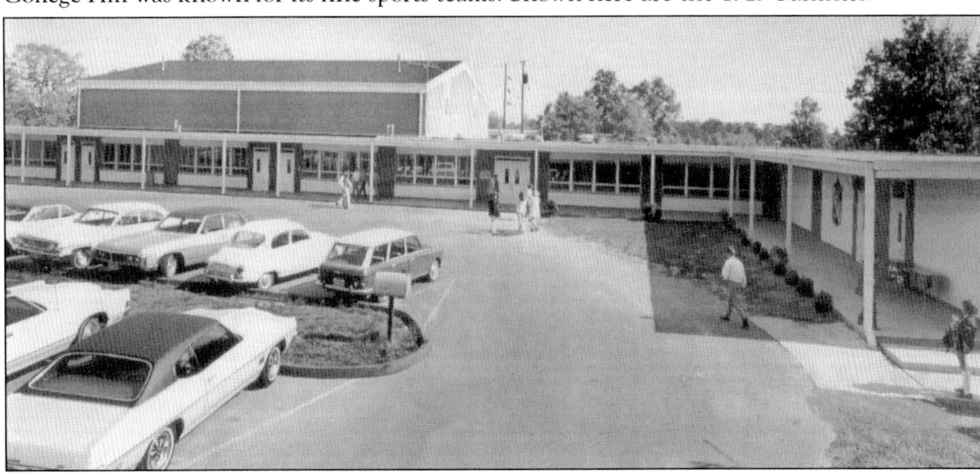

Cleveland Day School was chartered in 1963 to provide a nonsectarian, coeducational preparatory curriculum in grades 1 through 12. It was situated on a 65-acre campus off Blythe Ferry Road. The Day School closed in 1976.

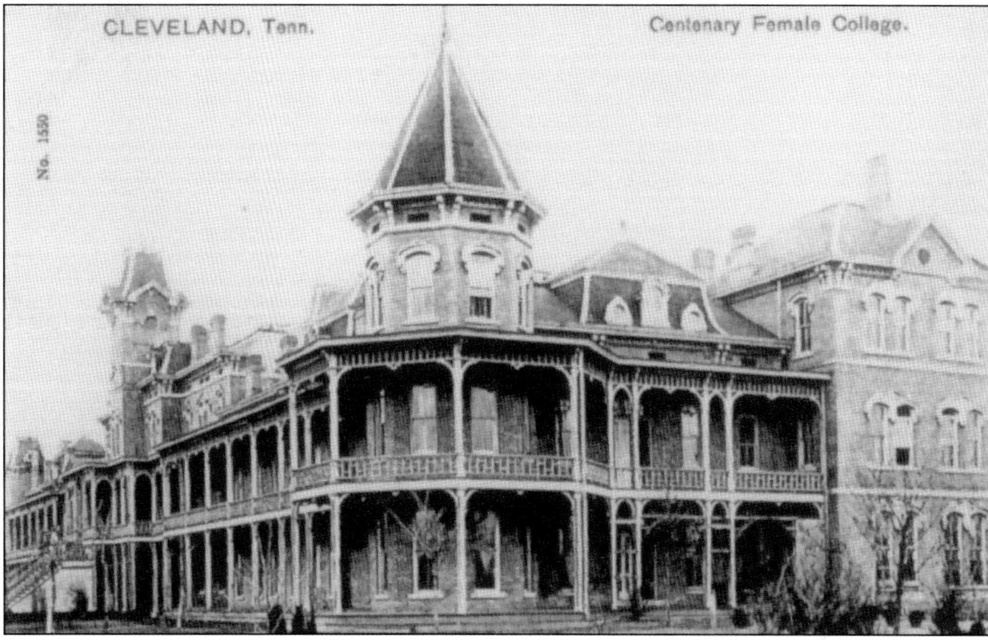

The year 1884 was the Centennial of American Methodism and the year George R. Stuart became pastor of Lea Street Methodist Church. Stuart and his father-in-law, David Sullins, were instrumental in the Holston Conference of the Methodist Episcopal Church, South, in opening an institution for females in Cleveland. The school was named Centenary in honor of the Methodist Centennial and opened in 1885.

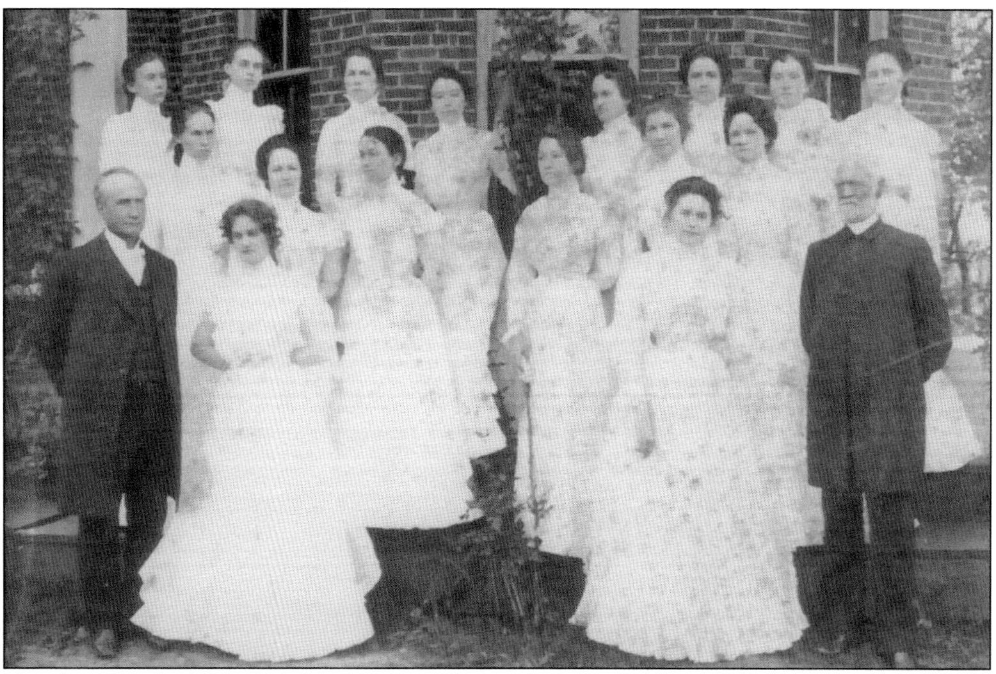

David Sullins was a Methodist minister who was instrumental in starting Sullins College in Bristol, VA, as well as Centenary Female College in Cleveland. Sullins is the bearded gentleman on the right.

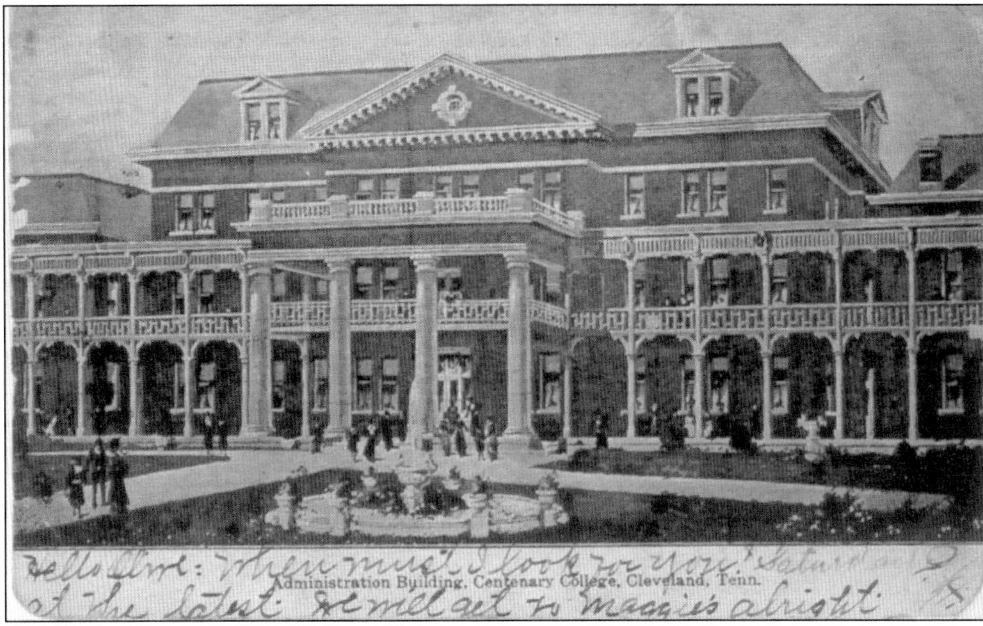

This postcard shows the administration building at Centenary Female College. It burned February 9, 1907.

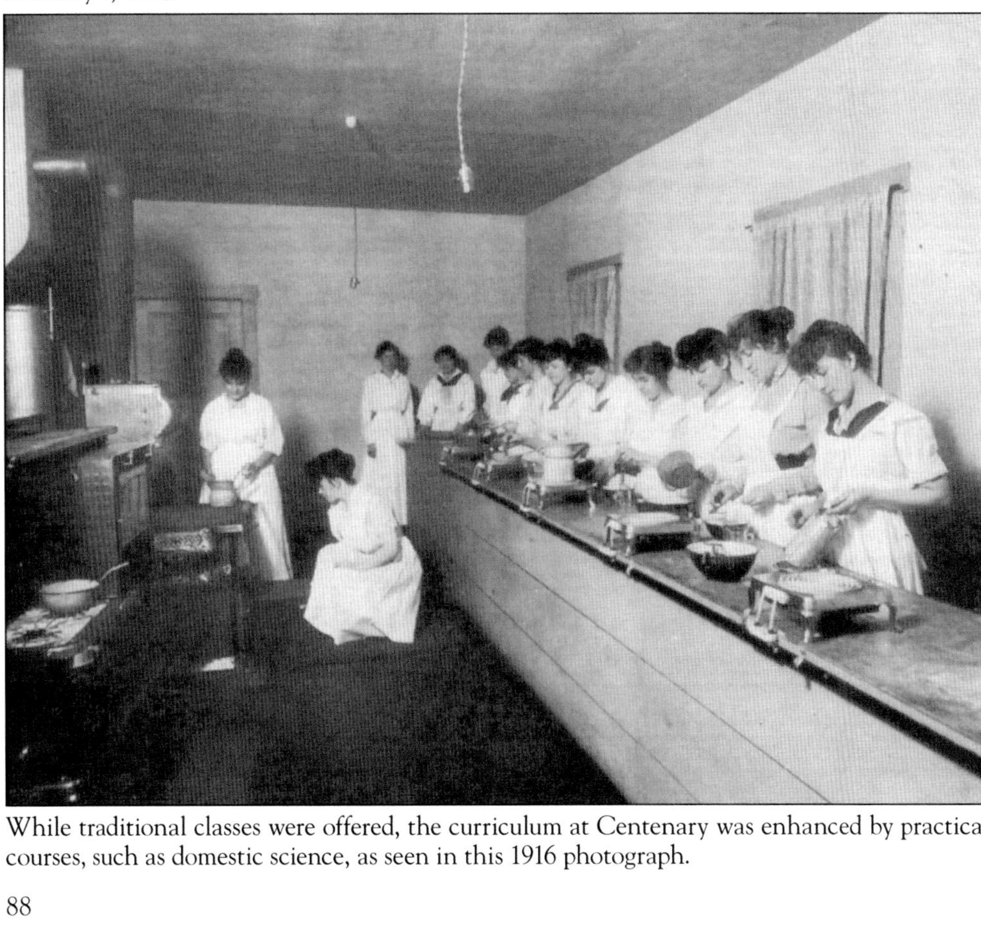

While traditional classes were offered, the curriculum at Centenary was enhanced by practical courses, such as domestic science, as seen in this 1916 photograph.

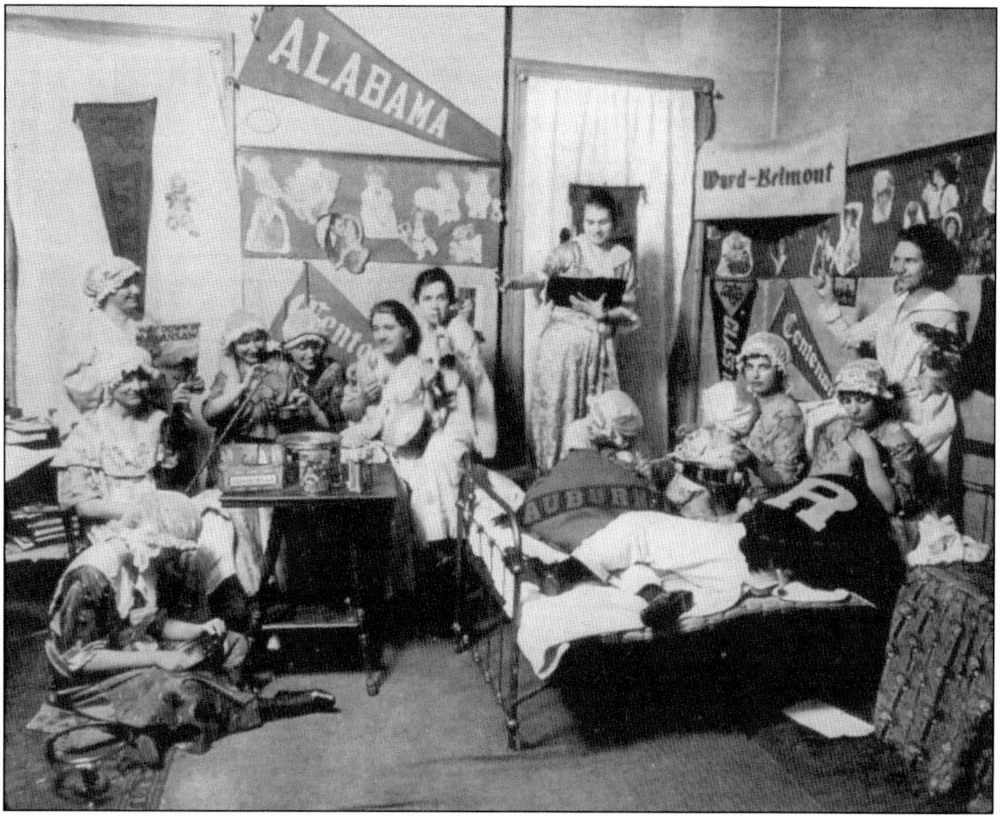

Centenary Female College was not all work and no play as seen by this photo of the Sunday Night Club. The club motto was "Don't leave until tomorrow what you can eat tonight."

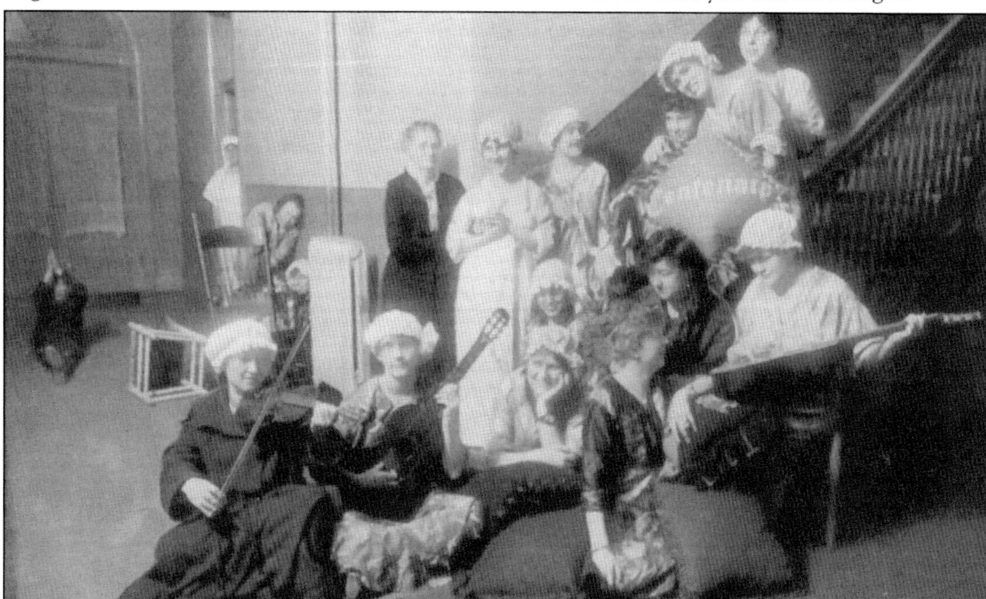

Each dormitory section was named, and the girls performed skits and musicals together. Pictured here is the Middle Building Group of Centenary College in 1916.

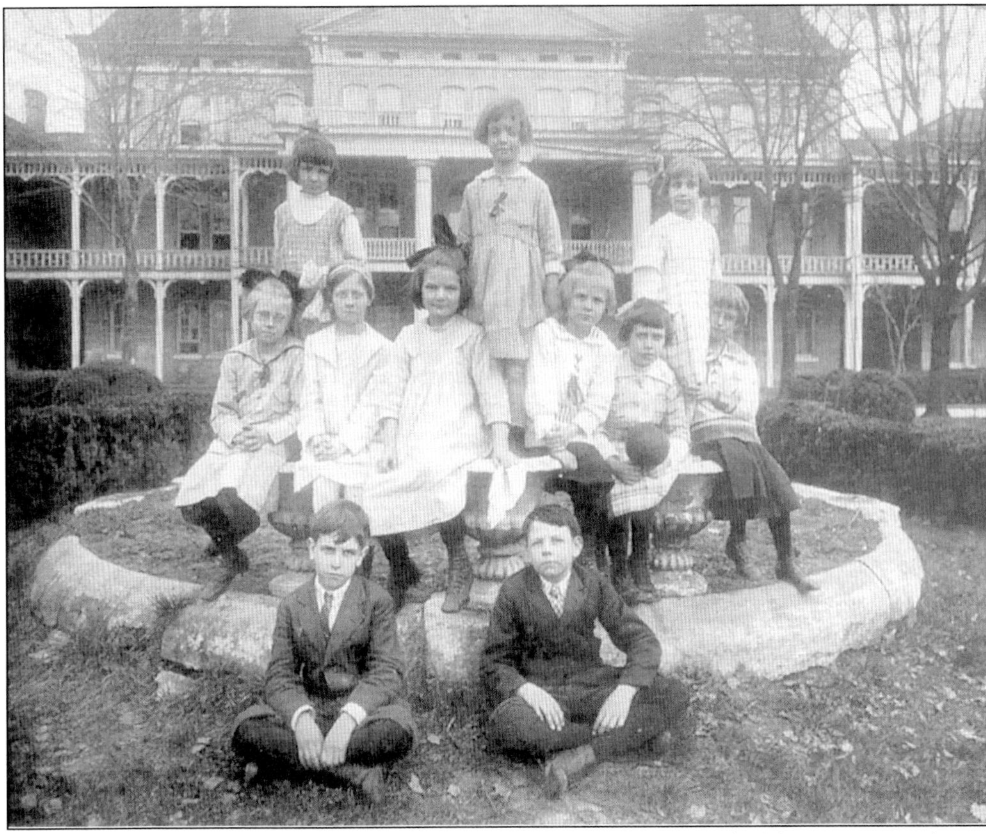

Centenary College also included a primary division. Pictured are several of the primary students.

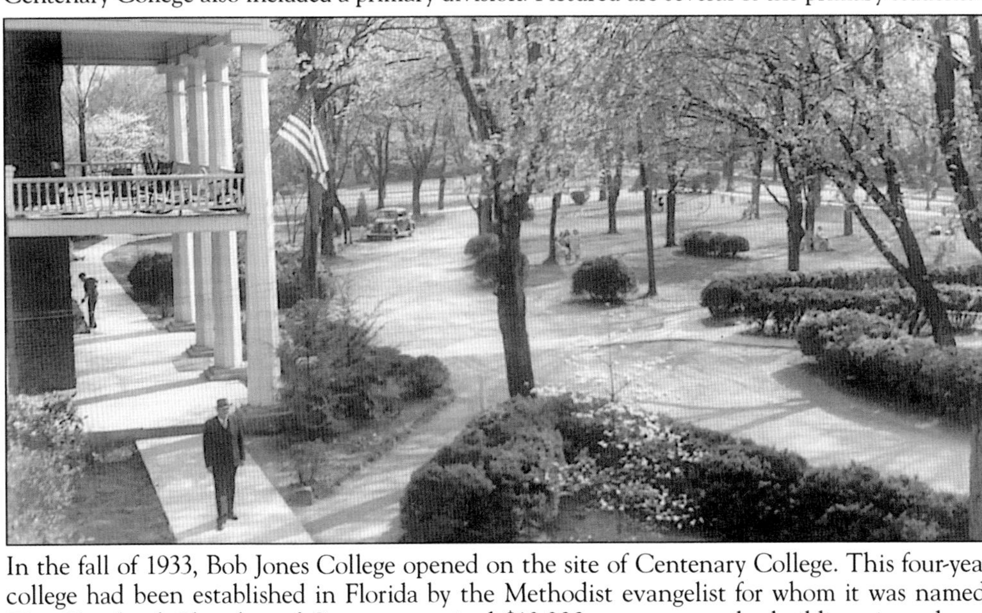

In the fall of 1933, Bob Jones College opened on the site of Centenary College. This four-year college had been established in Florida by the Methodist evangelist for whom it was named. The Cleveland Chamber of Commerce raised $10,000 to renovate the buildings in order to encourage Bob Jones to locate in Cleveland. Dr. Bob Jones Sr. is pictured here on the campus in Cleveland.

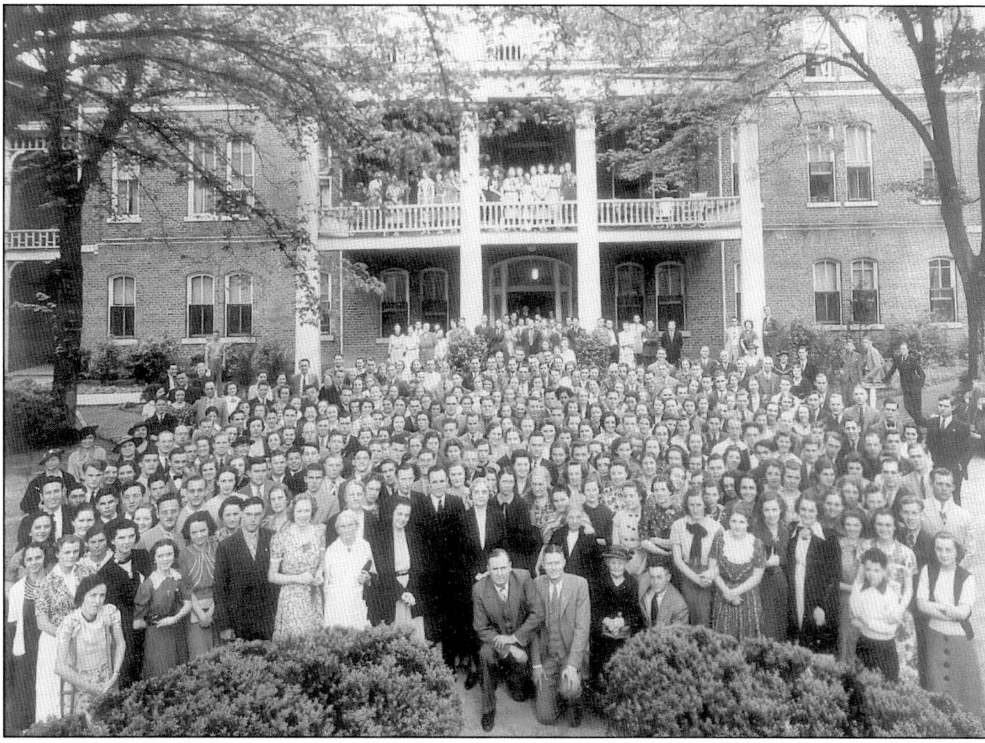

In 1936, Bob Jones College was the largest liberal arts college in Tennessee.

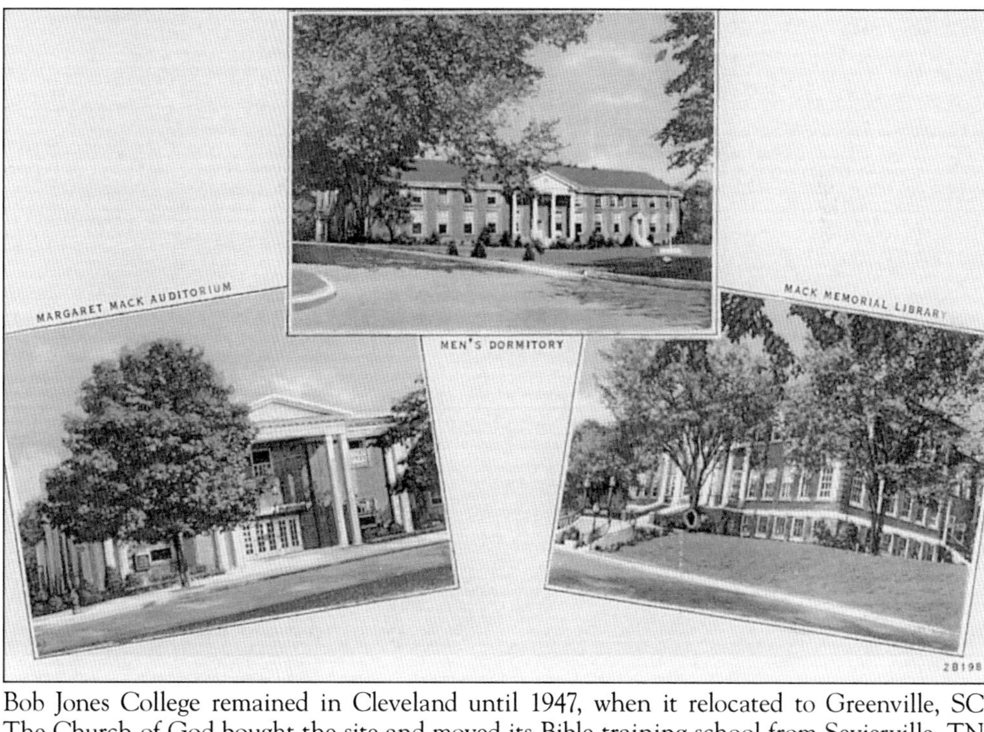

Bob Jones College remained in Cleveland until 1947, when it relocated to Greenville, SC. The Church of God bought the site and moved its Bible training school from Sevierville, TN, to Cleveland.

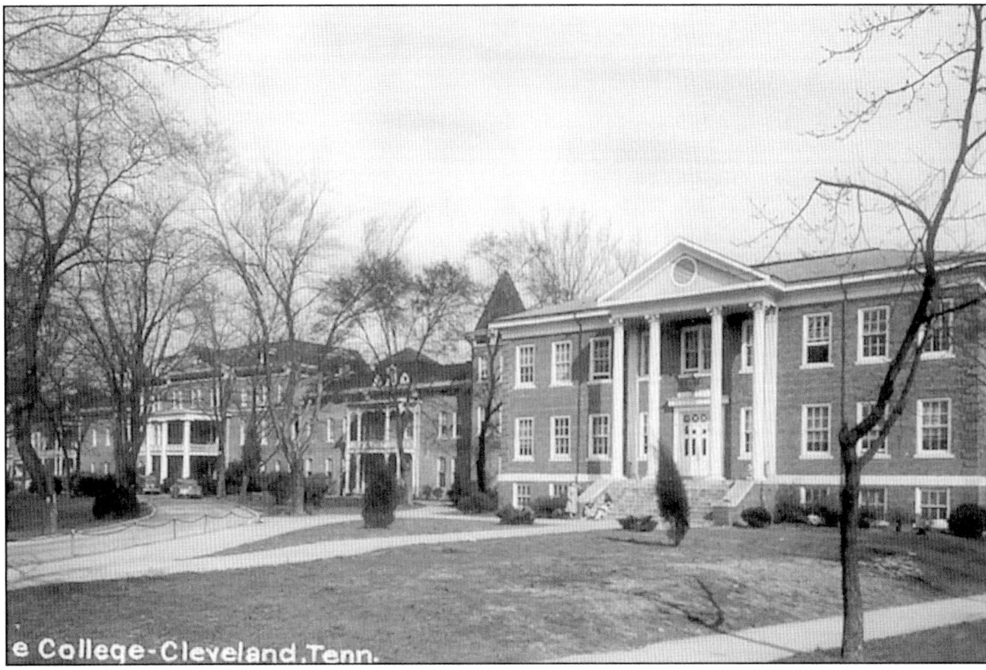

Lee College was named in honor of Flavius J. Lee, an early Church of God leader. The school evolved from a Bible training school to a four-year liberal arts college. In 1997 the college became Lee University.

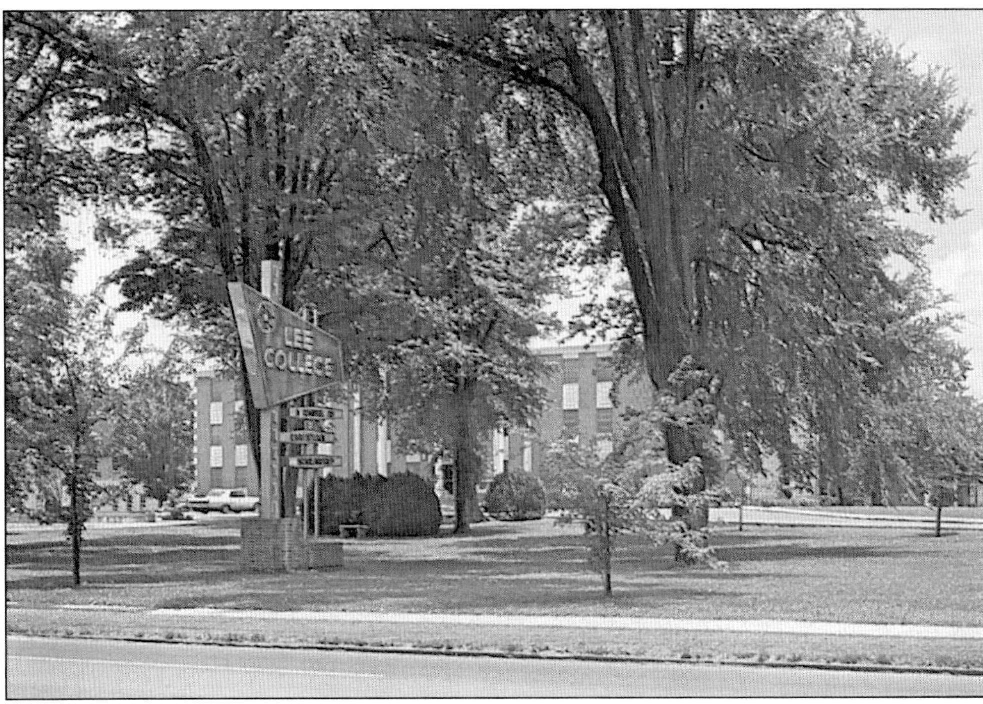

The Lee campus is beautiful with its green lawns and trees amidst majestic academic buildings.

Seven

MILITARY, FRATERNAL, AND CIVIC GROUPS

There were three reasons for the existence and popularity of male fraternal groups at the beginning of the twentieth century: insurance, entertainment, and male bonding. Social security covered the insurance need; radio and television fulfilled the need for entertainment; only male bonding was left as the key need to be addressed by fraternal groups, and even it was under attack by special interest groups in late-twentieth-century society.

—Steve Addison
Bradley County Historical Society member and local author

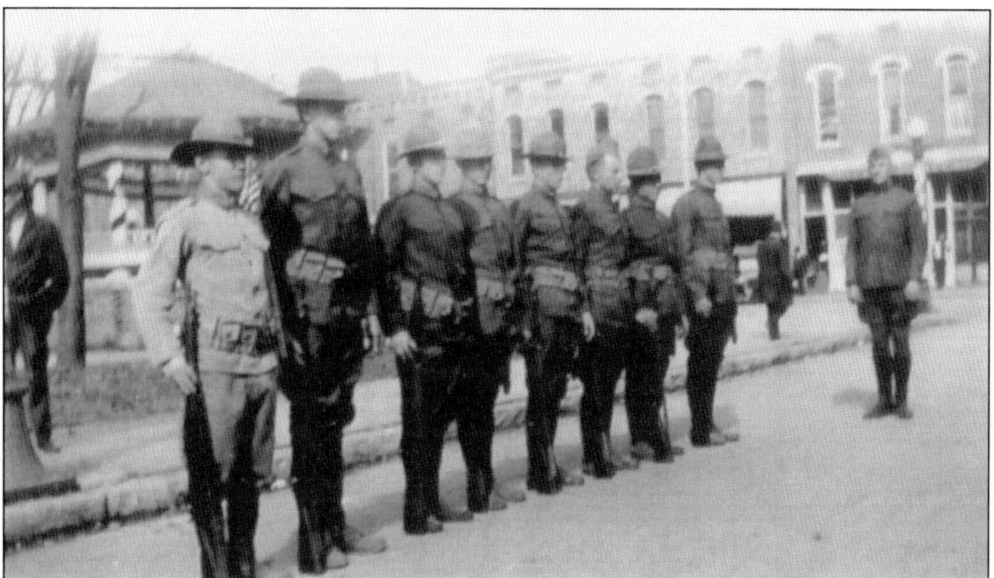

Veterans lined up on Armistice Day, November 11, 1920, on the courthouse square. The local American Legion post was organized in 1920 under the name of Bradley Post #81. Cleveland's first public fireworks display was a result of the Legion's activities.

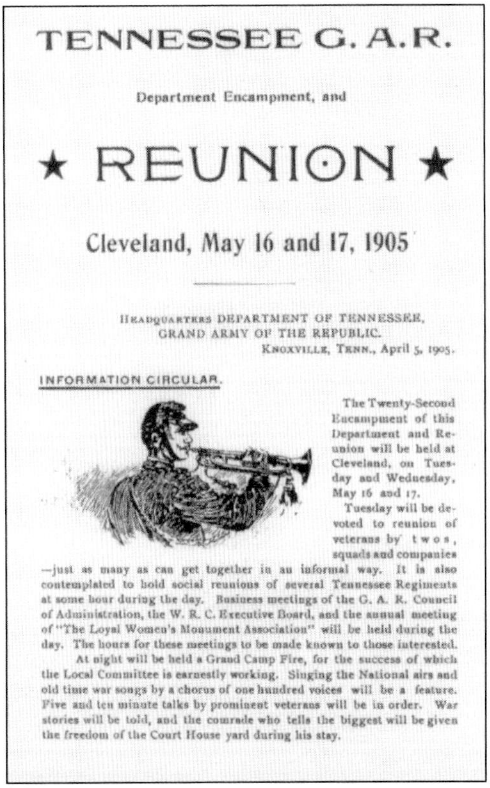

TENNESSEE G. A. R.

Department Encampment, and

★ REUNION ★

Cleveland, May 16 and 17, 1905

HEADQUARTERS DEPARTMENT OF TENNESSEE,
GRAND ARMY OF THE REPUBLIC.
KNOXVILLE, TENN., April 5, 1905.

INFORMATION CIRCULAR.

The Twenty-Second Encampment of this Department and Reunion will be held at Cleveland, on Tuesday and Wednesday, May 16 and 17.

Tuesday will be devoted to reunion of veterans by twos, squads and companies—just as many as can get together in an informal way. It is also contemplated to hold social reunions of several Tennessee Regiments at some hour during the day. Business meetings of the G. A. R. Council of Administration, the W. R. C. Executive Board, and the annual meeting of "The Loyal Women's Monument Association" will be held during the day. The hours for these meetings to be made known to those interested.

At night will be held a Grand Camp Fire, for the success of which the Local Committee is earnestly working. Singing the National airs and old time war songs by a chorus of one hundred voices will be a feature. Five and ten minute talks by prominent veterans will be in order. War stories will be told, and the comrade who tells the biggest will be given the freedom of the Court House yard during his stay.

The Grand Army of the Republic (GAR) of Tennessee had an encampment in Cleveland, May 16 and 17, 1905. Bradley County had many GAR veterans, as the county did not vote to secede in the Civil War. However, since Cleveland was initially under Confederate control, Union sympathizers often joined units that mustered out of the area.

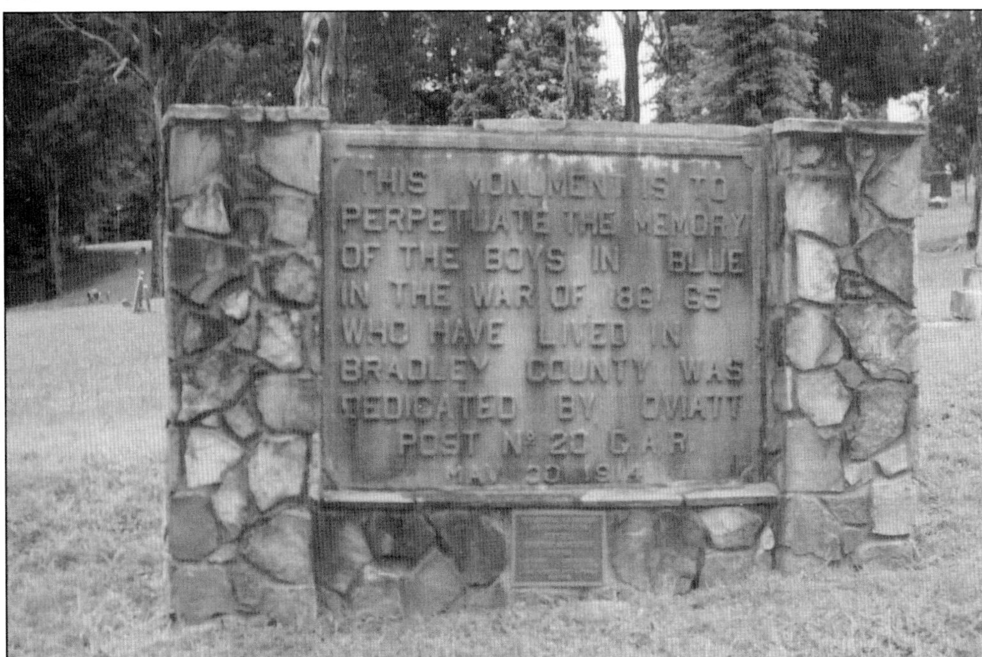

On May 30, 1914, the Oviatt Post No. 20 of the GAR dedicated a monument to the "Boys in Blue from Bradley County." Cleveland is one of the few towns in America with monuments to both Union and Confederate soldiers.

John D. Traynor, for whom the United Confederate Veterans (UCV) camp was named, was a son of John D. Traynor Sr., who located in Cleveland in 1836. John D. Traynor Jr., a captain in the Confederate army, was unmarried. He was born in 1841 and died August 15, 1890. He is buried at Fort Hill Cemetery.

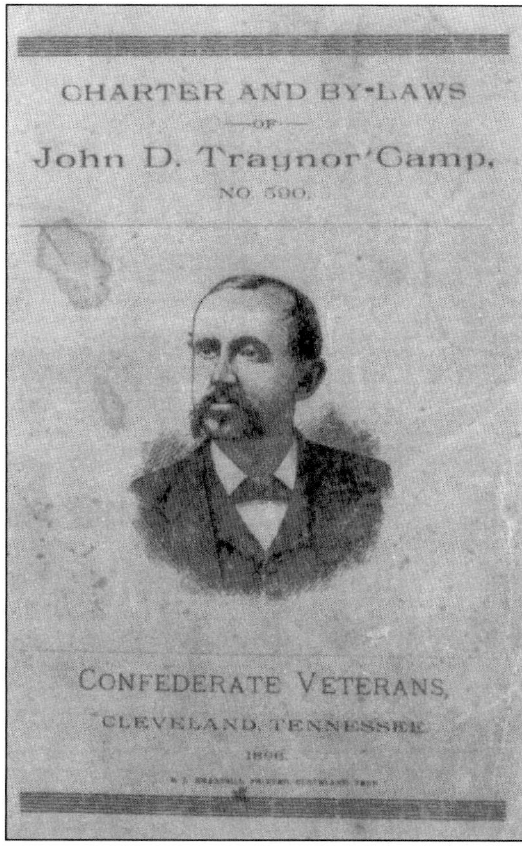

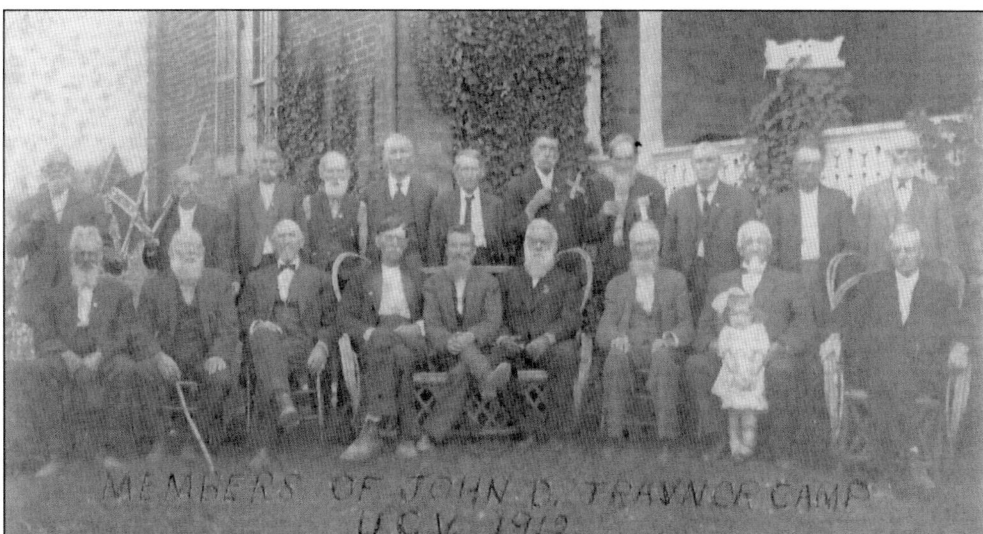

In 1894, the Bradley County Veterans Society received a charter from the Confederate Veterans Grand Lodge, which designated the new group the John D. Traynor Camp United Confederate Veterans, No. 590. The first officials under the charter were Dr. S.H. Day, commander; J.G. Stuart, first lieutenant; and G.B. Hayes, second lieutenant. This 1912 photograph of the members of John D. Traynor Camp UCV shows the aging veterans.

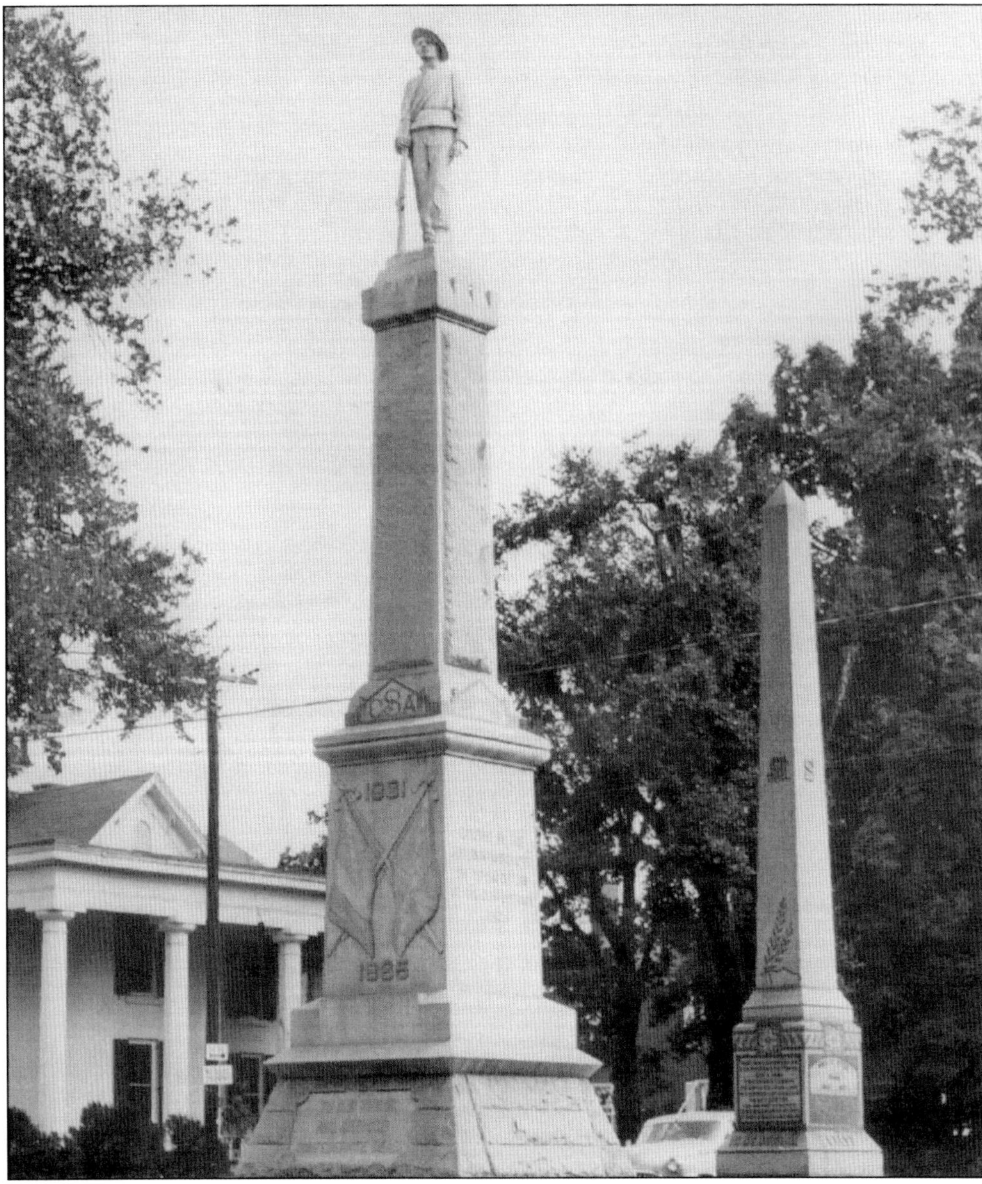

On October 5, 1906, by unanimous vote, the John D. Traynor UCV Camp agreed to begin raising money to erect a monument to our "Unknown Dead." In the previous year, on April 15, 1905, a chapter of the Daughters of the Confederacy (UDC) was formed under the leadership of Mrs. J.H. Hardwick. The Confederate monument was the first major project of the new UDC Chapter.

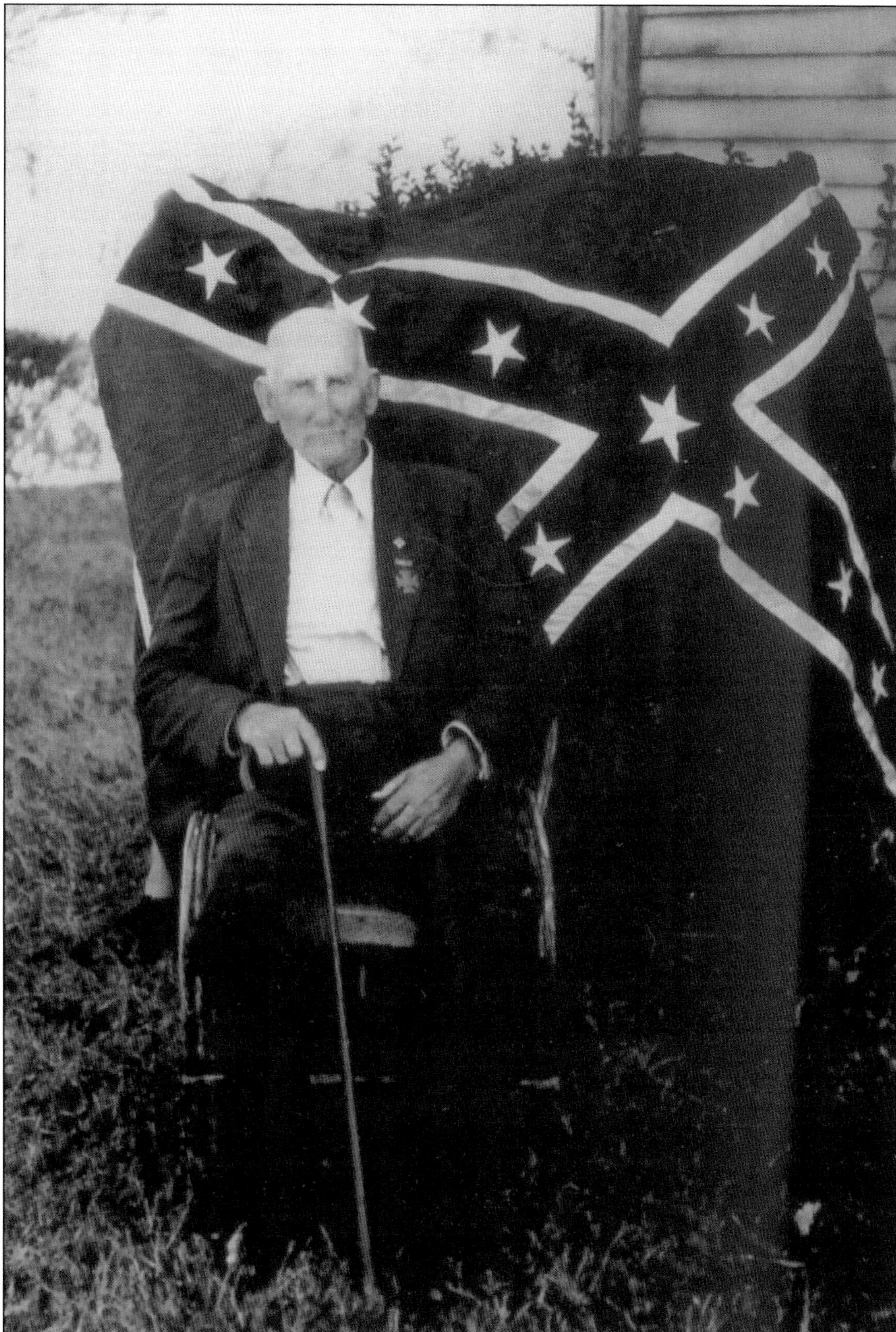

This 1938 photograph captures on film F.M. Gibson, the last surviving Confederate veteran living in Bradley County.

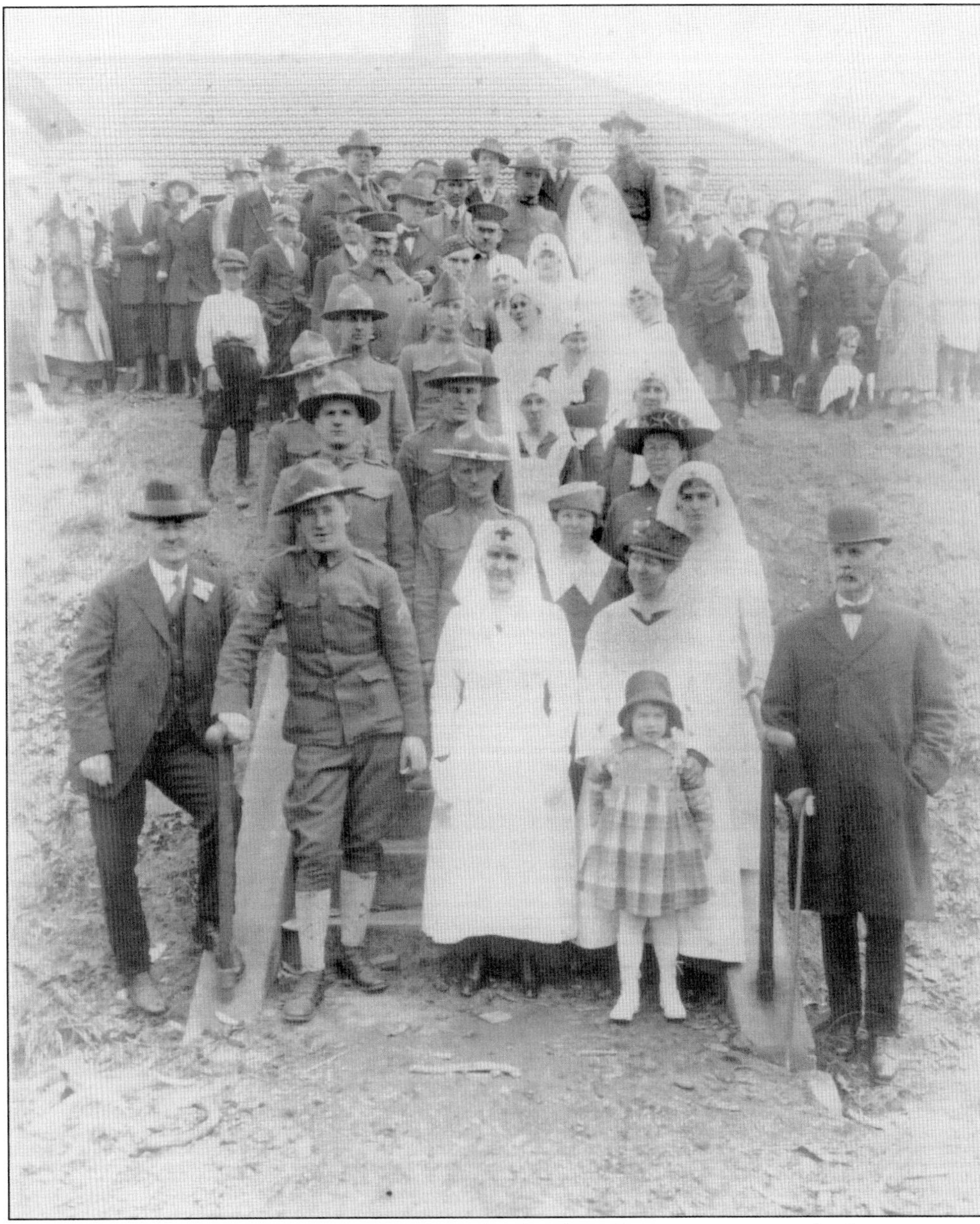

During World War I, troop trains stopped in Cleveland on their way east to embarkation points, and soldiers were served coffee and doughnuts by the ladies of the Red Cross. In the first row at the bottom of the steps leading up to depot are, from left to right, Frank J. Harle (sergeant of train), Miss Martha Lea (in Red Cross uniform), Mrs. O.A. Knox, little Elizabeth Bidwell, and Pastor Frank Porter.

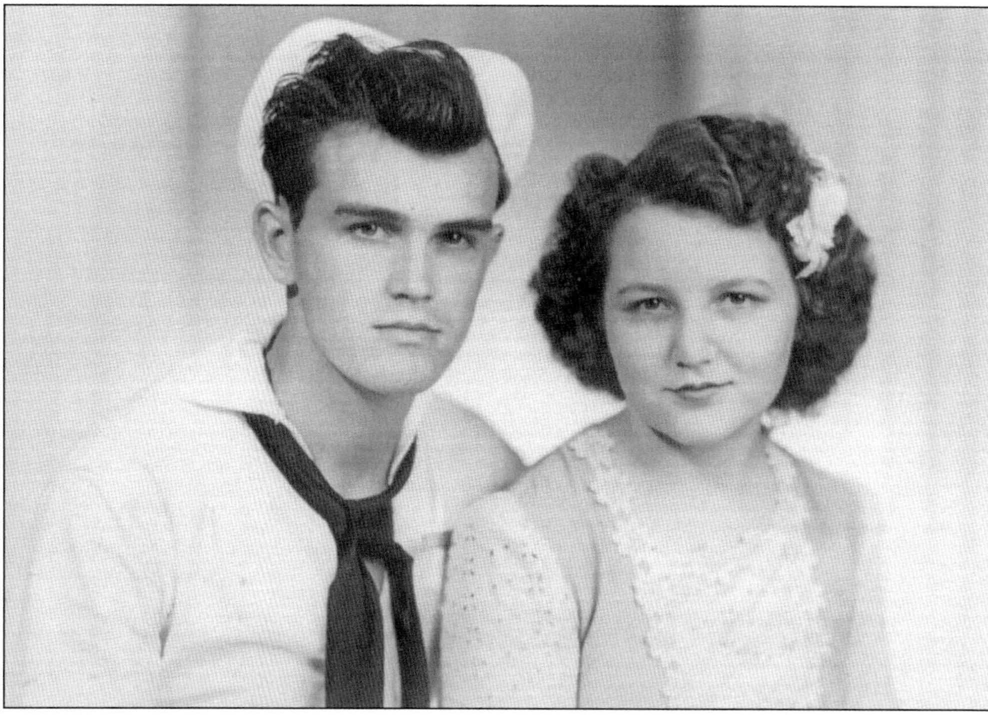

Jim Gibbons, fireman first class, served on the USS *Portland* (CA-33). He and his wife, Lorene Pendergrass Gibbons, are shown shortly after their wedding in June 1944, just before he returned to his ship in the European theatre.

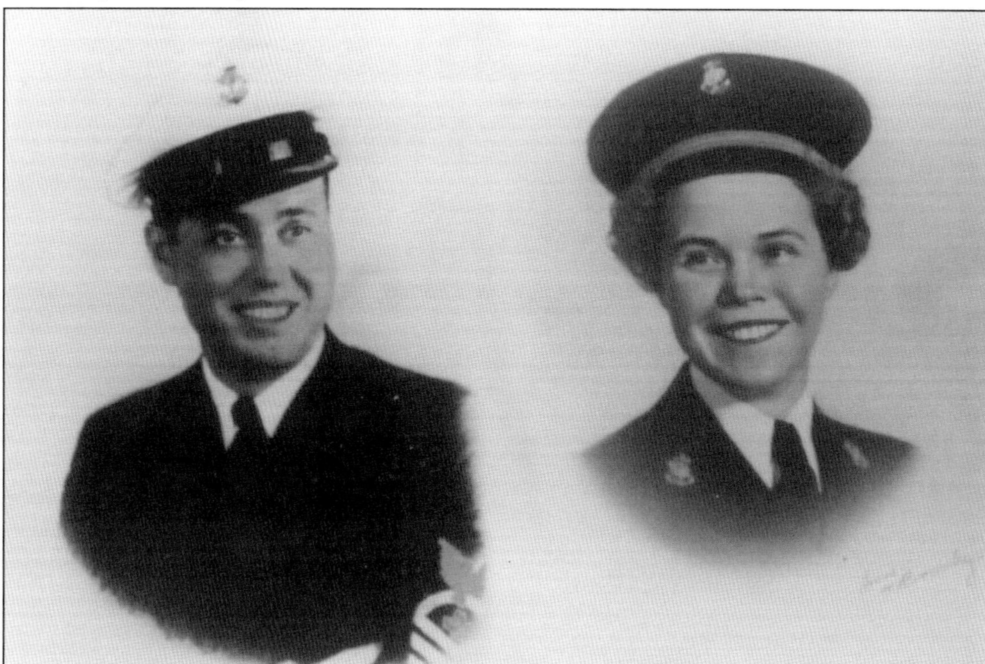

Pictured here are Master Chief Frank Climer, a Navy corpsman, and his future bride, Lieutenant Junior Grade Katherine Welsch, of the Navy Nurse Corps.

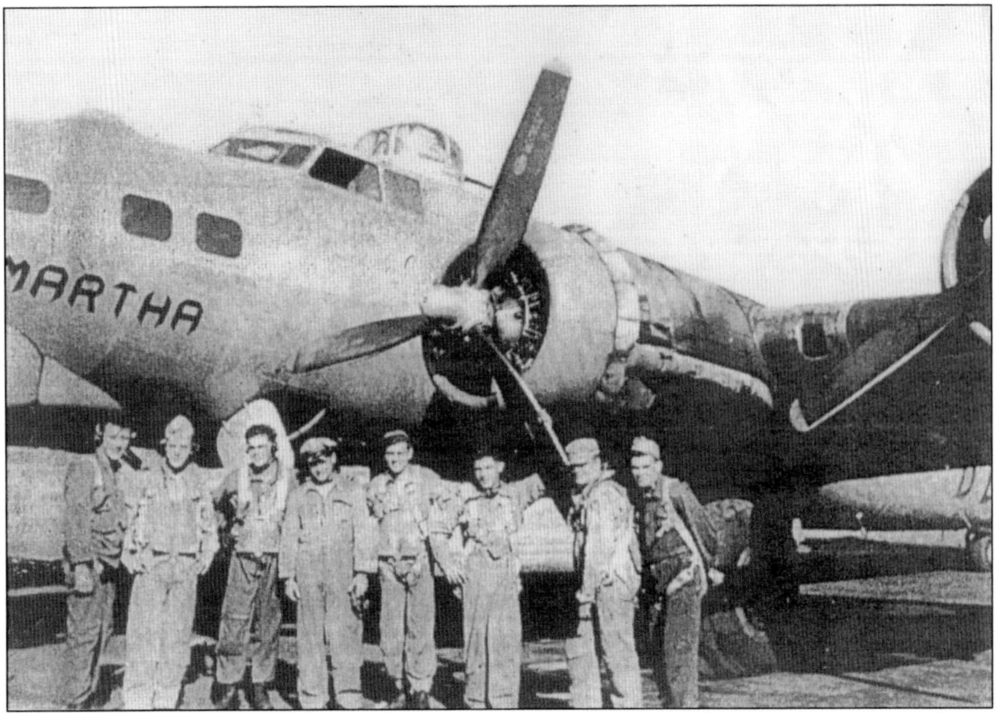

Bobby Taylor, shown fifth from left, served as flight engineer on a B-17 Flying Fortress, 457th Bomb Group, 8th Air Force, based in England. He flew 35 combat missions over Germany and was awarded six air medals.

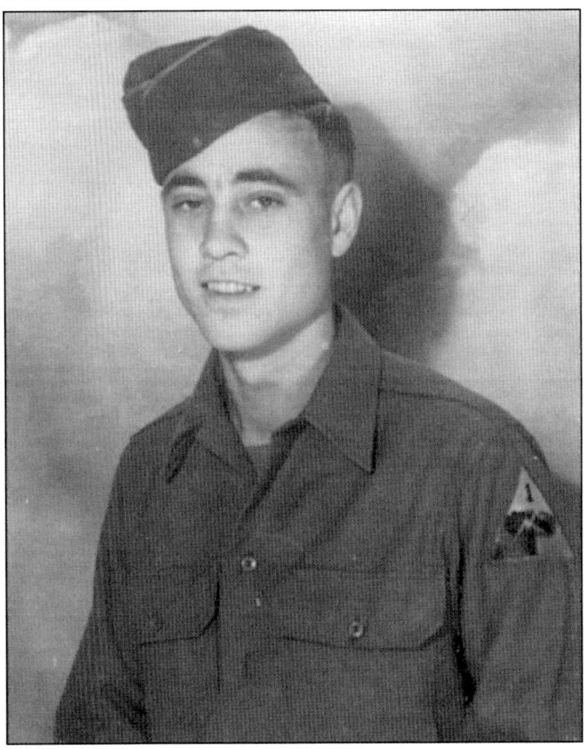

Bob Osborne was drafted in 1943 following his high school graduation. After serving two years overseas in Africa and Italy with the 1st Armored Division, he was discharged on November 3, 1945.

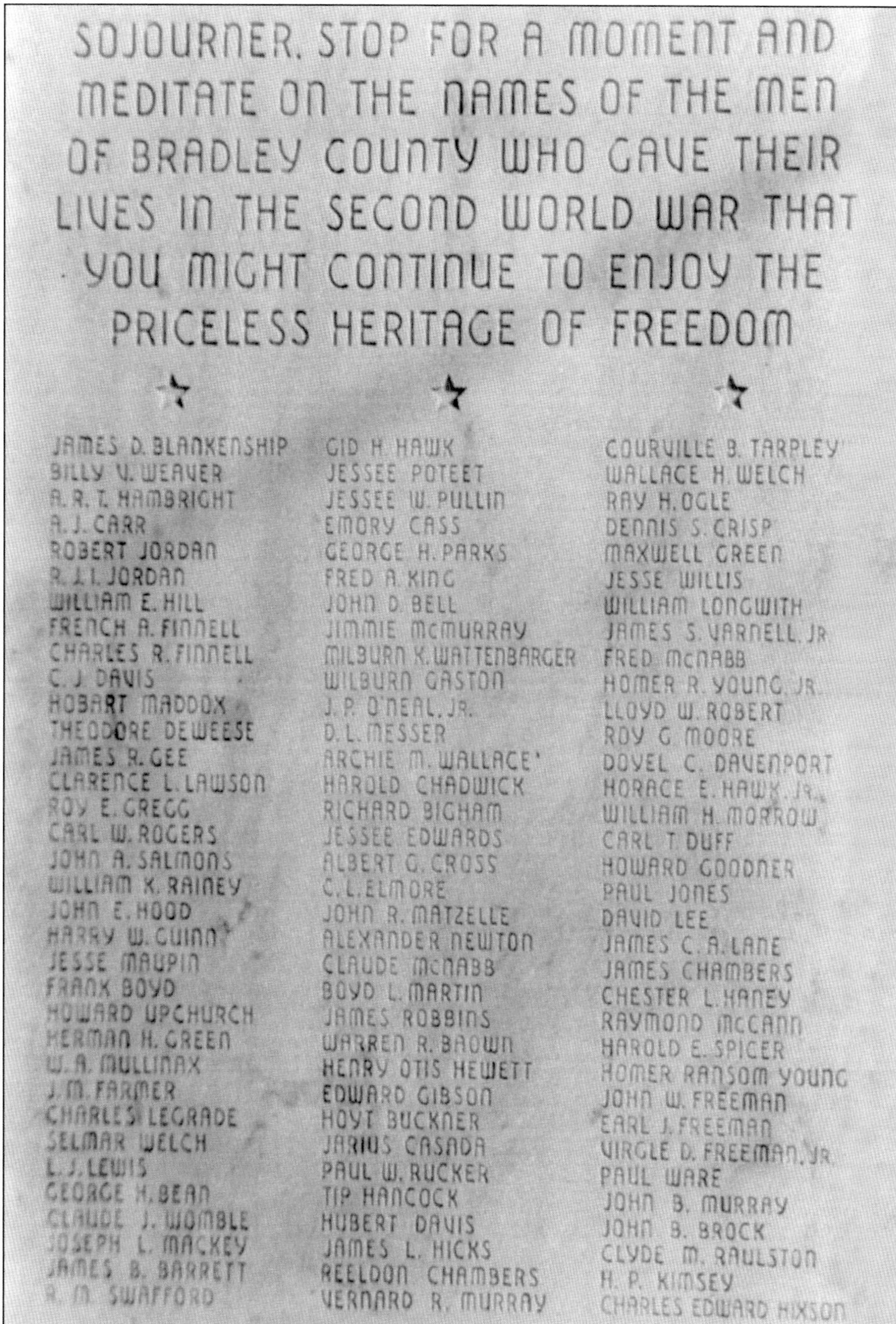

In World War II, the first reported casualty from Bradley County was Corp. James R. Gee, the 22-year-old son of Mrs. Cordie R. Gee. He was killed in a June 1942 plane crash.

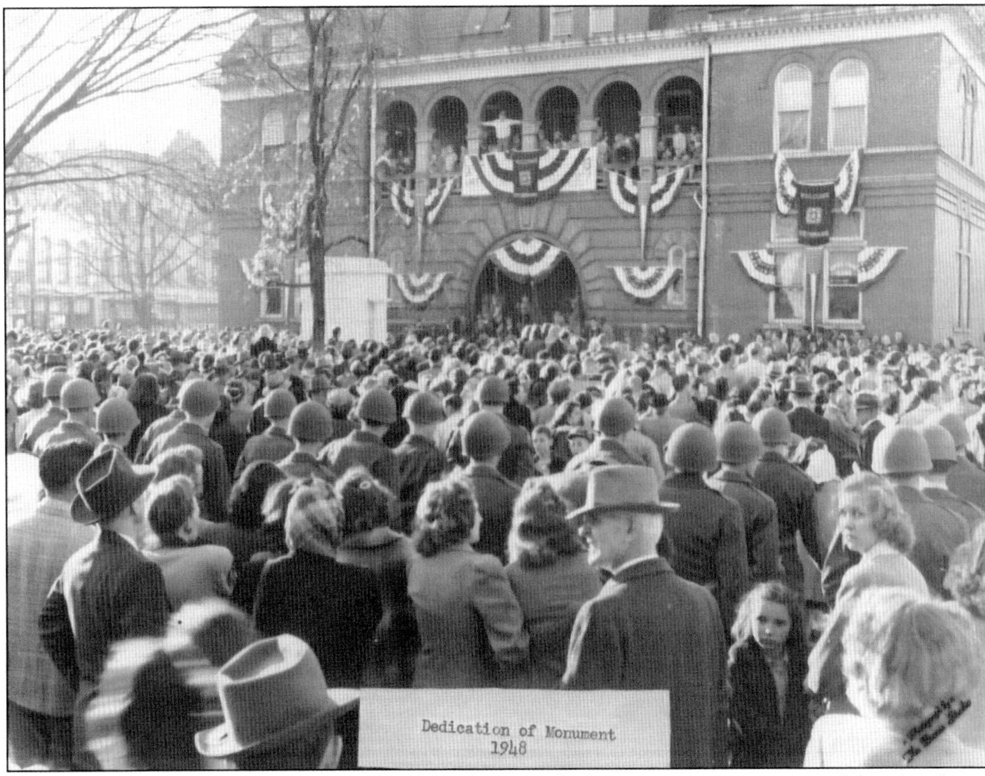

On November 11, 1948, Mayor Willard Parks unveiled a monument sponsored by the James Blankenship Post 2398 VFW to honor those from Bradley County who gave their lives in World War II.

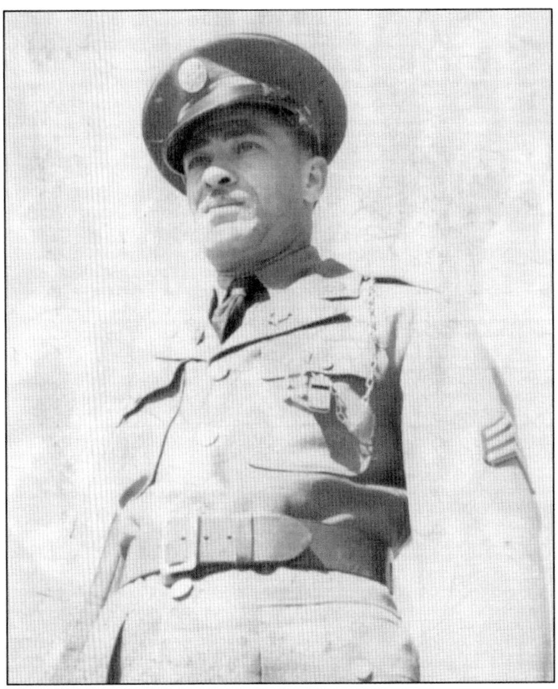

Sgt. Rufus Young served in the military police. He enlisted on October 26, 1948, and received an honorable discharge on September 26, 1952.

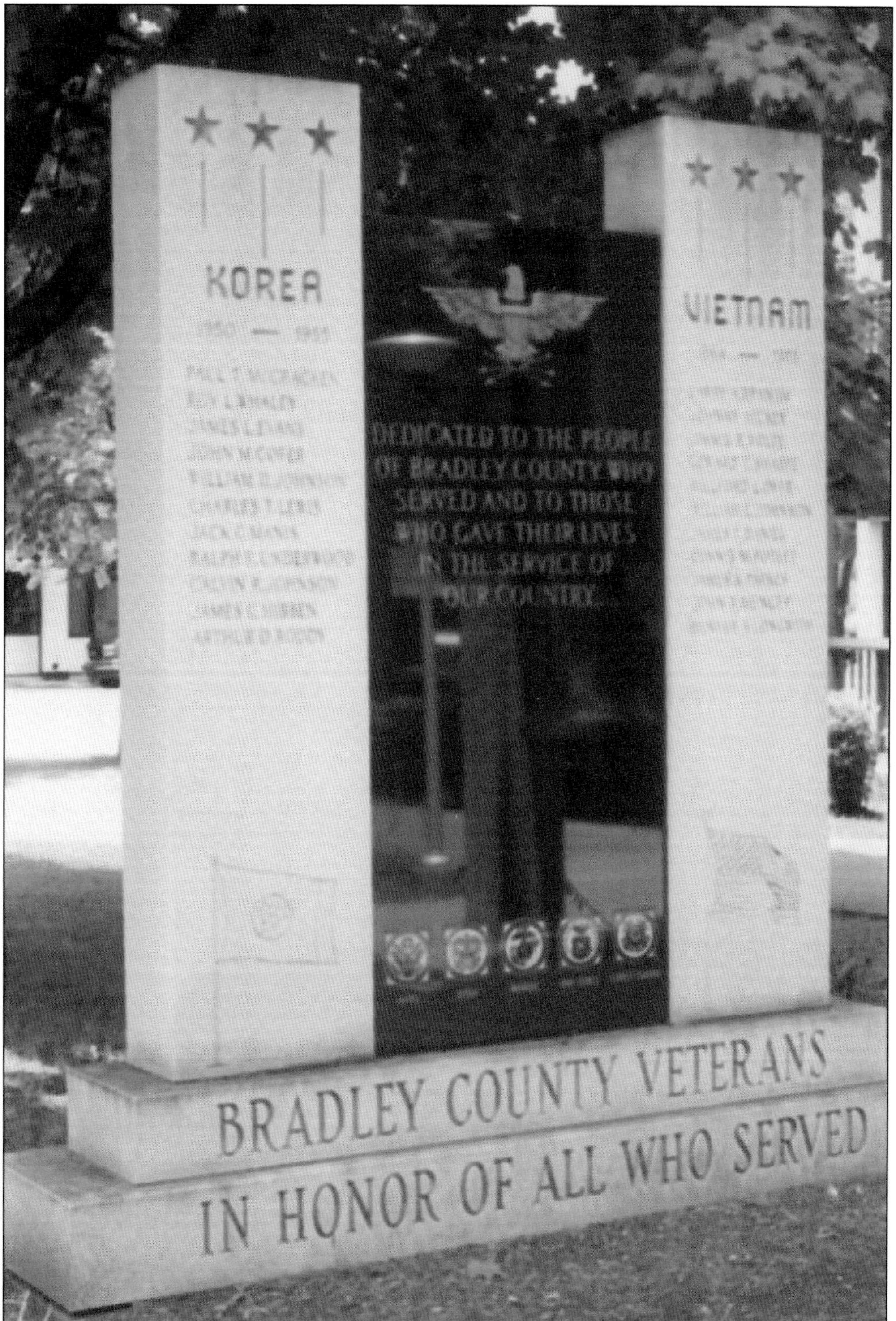

The names of veterans who gave their lives in Korea (1950–1955) and Vietnam (1964–1975) are inscribed on a beautiful granite marker on the courthouse square.

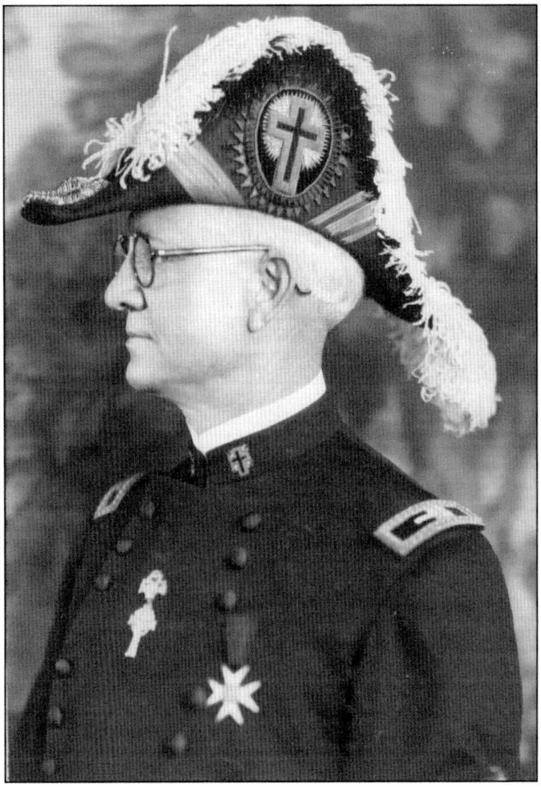

L.L. Woollen, a member of the Knights Templar, which is a body of Freemasonry, was the mayor of Cleveland in 1920 and 1921. Mayor Woollen led the fight against the Tennessee Electric Power Company and was successful in getting power rates for Cleveland reduced from 12.5¢ to 11¢ per kilowatt hour.

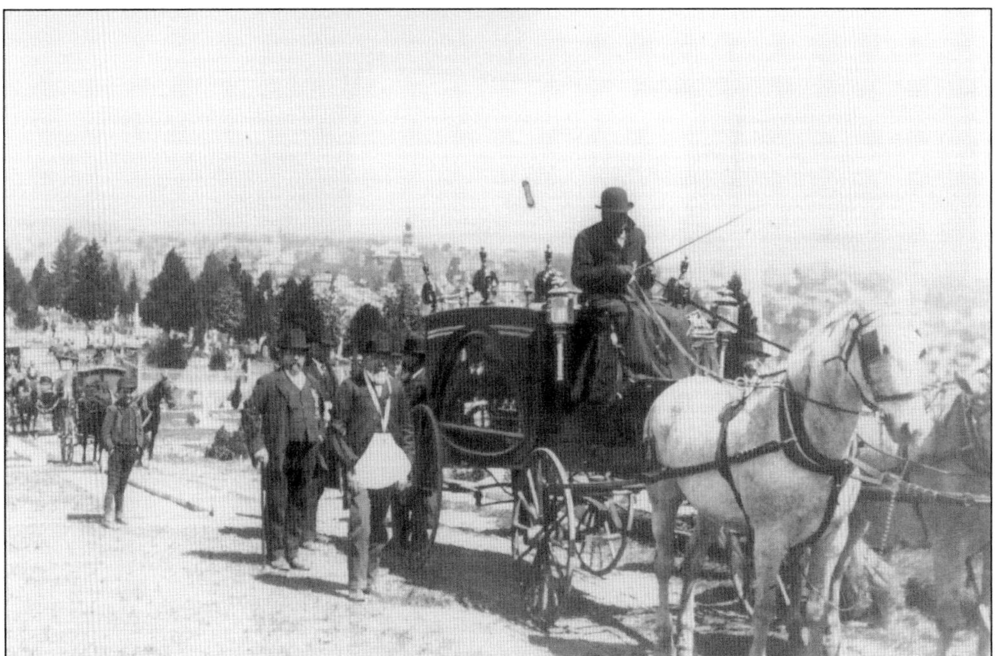

This is a Masonic funeral that took place at Fort Hill Cemetery about 1900. The horse-drawn, glass-sided hearse was followed by fraternal brothers as they paid their final respects to a departed brother.

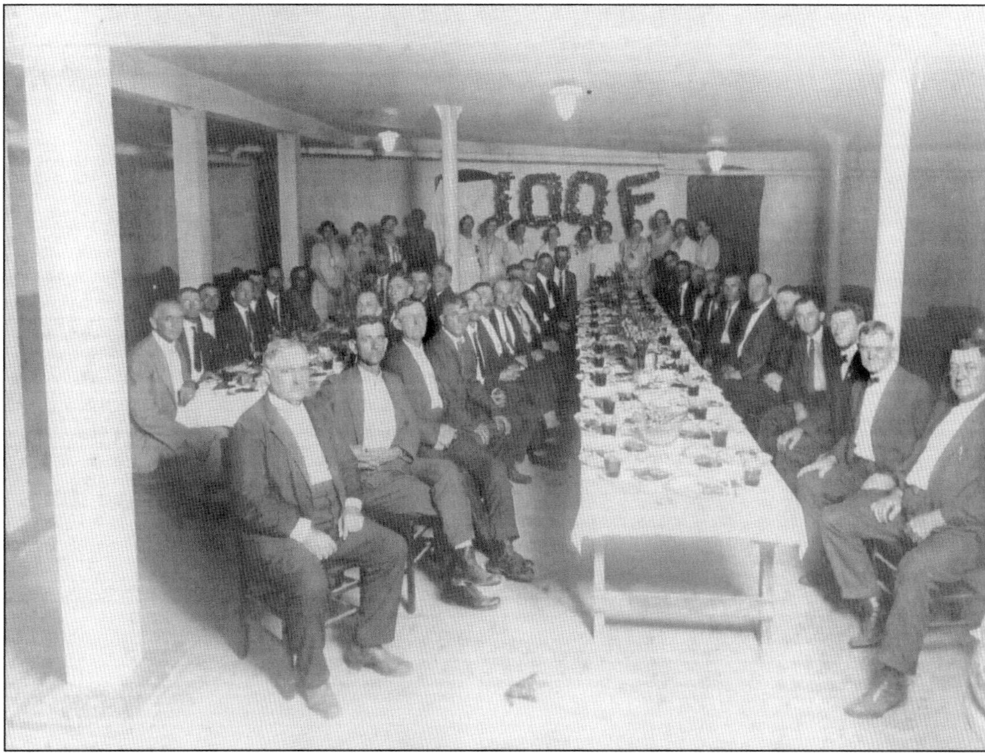

Pictured here is an Independent Order of Odd Fellows (IOOF) banquet held on December 2, 1922. The Odd Fellows is a fraternal group started by Thomas Wildey in Baltimore in 1819.

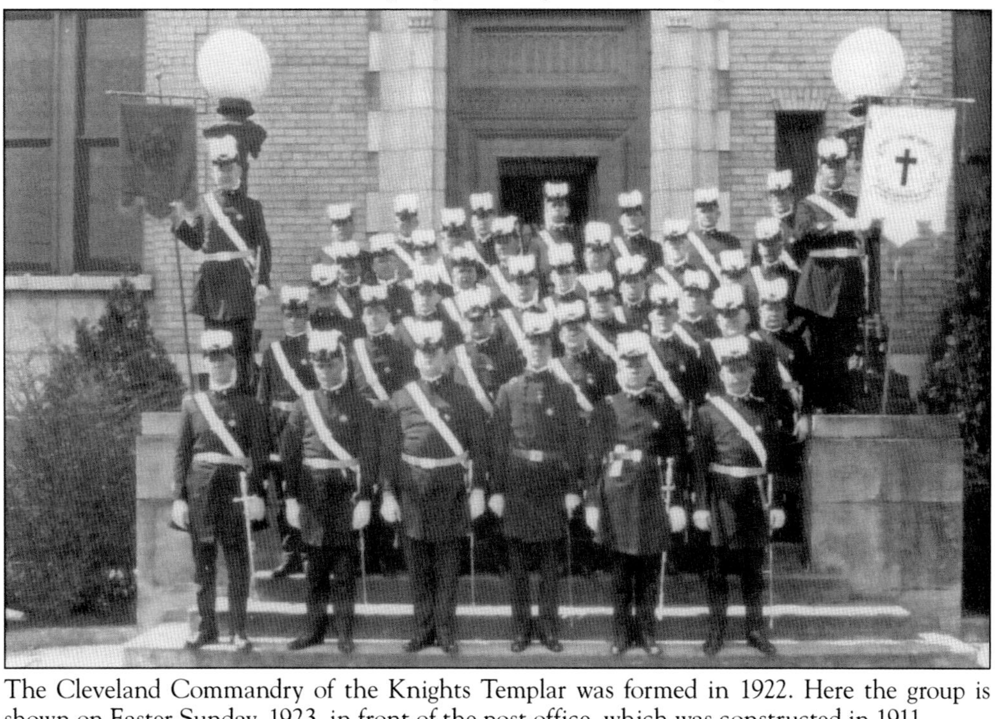

The Cleveland Commandry of the Knights Templar was formed in 1922. Here the group is shown on Easter Sunday, 1923, in front of the post office, which was constructed in 1911.

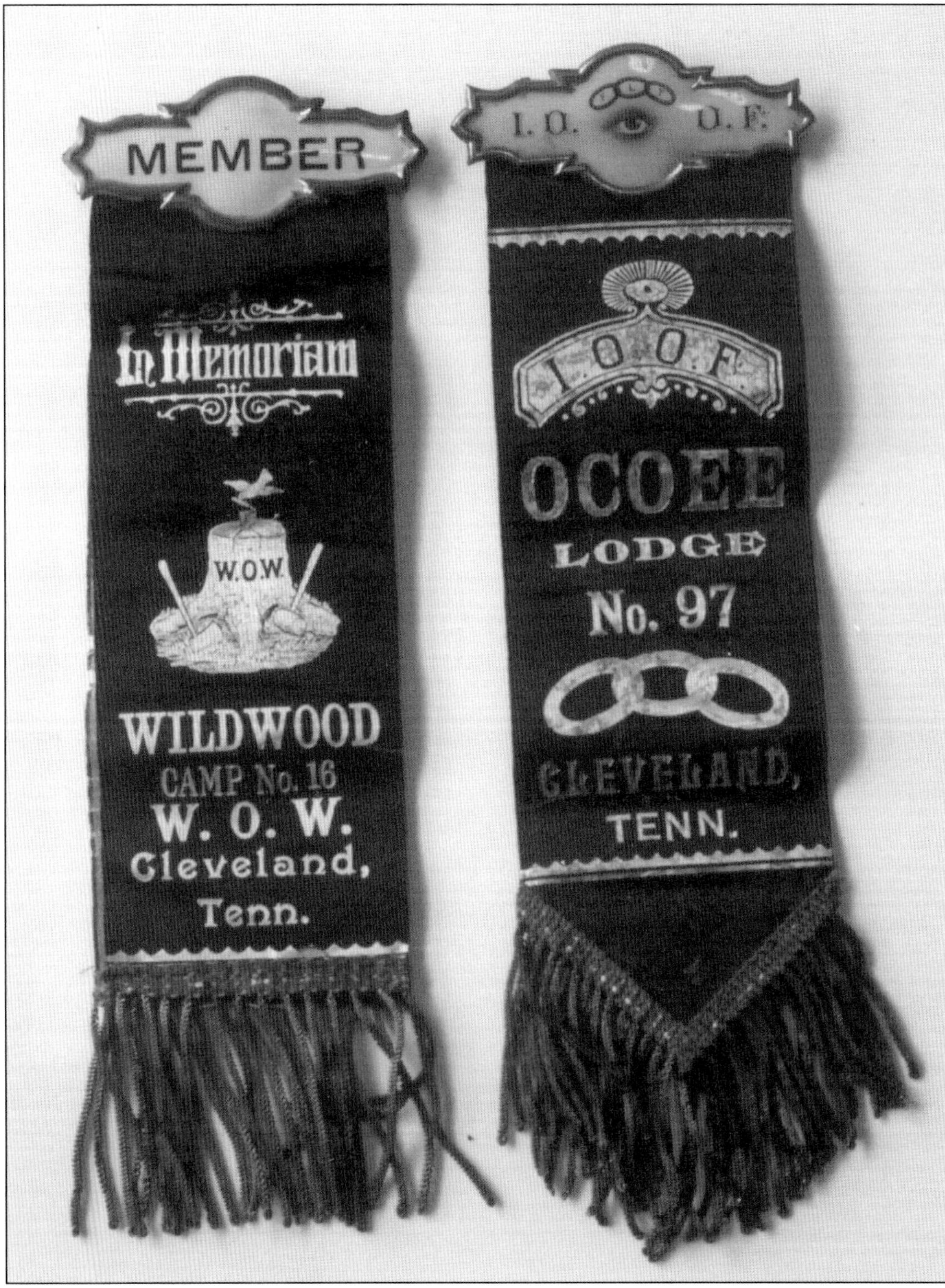

On the left is a memorial badge of Wildwood Camp No. 16, Woodmen of the World (WOW), a fraternal benefit society founded in 1890 in Omaha, NE, by Joseph Cullen Root. On the right is a badge for Ocoee Lodge No. 97 of IOOF, organized in 1856. Both lodges are still active today (2000).

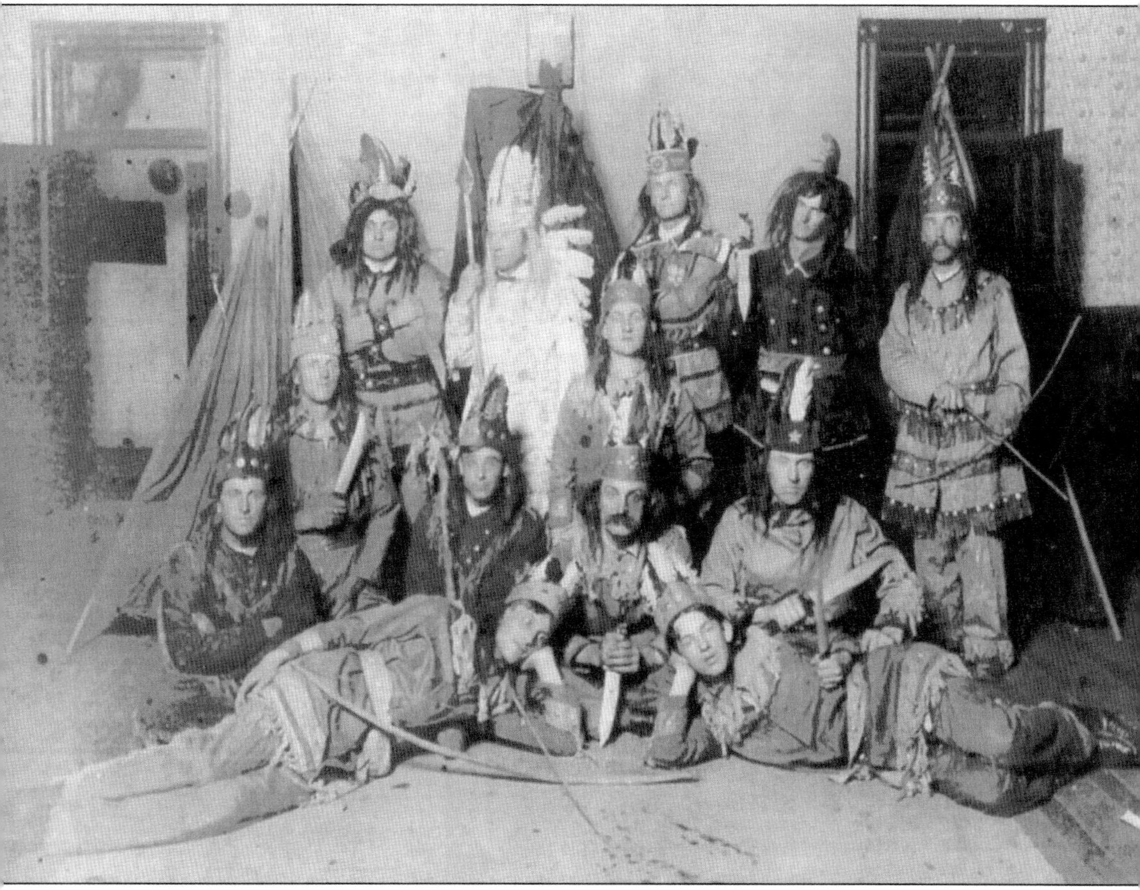

The Improved Order of Red Men (IORM), a fraternal body with the intention of preserving the history, customs, legends, and names of the aborigines, was founded in Baltimore in 1833. The Estanelle Tribe degree team of Athens came in March 1921 to organize a new IORM tribe in Cleveland. J.V. Dodd was installed as Keeper of Wampum, George Hain as Prophet, and C.R. Hozworth as Senior Sagamore.

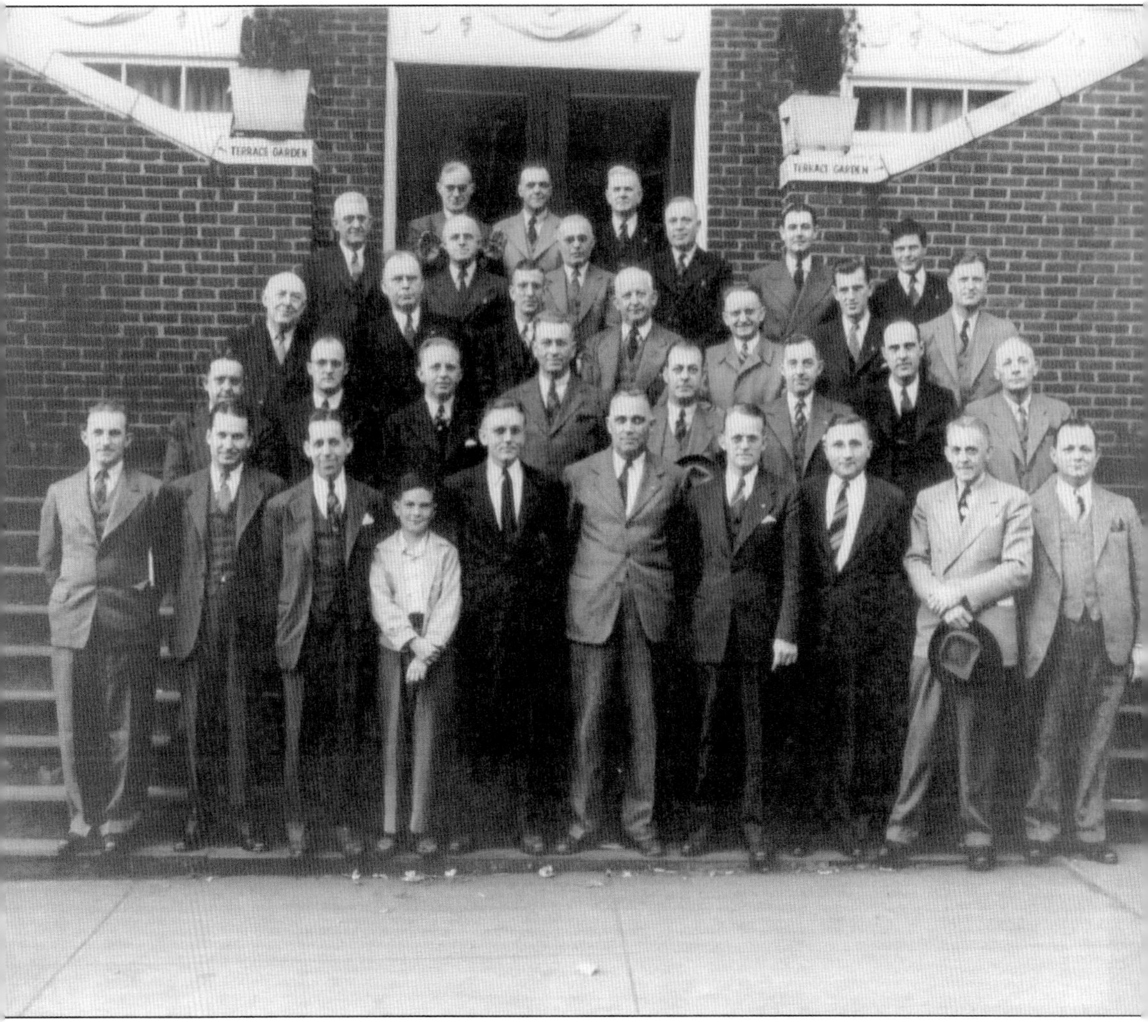

Several civic clubs have been active in Cleveland, including Civitan, Kiwanis, Lions, Optimist, Pilot, Rotary, Ruritan, and Sertoma. Organized in 1920, the Kiwanis Club is the oldest civic club in Cleveland. Shown here on the steps of the Cherokee Hotel are, from left to right, the following: (first row) Vaughn Hamilton, John Pinion (visitor), David McLain, Billy Hickey (visitor), Hays Davis, E.J. Vann, T. Lloyd McLain, Reverend Marvin Kincheloe, W.W. Byars, and Dave Hecklin; (second row) W.J. McReynolds, W.W. Smith, W.V. Gibson, Reverend W.A. Keel, Reverend Joe Grey, C.L. Wilson, Reverend Cordis Womack, and Bethel Brown; (third row) C.W. Harle, W.B. Parks, S.C. Pettit, Will Rogers, Alfred Cerpkey, C. Raulston McGhee, and Luther Hargis; (fourth row) E.E. Shouse, H.P. Bridges, R.R. Abel, ? Janskey, Zell Taylor, and J.L. Van Wagner; (last row) George Hardwick Jr., W.W. Jacobs, and R.T. Allen.

Eight

LEISURE

Everyone has deep in their heart the old town or community where they first went barefooted, got their first licking, traded the first pocket knife, grew up and finally went away thinking they were too big for that Burg. But that's where your old heart is.

—Will Rogers

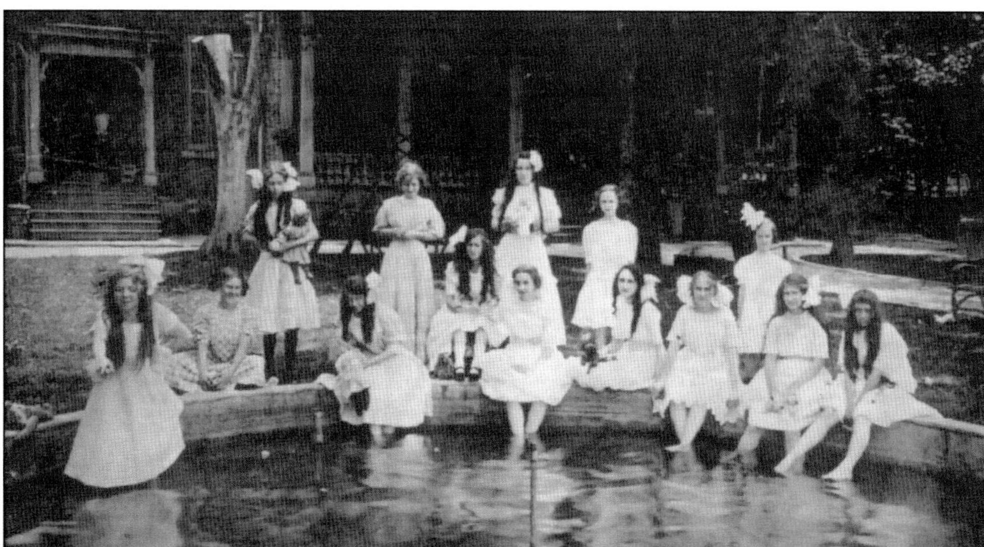

Captured on film around 1910, these girls are sitting on the edge of a fountain pool behind the P.M. Craigmiles house. Some have dolls or teddy bears and are barefoot, ready to wade in the pool.

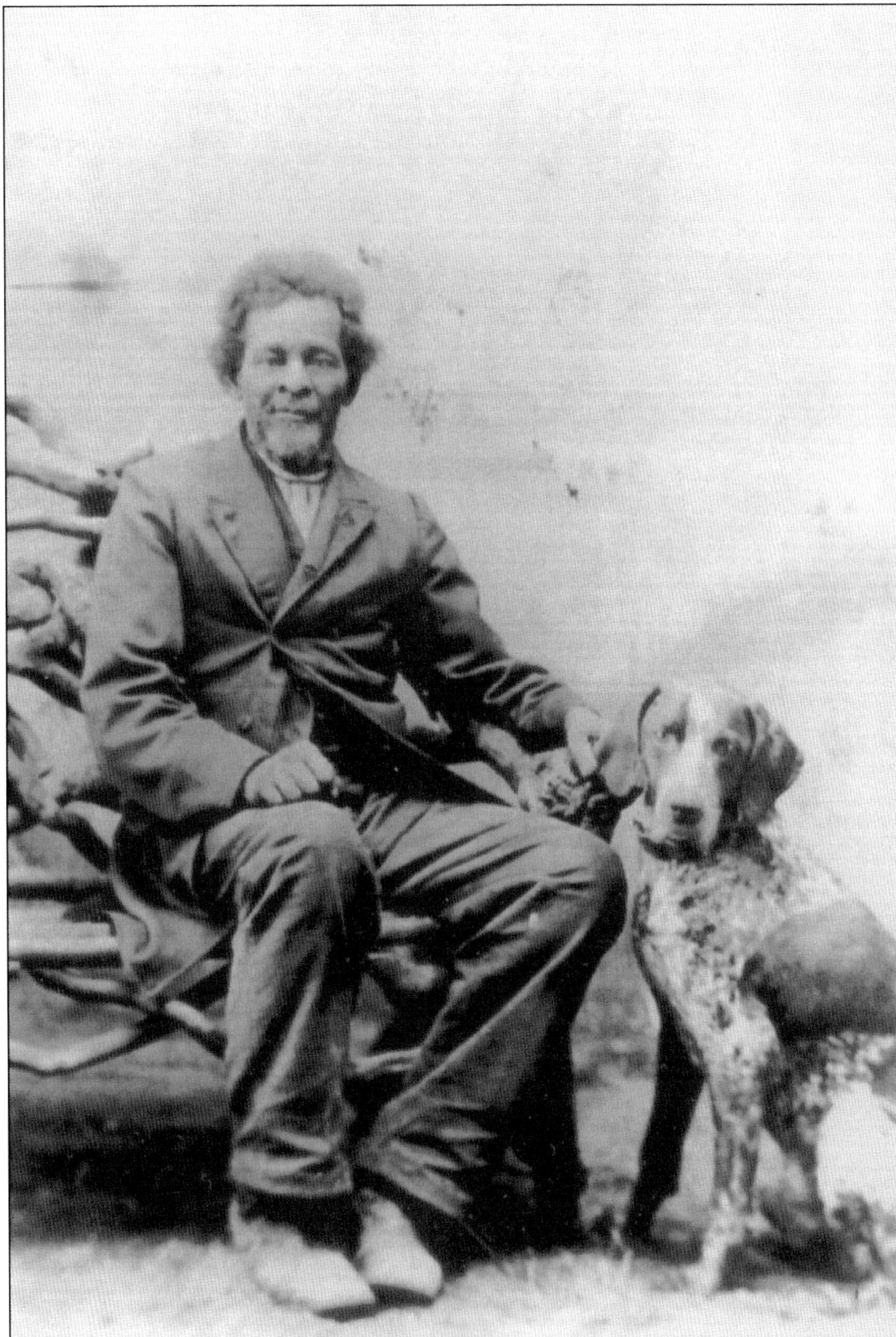

"Uncle Thompson" was the family slave who lived with the J.H. Hardwick family during the 1880s when the future industrialist, C.L., was young.

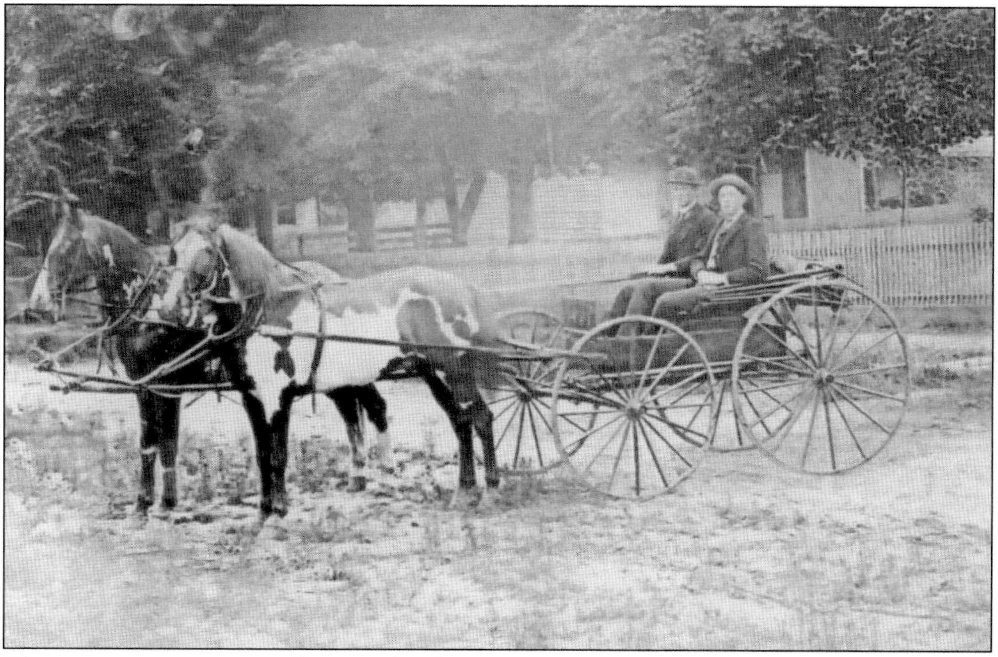

These two men are pictured here in their horse-drawn carriage.

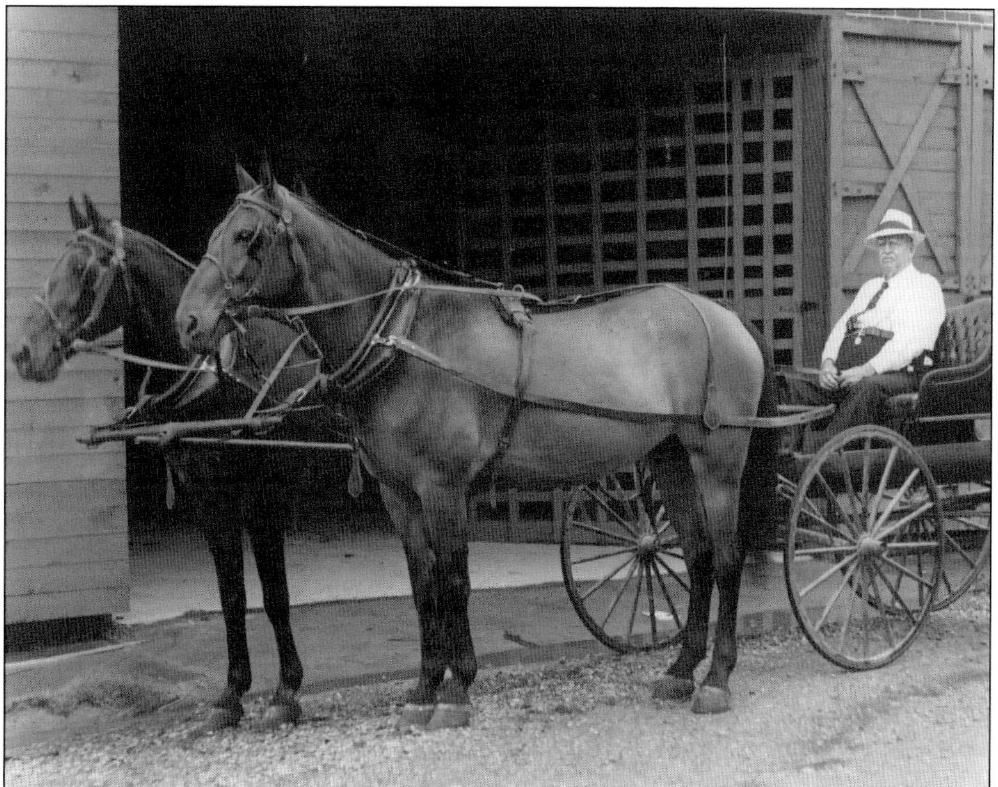

Lively stable owner Joe Hawk is ready for a carriage ride with two horses providing the "horsepower."

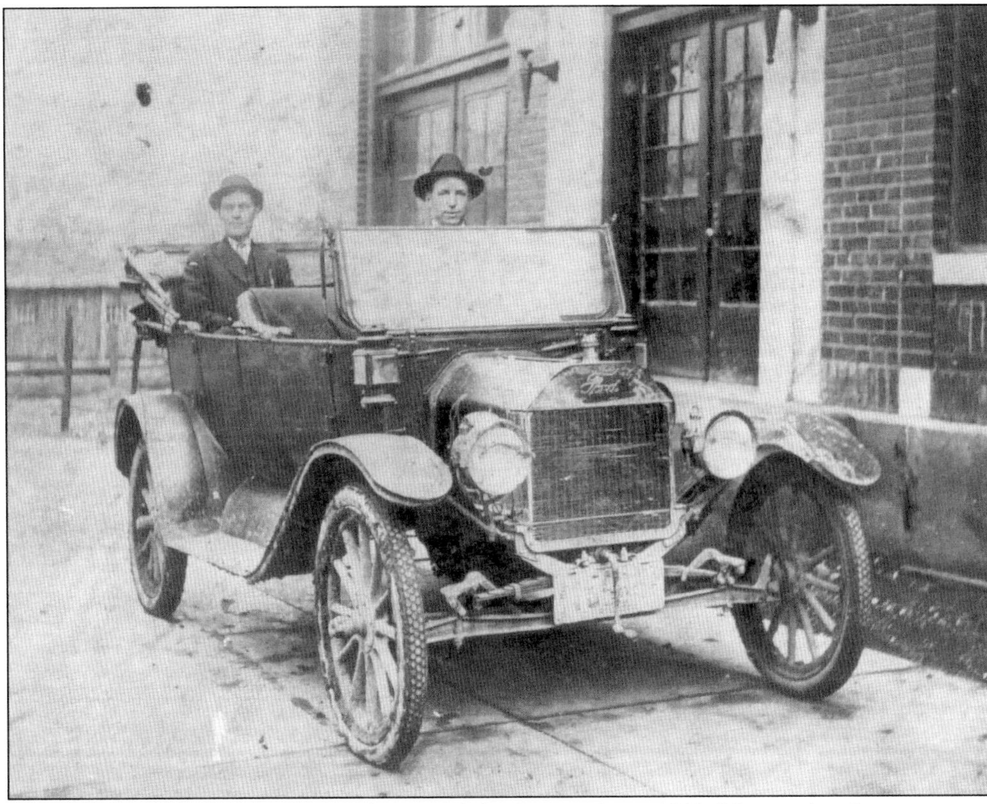

This "horseless carriage" is a Ford automobile shown about 1910. Notice the thin tires and crank on front.

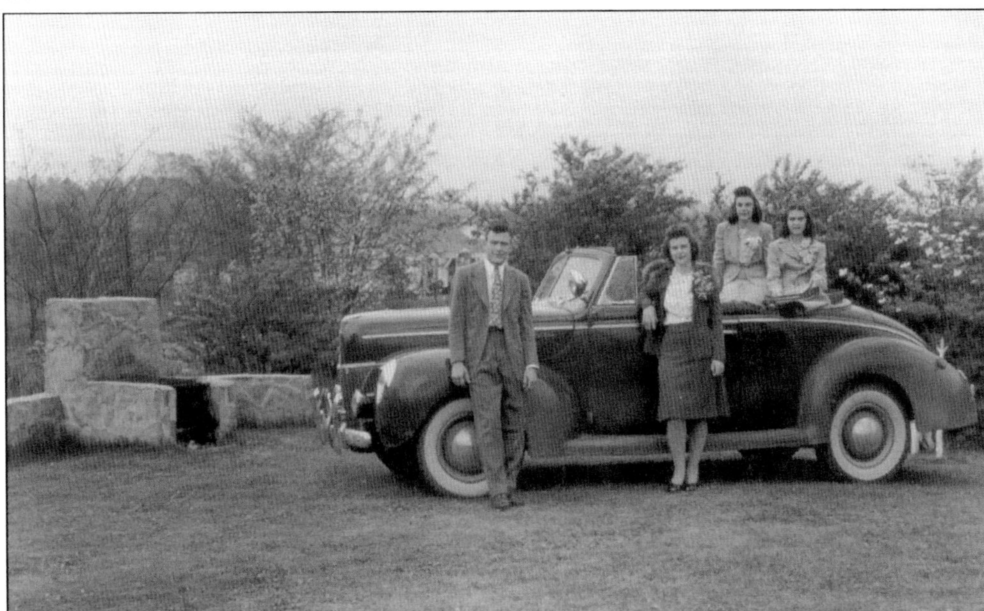

Pictured here with his 1940 Ford convertible are Jimmy Cooke and his three sisters, Elizabeth, Catherine, and Anna.

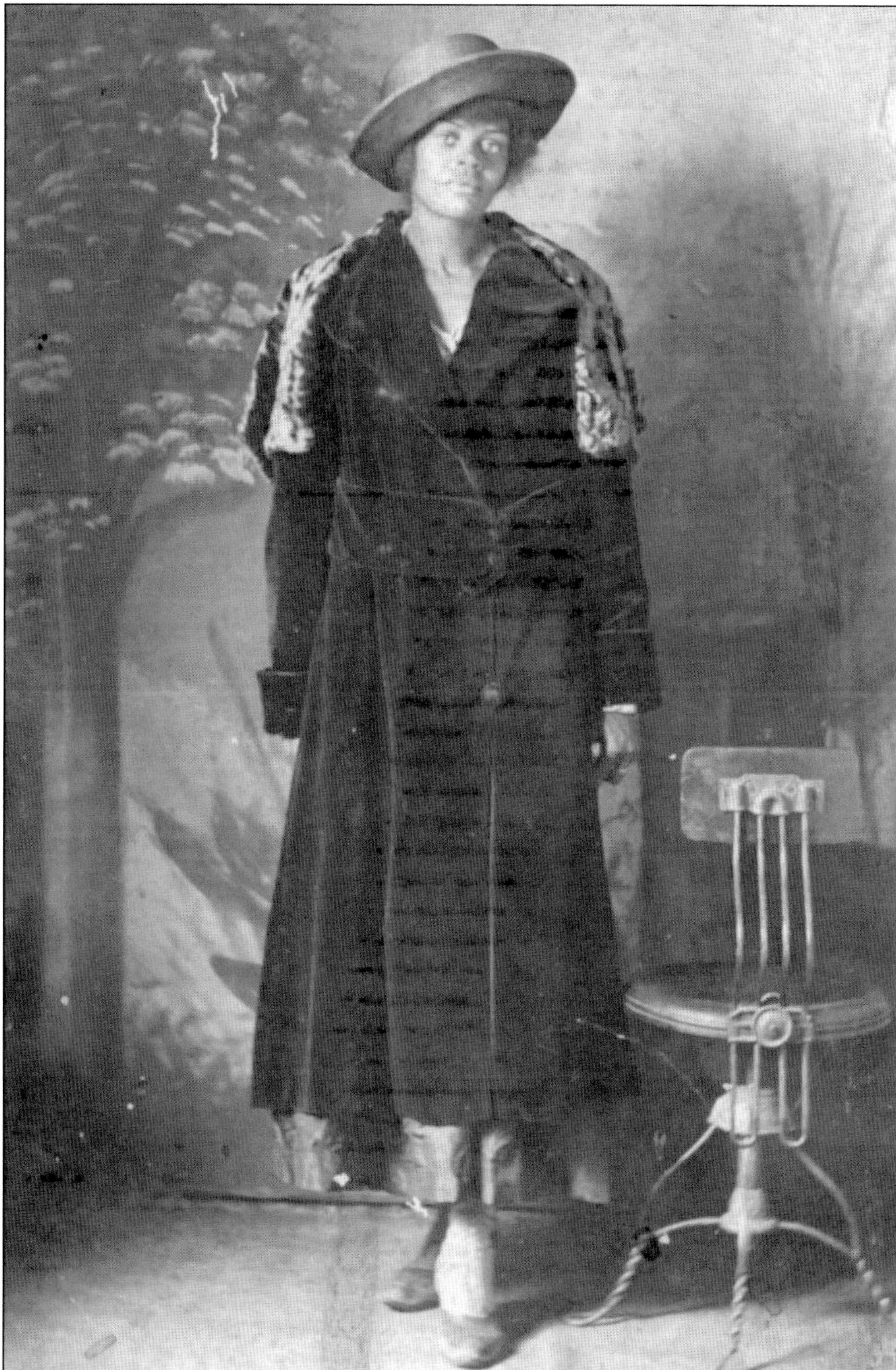

Lissie Pugh is shown here in a stunning outfit about 1900.

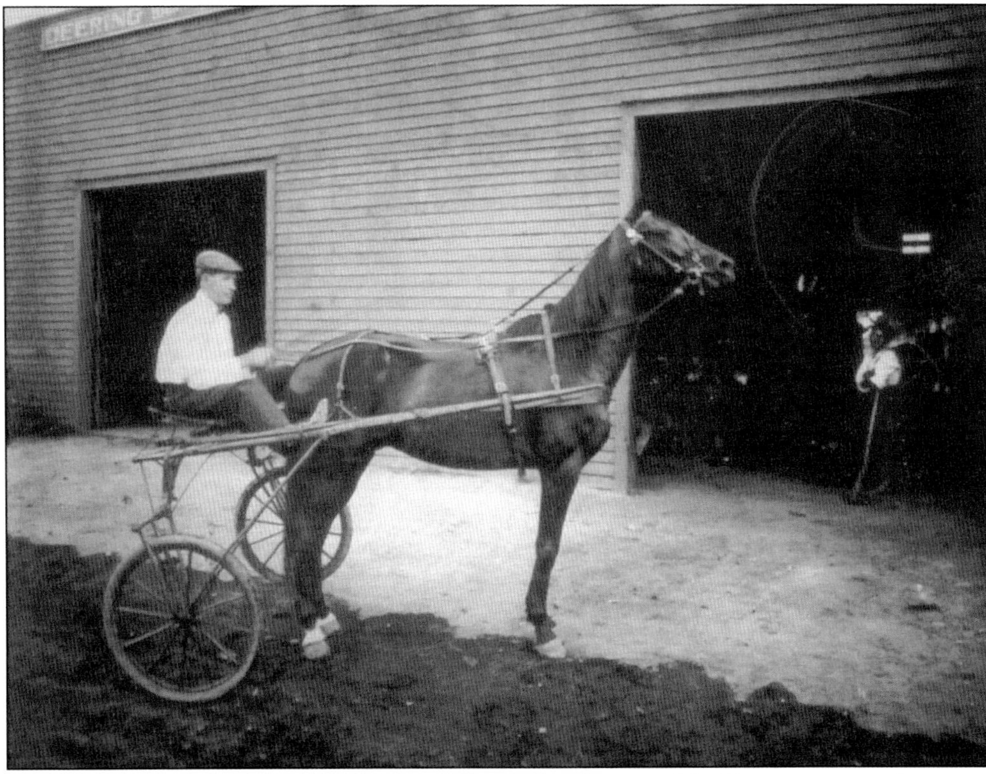

Ellis Callahan Haggard is shown in 1904 in front of his livery stable. He is sitting on the seat of the racing sulky.

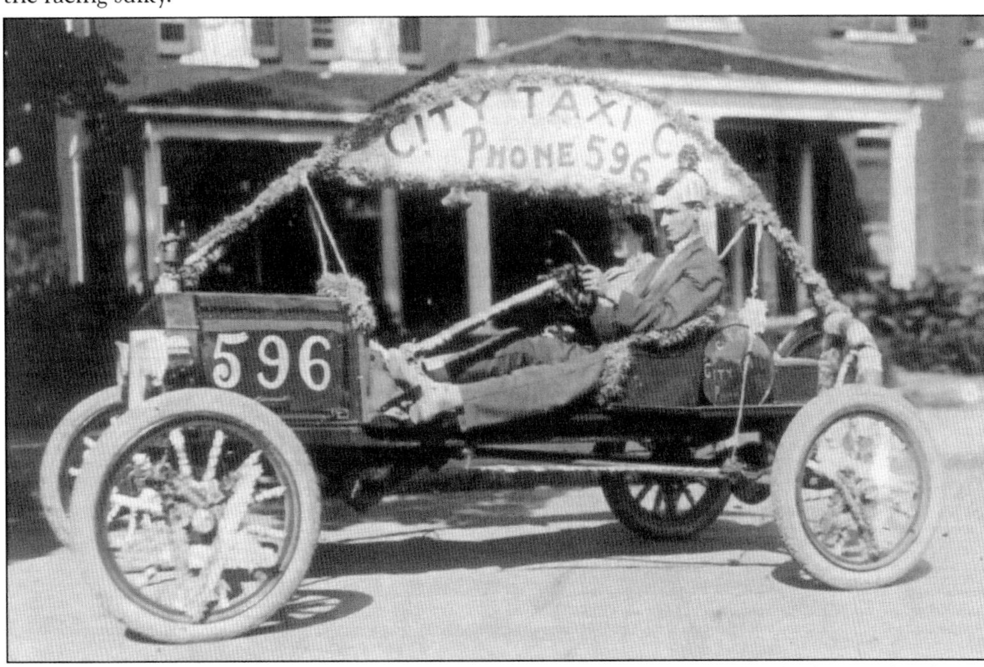

Pictured here is the City Taxi Company car participating in the Fourth of July parade of 1911. Note the wooden spoke wheels and three-digit phone number.

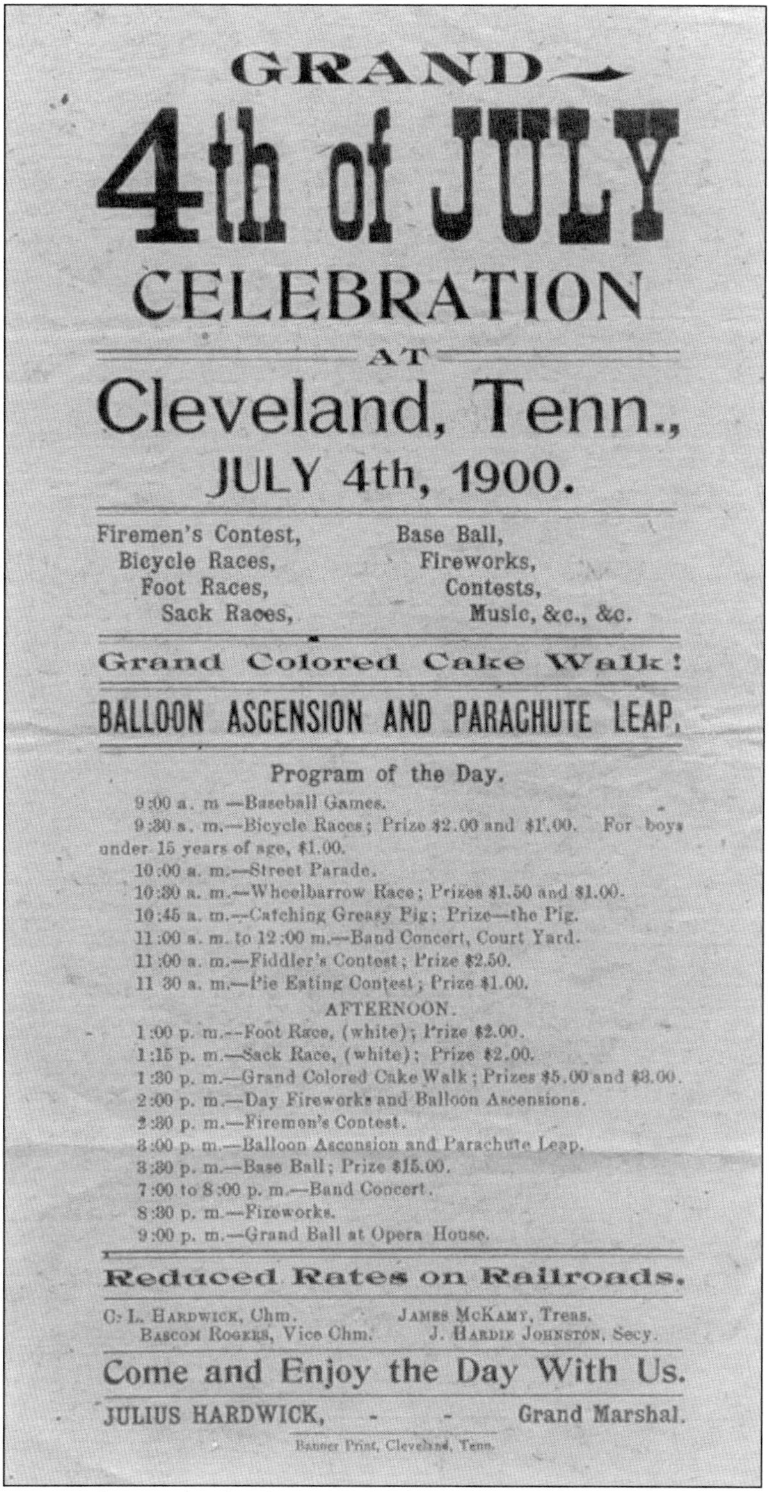

GRAND

4th of JULY

CELEBRATION

AT

Cleveland, Tenn.,

JULY 4th, 1900.

Firemen's Contest,
Bicycle Races,
Foot Races,
Sack Races,
Base Ball,
Fireworks,
Contests,
Music, &c., &c.

Grand Colored Cake Walk!

BALLOON ASCENSION AND PARACHUTE LEAP.

Program of the Day.

9:00 a. m—Baseball Games.
9:30 a. m.—Bicycle Races; Prize $2.00 and $1.00. For boys under 15 years of age, $1.00.
10:00 a. m.—Street Parade.
10:30 a. m.—Wheelbarrow Race; Prizes $1.50 and $1.00.
10:45 a. m.—Catching Greasy Pig; Prize—the Pig.
11:00 a. m. to 12:00 m.—Band Concert, Court Yard.
11:00 a. m.—Fiddler's Contest; Prize $2.50.
11 30 a. m.—Pie Eating Contest; Prize $1.00.

AFTERNOON.

1:00 p. m.—Foot Race, (white); Prize $2.00.
1:15 p. m.—Sack Race, (white); Prize $2.00.
1:30 p. m.—Grand Colored Cake Walk; Prizes $5.00 and $3.00.
2:00 p. m.—Day Fireworks and Balloon Ascensions.
2:30 p. m.—Firemen's Contest.
3:00 p. m.—Balloon Ascension and Parachute Leap.
3:30 p. m.—Base Ball; Prize $15.00.
7:00 to 8:00 p. m.—Band Concert.
8:30 p. m.—Fireworks.
9:00 p. m.—Grand Ball at Opera House.

Reduced Rates on Railroads.

C. L. HARDWICK, Chm. JAMES McKAMY, Treas.
BASCOM ROGERS, Vice Chm. J. HARDIN JOHNSTON, Secy.

Come and Enjoy the Day With Us.

JULIUS HARDWICK, - - Grand Marshal.

Banner Print, Cleveland, Tenn.

Holidays were great fun in Cleveland as is evident in this flyer for the Fourth of July celebration in 1900.

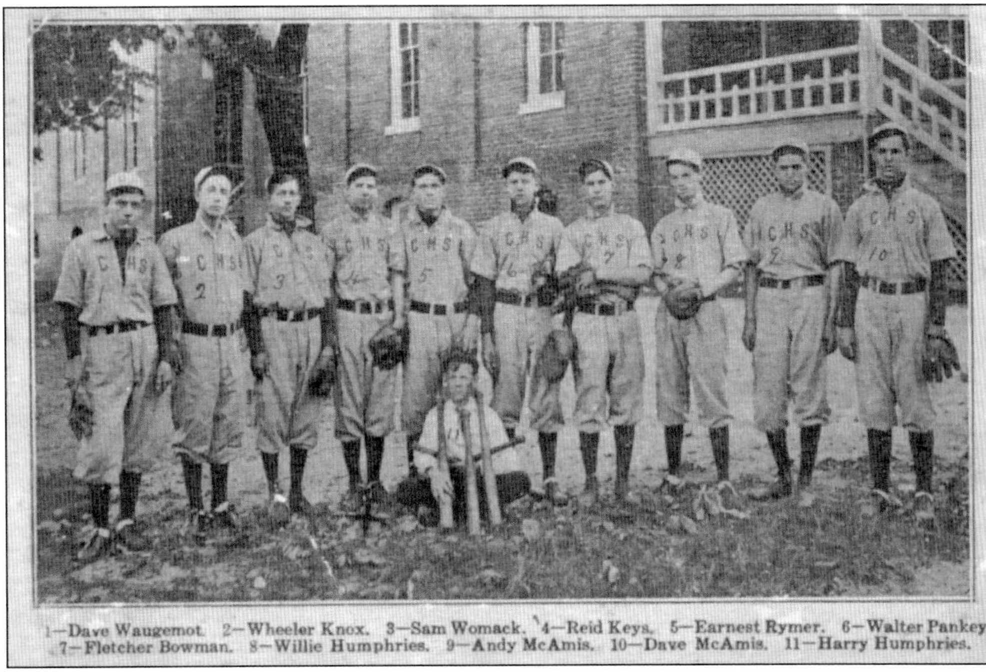

This postcard, mailed in 1911, shows the Cleveland High School baseball team. From left to right are Dave Waugemot, Wheeler Knox, Sam Womack, Reid Keys, Earnest Rymer, Walter Pankey, Fletcher Bowman, Willie Humphries, Andy McAmis, and Dave McAmis; (in front) Harry Humphries, the bat boy.

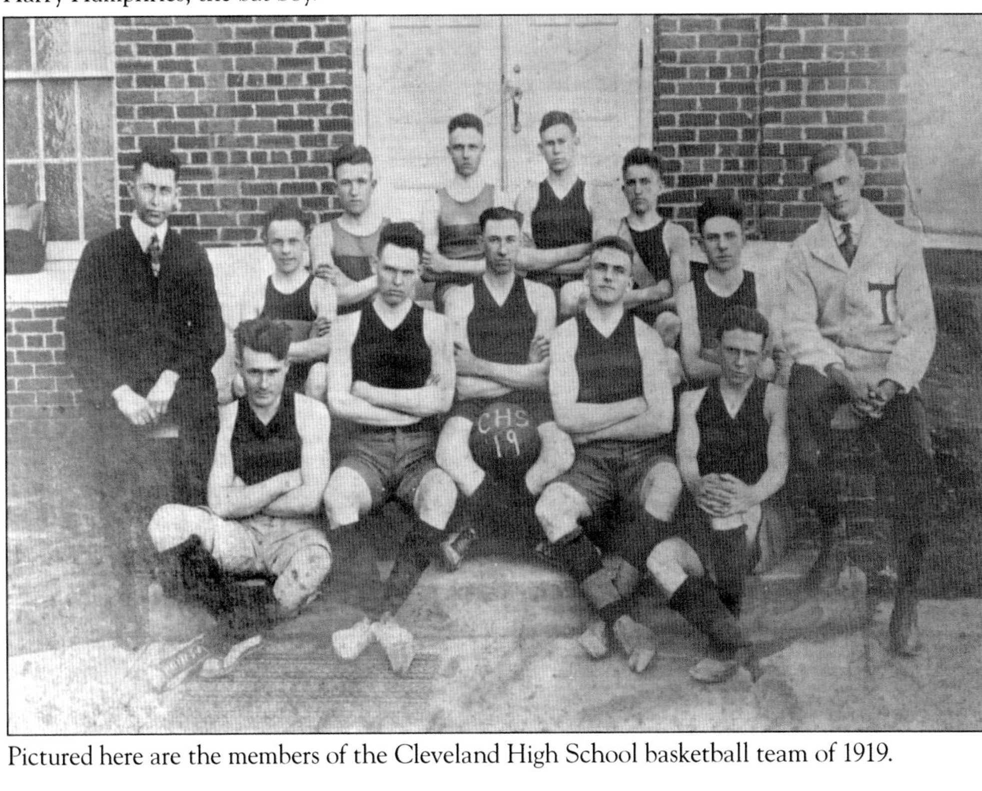

Pictured here are the members of the Cleveland High School basketball team of 1919.

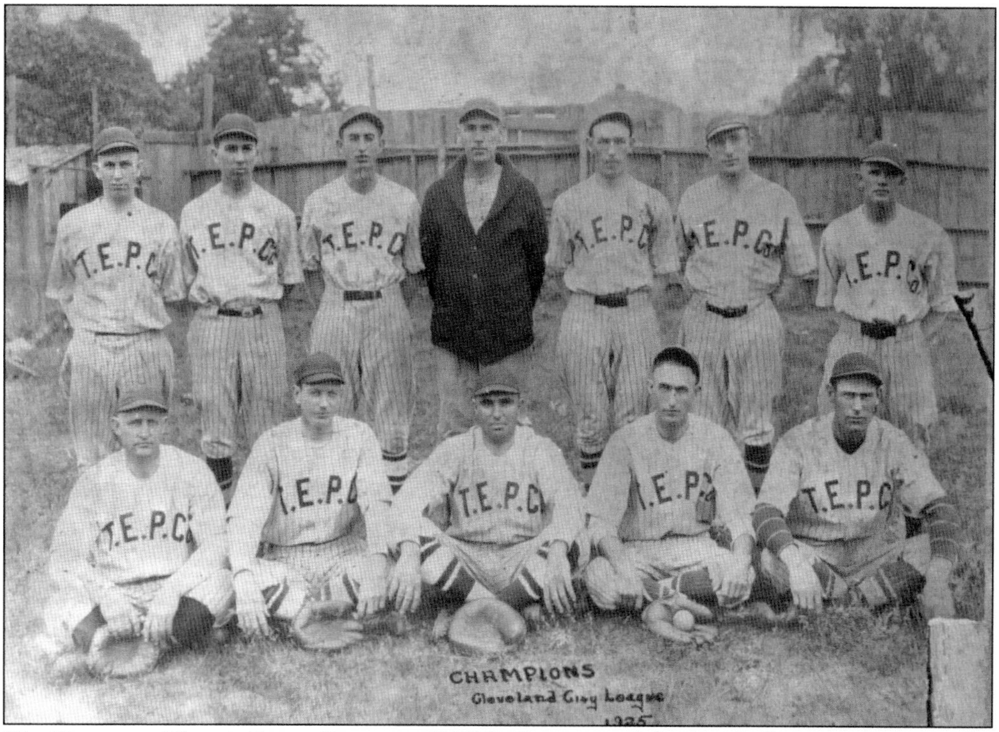

The Tennessee Electric Power Company (TEPCO) sponsored this baseball team, which was the champion of the Cleveland City League in 1925.

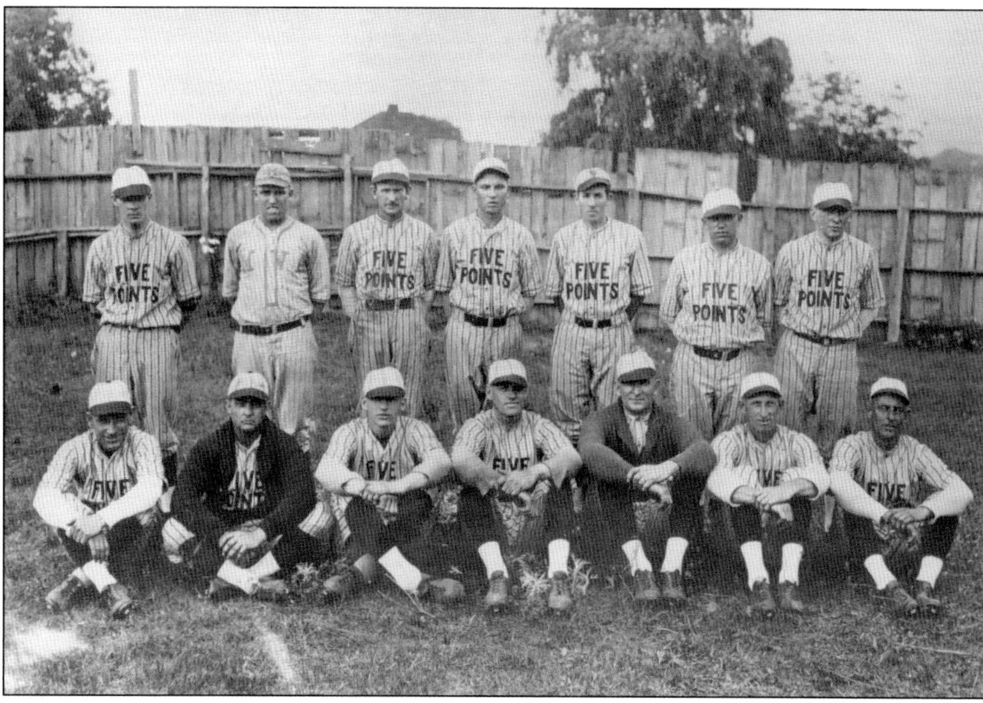

This is the Five Points baseball team about 1926. J.D. "Bud" Morelock (1896–1976) is seated in the center.

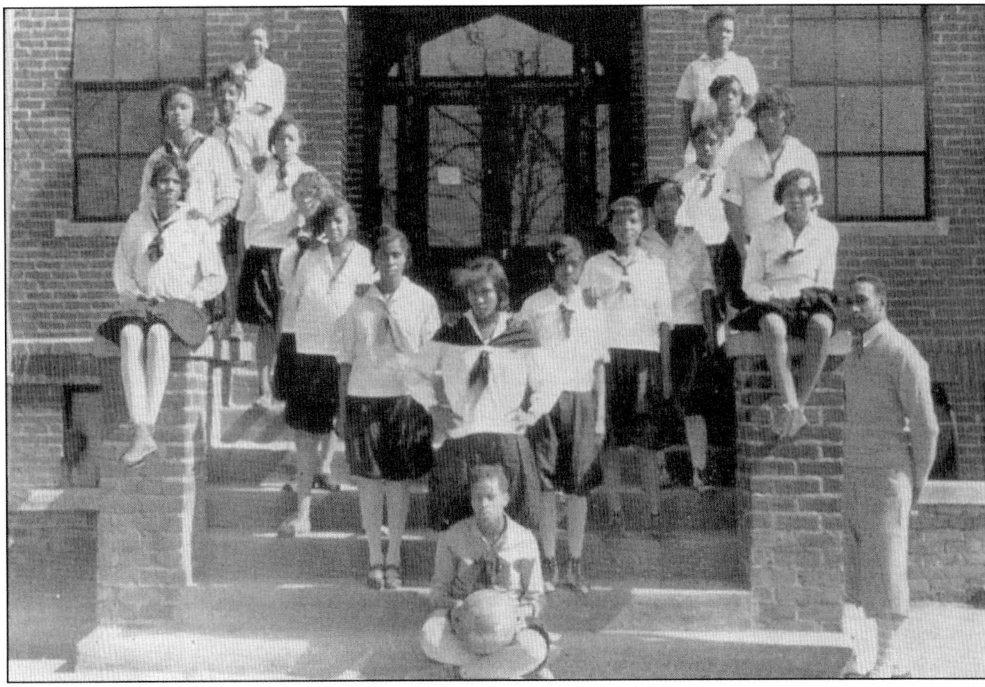

Shown here is the Girls Athletic Club of College Hill School in 1930.

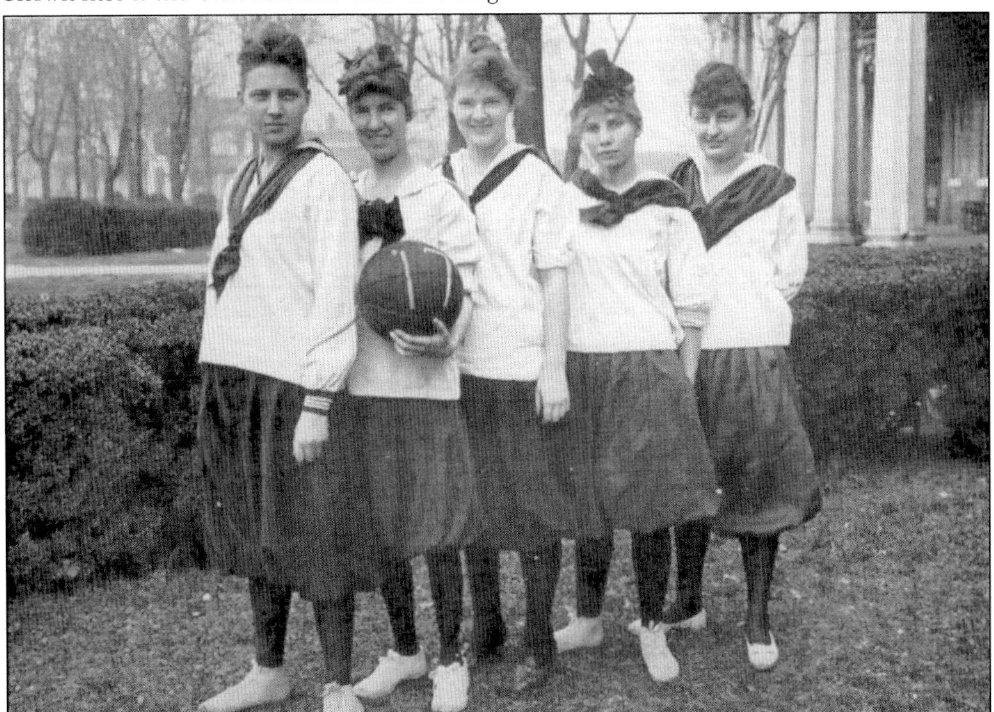

This is a 1917 photograph of the Centenary College junior basketball team. The uniforms consisted of black cotton stockings, middy blouses, and very full, black bloomers extending below the knees.

The Bloomer Girls were the first professional female baseball players. Shown is a broadside for their appearance in Cleveland in the 1890s. Pictured at bat is Maud Nelson, world-renowned Bloomer Girl pitcher who enjoyed a 40-year career in baseball.

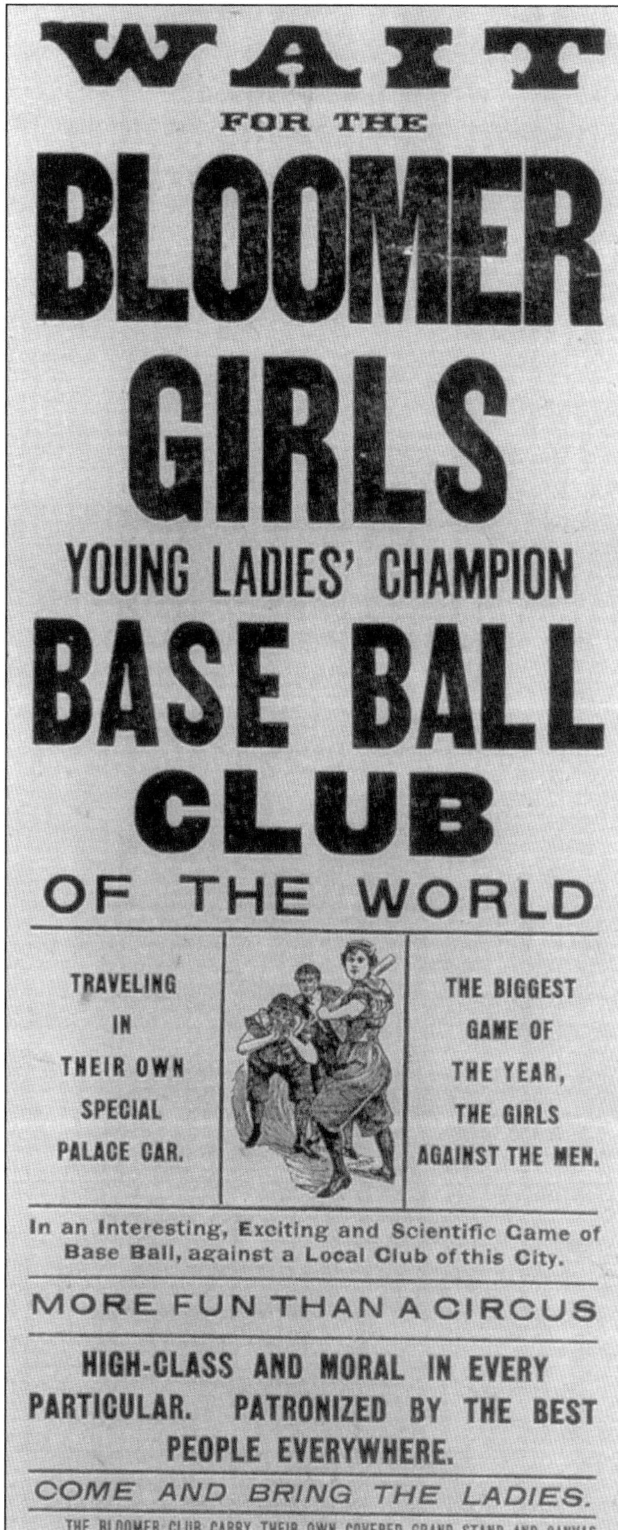

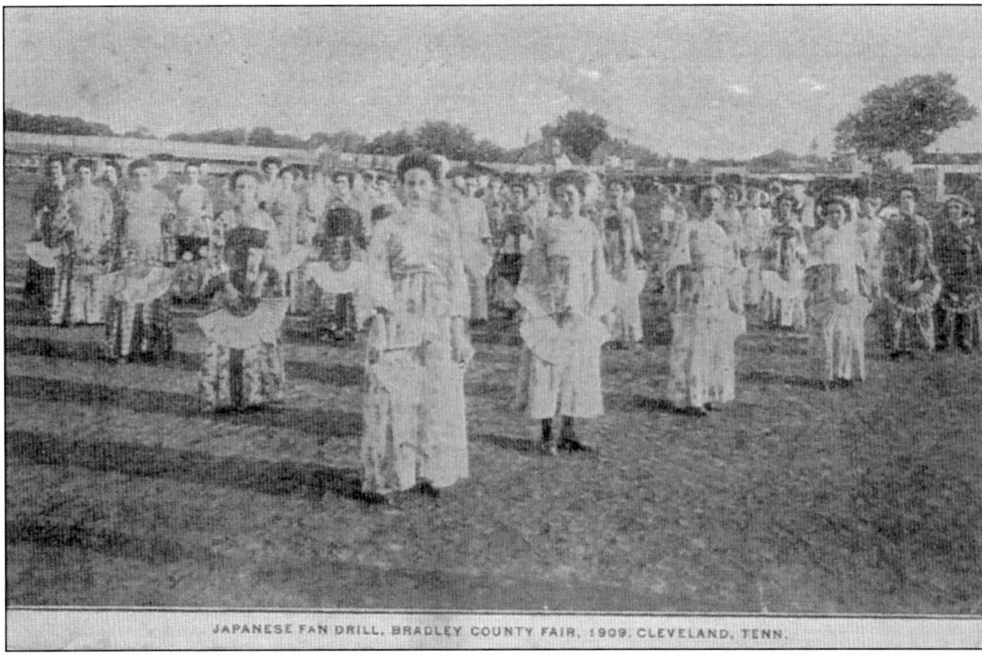

This postcard shows a Japanese Fan Drill at the Bradley County Fair of 1909.

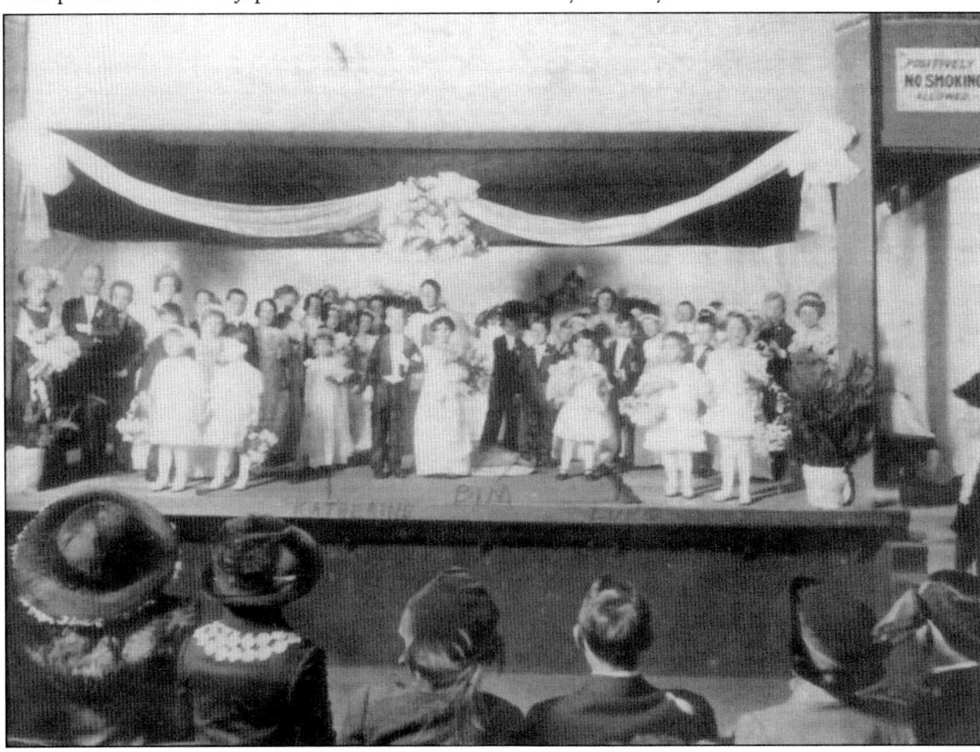

"Tom Thumb" weddings, with small children acting as members of the wedding party, were popular events in the early 1900s. Lifelong resident of Cleveland Rose Kinder Simbro related that her participation in such an event sponsored by her church was one of the highlights of her youth.

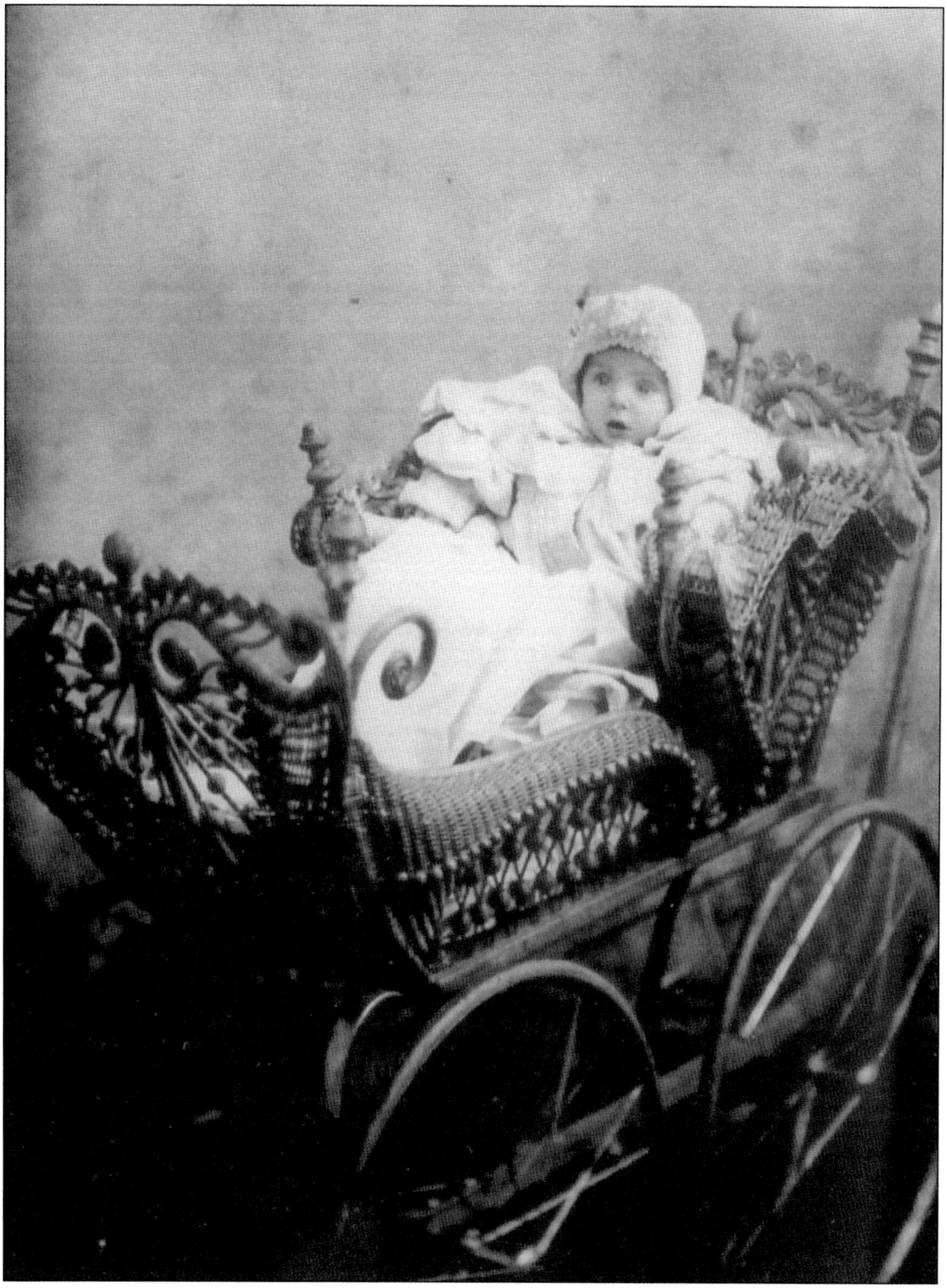

This pretty baby in the ornate wicker carriage is five-month-old Sharon Tipton in March 1897.

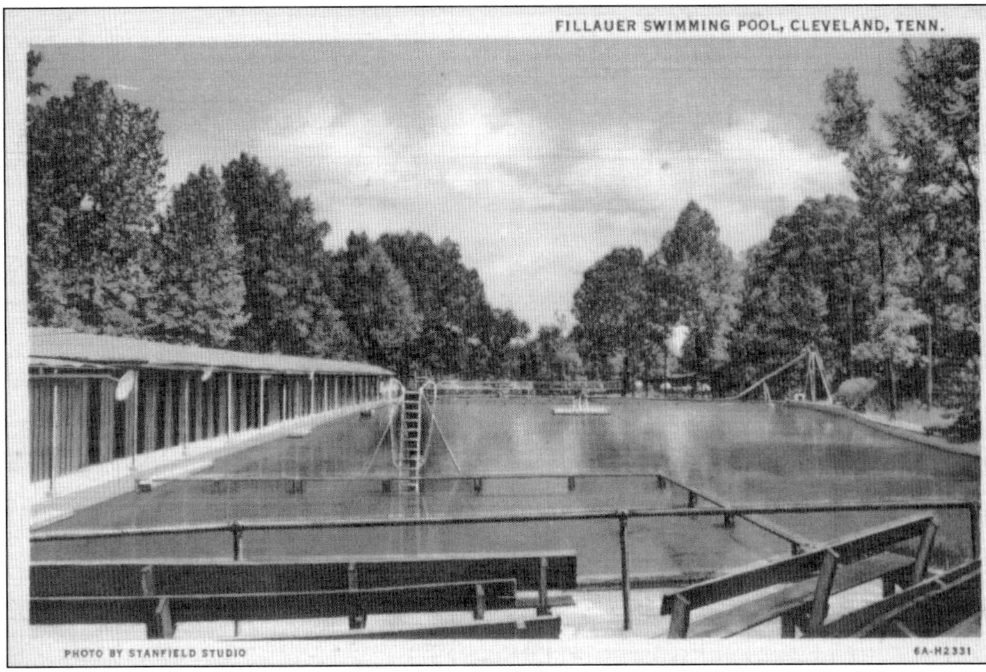

This postcard of Fillauer Swimming Pool was mailed in 1939. Home swimming pools were scarce at that time, and Fillauer, run by John Fillauer, was the only public pool in Cleveland.

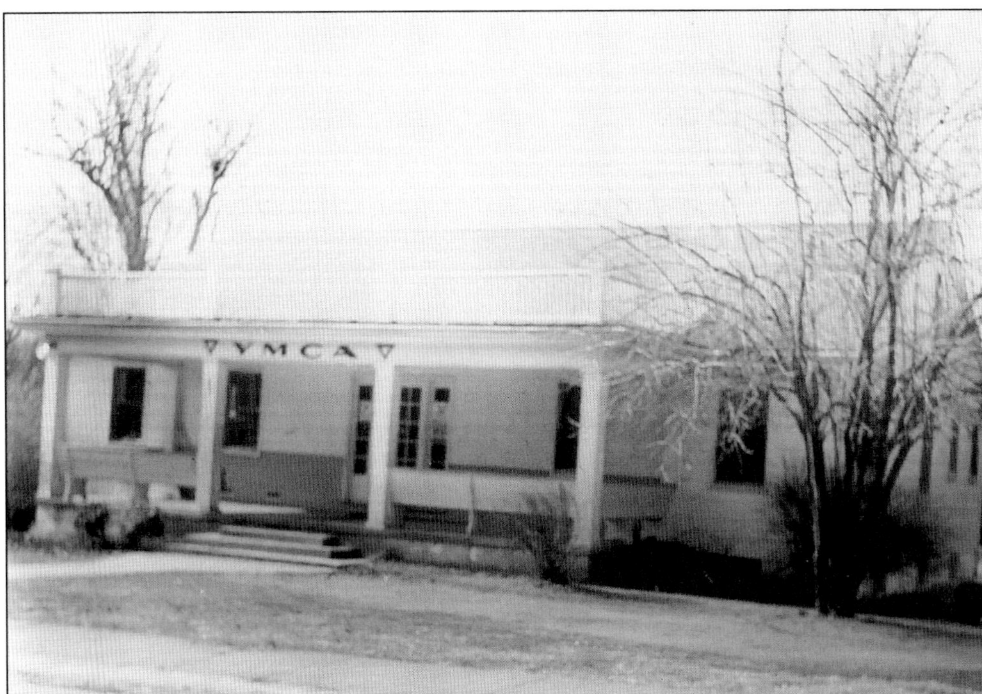

This is a photograph of the Cleveland YMCA in the 1950s. Located on Spring Street, it was the center of many activities for Cleveland's young people.

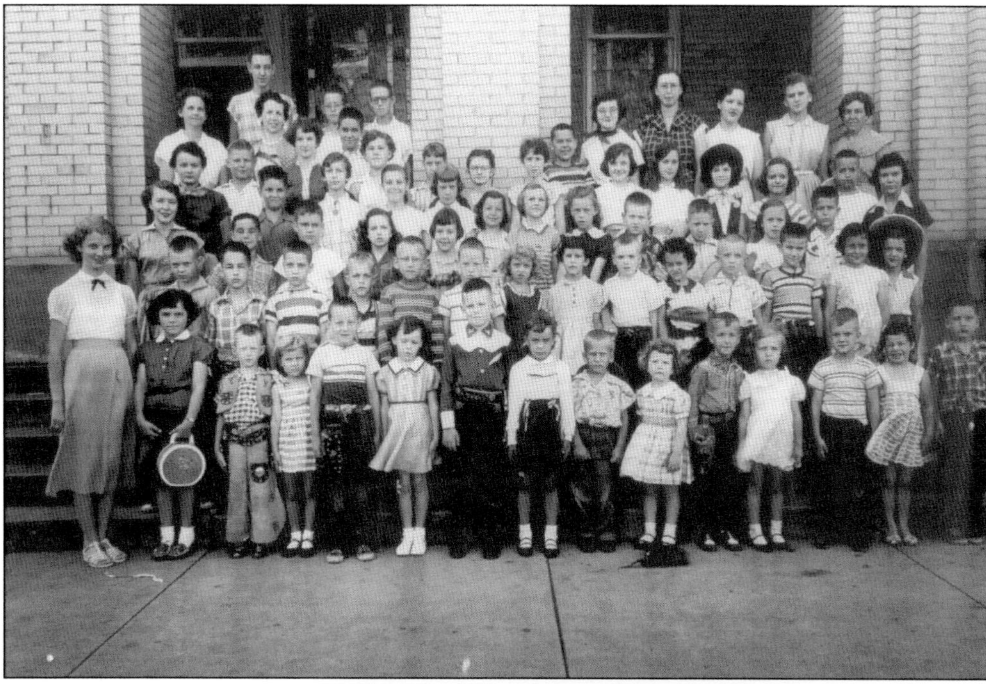

Cleveland children look forward to vacation Bible schools during the summer. This vacation Bible school at First Methodist Church in 1954 shows many of the children dressed in a Western theme.

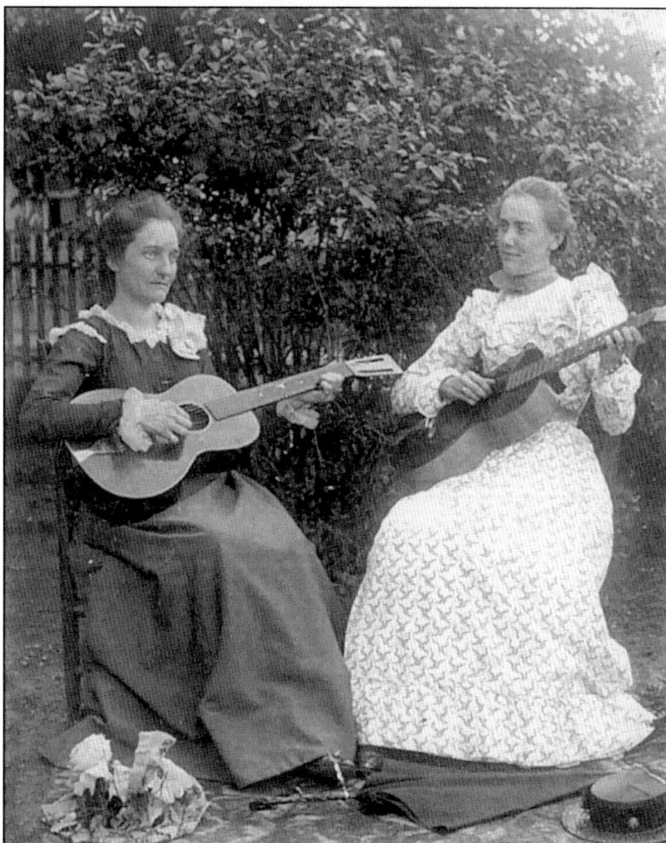

Music has always been a favorite pastime of Cleveland citizens. Pictured here on June 18, 1900, with their guitars are Fannie Atchley and Pearl Frazier. Notice their hats on the ground before them.

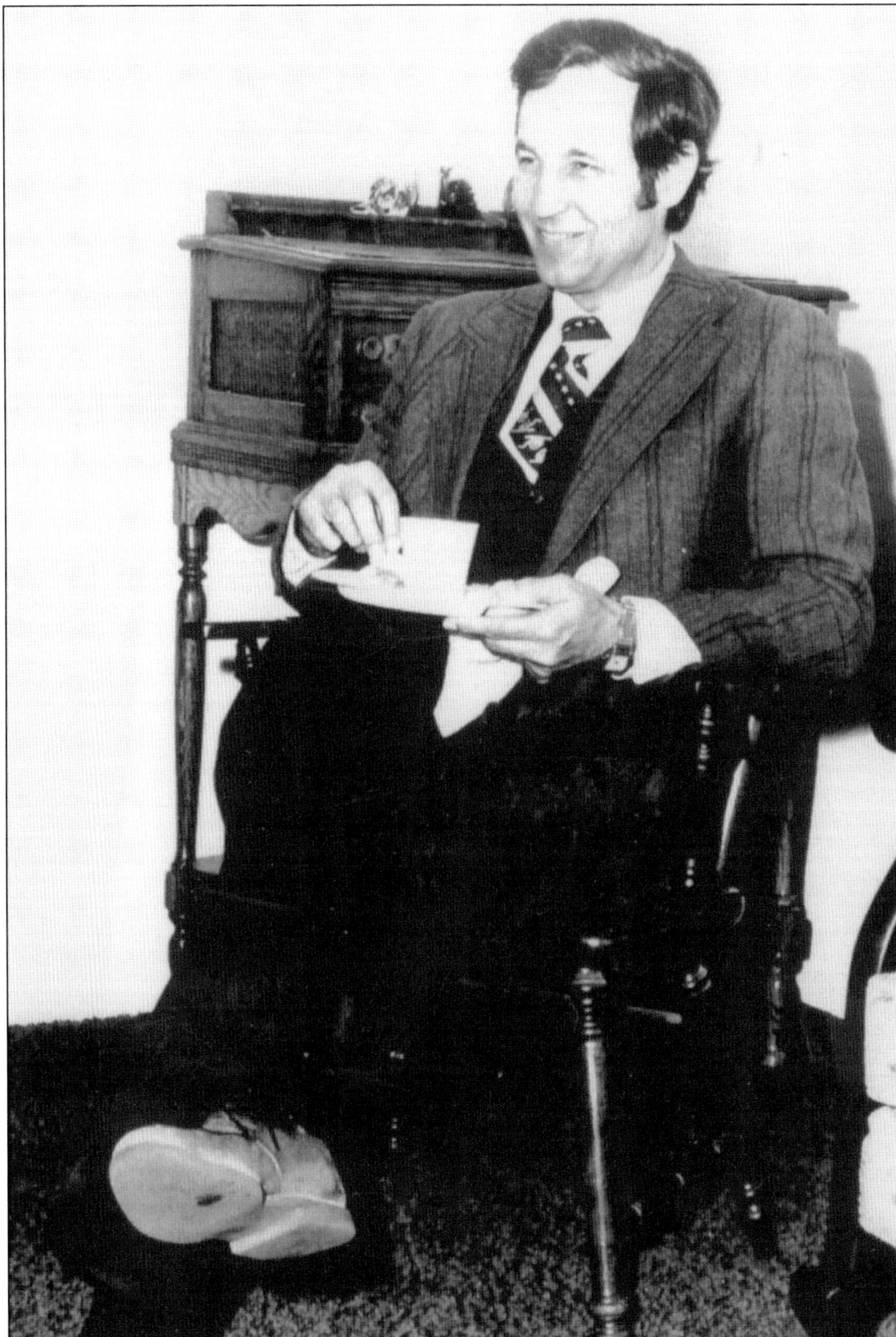

Shown enjoying a little refreshment is Dr. William R. Snell—Lee College history professor, Cleveland city historian, and author of *Cleveland the Beautiful.*

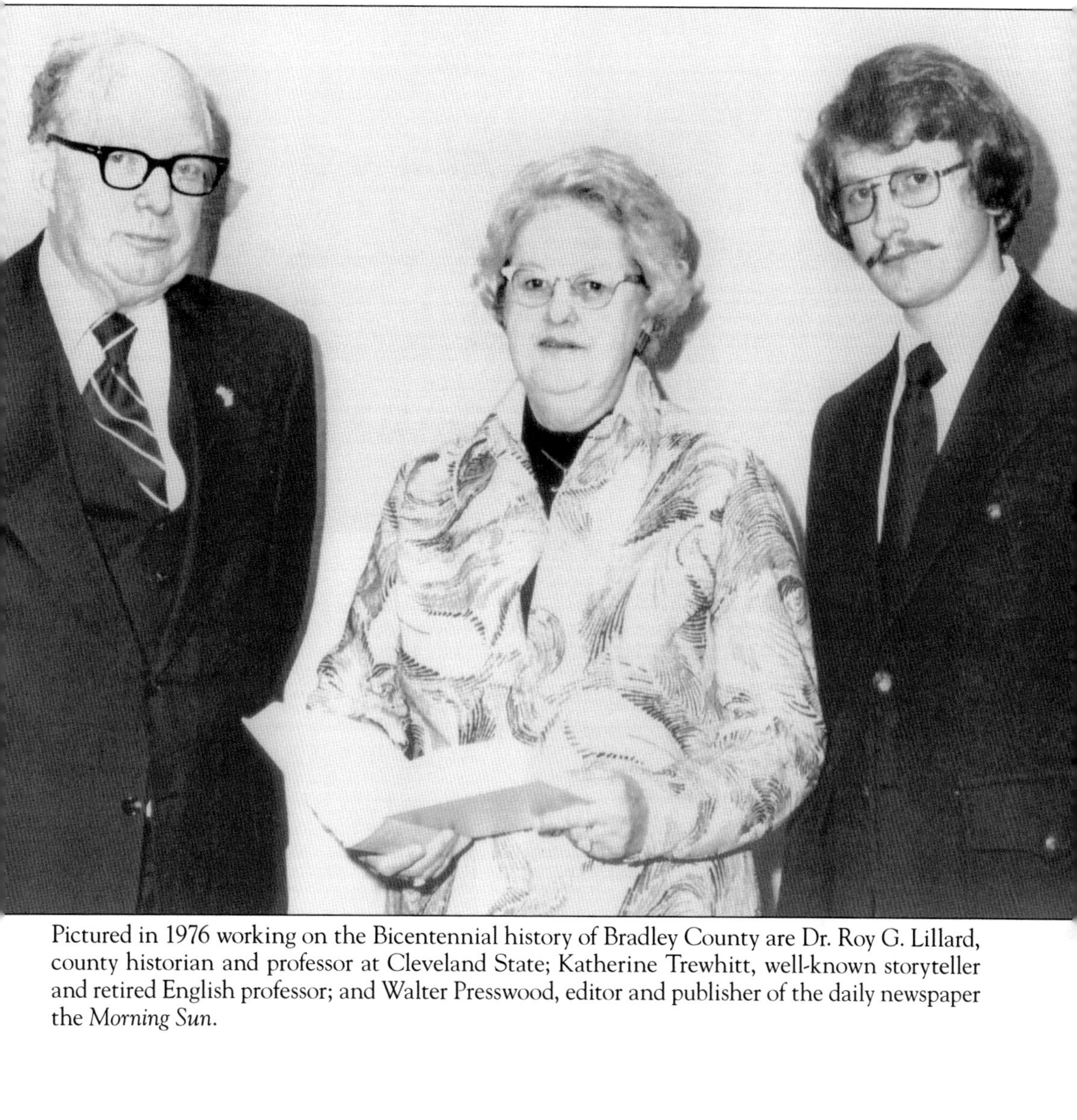

Pictured in 1976 working on the Bicentennial history of Bradley County are Dr. Roy G. Lillard, county historian and professor at Cleveland State; Katherine Trewhitt, well-known storyteller and retired English professor; and Walter Presswood, editor and publisher of the daily newspaper the *Morning Sun*.

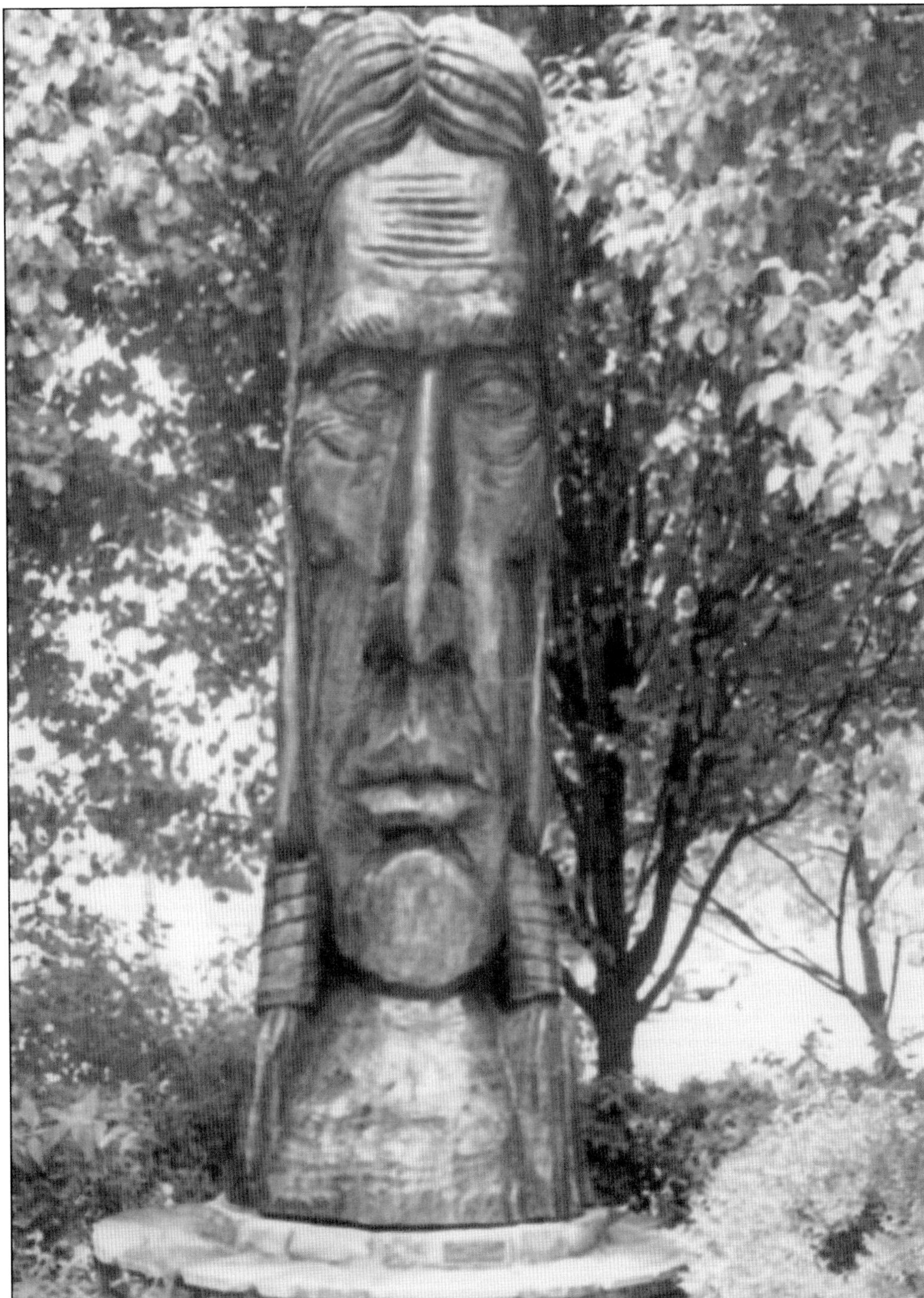

Peter Wolf Toth, Hungarian-born, escaped from his homeland and became a United States citizen. He determined to sculpt a statue in every state to honor American Indians. He began the process in California in the winter of 1972. The *Cherokee Chieftan* in Cleveland, his ninth, was completed in December 1973. Located in Johnston Park, the sculpture is a reminder of Cleveland's beginnings and evolution over the past 164 years.

BIBLIOGRAPHY

Coleman, George W. *Life and Addresses of G.W. Coleman*. Cleveland: G.W. Coleman, 1927.

Conner, John. *Reflections Past and Present: A Pictorial History of Bradley County 1836–1991*. Cleveland: Bradley County Historical Society, 1991.

Finley, James D. *Brotherhood in Bradley County 1847–1995*. Cleveland: J.D. Finley, 1997.

Harle, Louise. *I Remember Tall Tales and True of Cleveland and Bradley County*. Cleveland: Louise Harle, nd.

Lillard, Roy G., ed. *The History of Bradley*. Cleveland: Bradley County Chapter, East Tennessee Historical Society, 1976.

Morelock, Ann, and Trewhitt, Katherine, ed. *History of the First Cumberland Presbyterian Church, Cleveland, Tennessee 1837–1987*. Cleveland: First Cumberland Presbyterian Church, 1989.

Murray, Melba Lee. *Bradley Divided: Bradley County, Tennessee During the Civil War*. Collegedale, TN: the College Press, 1992.

Snell, William R. *Cleveland the Beautiful: A History of Cleveland, Tennessee 1842–1931*. Nashville: Williams Printing Co., 1986.

Snell, William R. and Robert L. George, ed. *From War to Peace: World War II and the Postwar Years, Bradley County, Tennessee, 1940–1950*. Cleveland: Bradley County Historical Society, 1986.

Snell, William R., ed. *Hard Times Remembered: Bradley County and the Great Depression, Selected Essays and Recollections*. Cleveland: Bradley County Historical Society, 1983.

Snell, William R., ed. *Myra Inman: A Diary of the Civil War in East Tennessee*. Macon, GA: Mercer University Press, 2000.

Strout, Shirley Kreasan. *The History of Zeta Tau Alpha (1898–1928)*, Volume I. Menasha, WI: The Collegiate Press, 1956.

Trewhitt, Katherine L., ed. *History of Broad Street United Methodist Church, Cleveland, Tennessee, 1836–1984*. Collegedale, TN: the College Press, 1984.

Wooten, James Morgan. *A History of Bradley County*. Cleveland: Bradley Post 81, the American Legion, 1949.

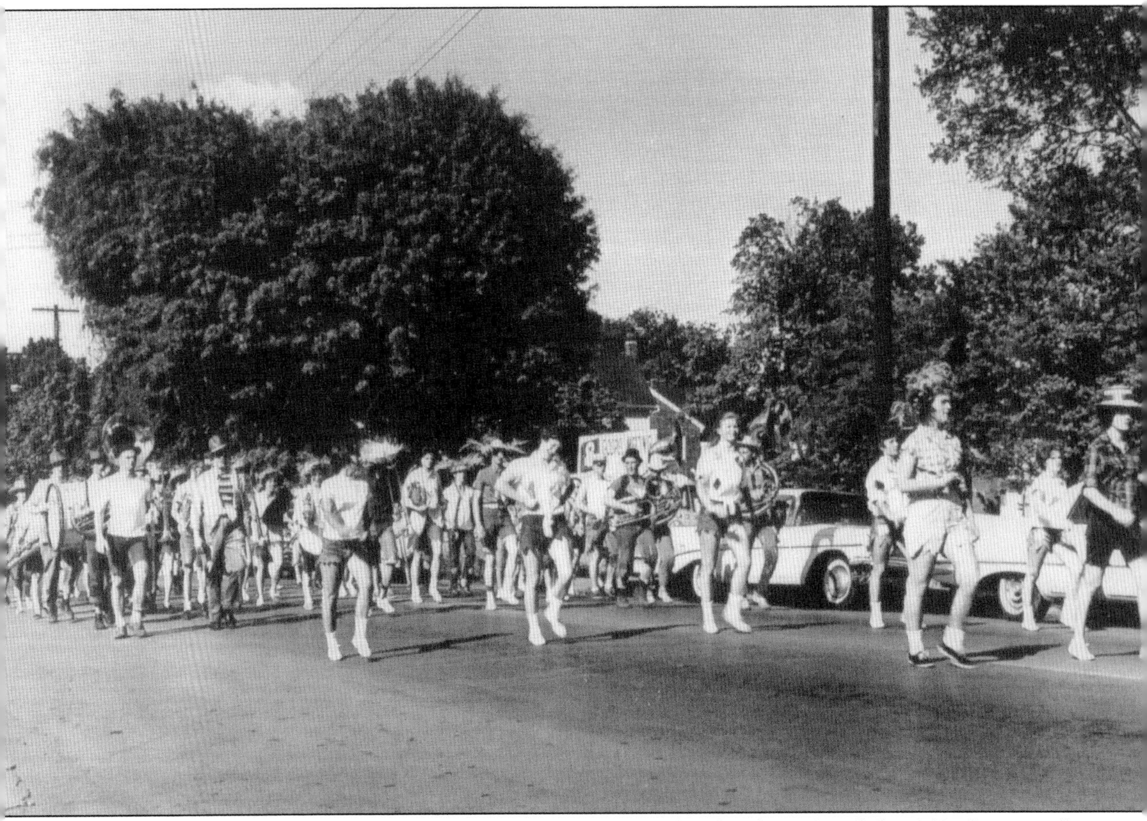

This Sadie Hawkins Day parade held in downtown Cleveland on April 5, 1962, features the Bradley County High School band.

About the Author

Robert L. George received a B.A. degree from Vanderbilt University and a M.B.A. degree from the University of Tennessee, Chattanooga. A Certified Public Accountant practicing in Cleveland, he is a member of the East Tennessee Historical Society and current president of the Bradley County Historical Society. George has served on the Holston Conference of the United Methodist Church Commission on Archives and History for eight years. He is currently treasurer of the Holston Conference Historical Society, treasurer of the Southeast Jurisdiction Historical Society, and a member of the Southeast Jurisdiction Commission on Archives and History.